Real travel writers, I had noticed, walk, cycle, row, hitchhike with a beer fridge, or in one particularly eccentric case swim, everywhere. You need a slow and unenclosed mode of travel to see what there is to see, and to interact with people along the way. A certain amount of discomfort and challenge are probably necessary to give narrative interest to the travel.

To be intimate with a river you must be close to it and flow at something like the river's pace. I was going to row; stopping to walk around anywhere that looked interesting.

In the end I decided I wanted to row and travel the rivers with some degree of difficulty because I wanted the intensity of experience and adventure that travel to new and unfamiliar places can bring. Rowing a small boat, nosing into little creeks and bays, would, I hoped, make my local suburban river a new and unfamiliar place.

Nick Burningham grew up in a small farming village in southern England in an entirely non-nautical family, but was always obsessed with sailing ships and boats. In 1973 he left England for Australia to help his parents get over his disappointing academic results.

After a short career beachcombing in north Queensland he went to Indonesia to investigate the engineless sailing craft still operating there, and over the following decade owned and sailed on several Indonesian perahu. A cargo of floor tiles and stone statues he carried from Bali to Darwin in 1980 on his *Hati Senang* was probably the last cargo carried internationally by a British registered, engineless, sailing vessel.

More recently Burningham has written numerous academic papers about traditional watercraft of South-East Asia. He has also designed and supervised the construction of several replica sailing vessels, including the *Duyfken*.

Messing about in Earnest

Mr Tablecloth Sail and Earnest on Blackwall Reach

Messing about in Earnest

Nick Burningham

Fremantle Arts Centre Press

Australia's finest small publisher

The remains of the 'convict fence' on the Canning River,
from the Rossmoyne shore

Contents

Maps

Acknowledgements

I could not be solely responsible for this book. Several of the guilty parties are named in the text and to them I extend my thanks. The Peter who helped me take *Earnest* to the river was Peter Kirby

Ray Coffey of Fremantle Art Centre Press demonstrated his faith in my Swan and Canning project by putting me to work building cupboards and bookcases, thus funding the stale gray bread, mousetrap cheese and plonk to provision my river voyages. Mar Bucknell, who read a draft manuscript, offered much useful criticism, suggestions and a warmly generous appraisal.

To the staff of the Alexander Library and Fremantle Library my thanks. And also to my good friend Ross Shardlow, Australia's finest marine artist whose illustrations combine inspired artistry with meticulous research and a seaman's love of ships and boats. His drawings appear on pages 33, 36, 42, 146, 282 and 376.

Every effort has been made to locate the copyright owners and seek permission for the use of material quoted in this book. The publisher would appreciate advice of ownership in cases where efforts have not been successful.

My gratitude to Sir Henry Semaphore who taught me to scull at Eton.

There is, doubtless, some uniquely deserving person whom I have forgotten to thank. A small compensation for this unforgivable omission: you may be sure that my delicate conscience will be wracked by a remorse as chilling as dread whenever I think of you until my dying day; a day to be hastened by the sickening shame you have innocently brought upon me.

Nick Burningham
Banyuwangi
5 July 2003

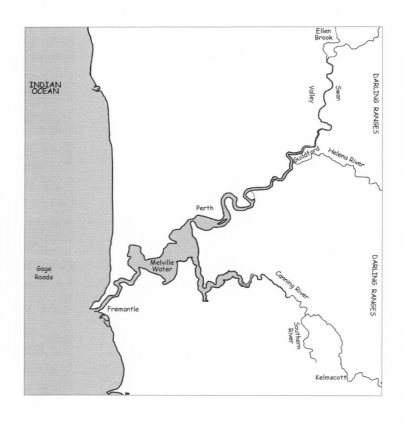

The Swan and Canning Rivers

Prologue

GOING NOWHERE IN EARNEST

I had returned to Perth from a long voyage on a sailing ship, earning wages appropriate to the age of sail, to find that middle-aged men were still unemployable in the real world. I could keep myself alive by 'dis-saving', odd jobs, very occasional consultancies and spending any payments finally received for a few magazine articles written two or three years back — so long as I subsisted on rice, lentils and cask wine.

The layabout lifestyle suited me well enough but to preserve a modicum of self-respect I needed to pretend to do something more estimable. I don't remember when I came up with the idea of investigating and writing about the Swan and Canning rivers. Probably it was at a dinner party where I was drinking more than my fair share of the wine. Somebody was polite enough to say that it sounded like a good idea.

Perth, the capital city of Western Australia, like all Australian state capitals, is the home of a large proportion of the state's population. And like all the other Australian state capitals it is a coastal city, but it is the Swan River, not the coast, that is the soul of the city. The river runs right through the middle of the greater metropolitan area. The Canning River, the Swan's major tributary, also runs most of its course through the greater metropolitan area, but it is much less regarded, almost a secret river.

The eighth of March 2002 was the one hundred and seventy-fifth anniversary of the beginning of Captain James Stirling's expedition up the Swan River. Stirling and the botanist Fraser who accompanied him liked what they saw. Stirling's crusading enthusiasm combined with Fraser's supposedly expert appraisal of agricultural prospects quickly led to Britain taking possession of Western Australia and the founding of the Swan River Colony by several shiploads of optimistic, largely self-funded pioneers.

The anniversary would have been an appropriate day to re-launch the little boat that I'd been repairing and intended to use for my own Swan River expeditions. Unfortunately I was not quite ready. The boat was ready to float but the oars and a couple of other important details were not finished. On that anniversary day I bought a pair of padlocks and some chain so that I could secure the boat to a convenient tree or railing on the banks of the river with the oars, rudder and sail chained into it. I was still sewing together some mosquito net to form a tent over the boat so that I could sleep in it when that seemed the most opportune thing to do.

During investigation of the lower reaches of the river, near Fremantle where I live, I could return home each evening, but from Perth Water onwards that would not be practical. The winds would not often favour an evening return to Fremantle, where the river meets the sea. Most days there is an easterly breeze off the land during the night and the morning and a sea breeze from the south-west during the afternoon and the first part of the night.

Perth Water is only half an hour away from Fremantle by road or rail, so if I found a safe place to lock the boat I could still get home. Using my small, fairly slow, rowing boat I intended to travel slowly and quietly and wouldn't cover distance too easily.

There were a number of reasons for that. Real travel writers, I had noticed, walk, cycle, row, hitchhike with a beer fridge, or in one particularly eccentric case swim, everywhere. You need a slow and unenclosed mode of travel to see what there is to see, and to interact with people along the way. A certain amount of discomfort and challenge are probably necessary to give narrative interest to the travel. Thus, a motorboat would not do at all, moreover, anything other than a small, lightweight boat or a canoe would not be able to get into some of the creeks and backwaters I wanted to visit. While a larger motorised boat would be more convenient for making miles, a small rowing boat would be much easier to beach and to drag over shallows and around obstacles such as the Kent Street Weir on the Canning River.

Fast modes of travel, such as cars and speedboats, are useless for getting to know intimate landscapes. Perhaps one can appreciate wide open spaces such as prairies and deserts from a car, but for more compact landscapes they are a dead loss. I used to visit the island of Bali frequently and often travelled the road up and down the south-east coast. I thought I knew it well until, with a friend, I cycled the same road and realised that I had never really seen it at all. A couple of years later I walked part of the same road and discovered that I had seen very little while hurrying through on a ten-speed bicycle.

To be intimate with the river you must be close to it and flow at something like the river's pace. What's more, the Swan River simply isn't long enough for motorboating. I'd run out of river in two or three days.

So, I was going to row; stopping to walk around anywhere that looked interesting. I wasn't entirely sure how I was going to spend the nights. I had phoned the police and asked if I could be arrested for vagrancy if I slept in or beside my boat in a park on the banks of the river. The police assured me that they don't bust people for simply sleeping in a park.

Sleeping in the bottom of the boat under the thwarts would not be at all comfortable; there is only just enough room to lie down. I would take a tent but suspected that camping in urban parks does contravene some by-laws, so if I used a tent it could only be in the most secluded places, pitching the tent at dusk and taking it down at first light. My hope was that good honest rowing and walking would make me tired enough to sleep anywhere so long as I could keep the mosquitoes off.

In the end I decided I wanted to row and travel the rivers with some degree of difficulty because I wanted the intensity of experience and adventure that travel to new and unfamiliar places can bring. Rowing a small boat, nosing into little creeks and bays, would, I hoped, make my local suburban river a new and unfamiliar place.

That was the way I rationalised it before setting out, though I realised that after a few days of rowing and sleeping rough within an hour or two's travel from home I might view things rather differently.

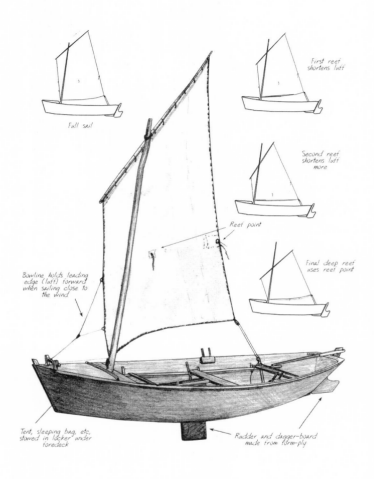

First reef
shortens luff

Second reef
shortens luff
more

Reef point

Final deep reef
uses reef point

Full sail

Bowline holds leading
edge (luff) forward
when sailing close to
the wind

Tent, sleeping bag, etc,
stowed in locker under
foredeck

Rudder and dagger-board
made from form-ply

Earnest

Chapter 1

SETTING OUT IN EARNEST

A week after the Stirling one hundred and seventy-fifth anniversary, with the oars varnished and most things sort-of-finished-ish to the nearly-good-enough standard I like to set as a benchmark, I asked my friend Peter to help me take the boat to the water.

Among Peter's several successful enterprises is the affixing of gyprock (plasterboard) to walls and ceilings so he has a roof-rack the whole length of his Holden king-size station wagon, with rollers at the ends — ideal for transporting scruffy plywood boats that look as if they've been cobbled together from bits of plasterboard.

Peter had intended to bring along his own sailing canoe and make a family picnic on the shores of the Swan River's Blackwall Reach, but he'd forgotten to mention it to his family and, on the appointed day, he was nursing a well-earned hangover, so launching festivities were scaled down. Nevertheless, Peter brought along his daughter Ella and her friend Rachel, and also (Peter has reminded me) his rat-like dog.

Ella, who appears to be about fourteen — which is curious since I remember her being an infant about eight years ago — has ambitions to be a film-maker and Peter thinks that recording my river escapades on video and stills would be a worthwhile experience. Ella and Rachel were very helpful with wrestling the boat out of the back garden and onto the roof-rack, and also with unloading the boat and all its gear at Blackwall Reach. Not only that, they were thoroughly polite about it which strikes me as remarkably mature. Presumably they regarded me, my boat, all its homemade gear, and the whole project as appallingly naff, or whatever the current equivalent of naff is, but they never showed a sign of it.

We put the boat in the water and I stood in it. There was no sign of any leaks! I got the oars and rowed around for the cameras. Then we shipped mast, sail, centreboard and rudder, and — after I'd sorted out a small problem where the wine-bottle-cork bung in the stern obstructed the pin that holds the rudder to its gudgeons (hinges) — shipped the rudder again and then the tiller. I sailed out across the river and back to the beach to make a small alteration to the rigging, then Peter sailed across the river and back to clear his head.

When Peter returned to the beach there was a bit of water

sloshing around in the flat bottom of the boat, but everything seemed more or less okay, so he took his hangover home and I went for a longer sail to practise the close investigation of the river's banks.

By the time I rounded Chidley Point at the end of Blackwall Reach, there was obviously somewhat more water sloshing around inside the boat. I'd been running downwind so no water could have splashed in over the rail. In the stern I could see that water was trickling in through the bung that I'd chopped short, so I dropped the little lugsail and rowed into the tiny beach at Green Place.

I had come prepared for a few leaks. Under a thwart I'd stuck a lump of the wax that encases certain Dutch and northern-French cheeses (the best wax comes from those little French *Bon Belle* cheesettes). This cheese wax is ideal for stopping leaks, even in relatively large vessels where you have to dive under the hull to reach the leaking seams. You can use it successfully from the inside or outside of the hull and the seams don't have to be dry. A more traditional sticky mix can be prepared by heating together ten parts of beeswax with one part of copra (coconut) oil, but don't expect to ever use the saucepan for food again.

Leaving Green Place with my bung waxed I didn't reset the sail because I wanted to row along slowly, very close to the shore. From Green Place to the little coombe called The Coombe (coombe is the Sussex name for a small steep valley) the land rises steeply from the river, with sensational views over Melville Water. It is reputedly the most expensive residential land in Perth and it is crowded with big, ostentatious houses. The best way to see The Coombe is to row along right underneath it, about ten metres from the shore — that way you see a few terraced gardens draped with clouds of bougainvillea and bits of the houses nearest to the water. The effect is exquisite. If you doubt that, or if you know the precinct I'm referring to and think 'exquisite' a bit hyperbolic, please read on — there is a rational explanation a few paragraphs below.

When I'd previously sailed my little boat on this part of the river a few years ago, the steep shore had been scarred by a quarry-like construction site that made no sense to me unless someone was building a relatively small house with hugely expansive driveways and multi-level car parks all over the gardens. Now it makes sense. They had been creating Roman ruins as foundations for a couple of faithfully recreated Tuscan or Umbrian farmhouses of attractive and human proportions. Trees and creepers are now melding the whole ensemble into the landscape and the effect is truly admirable.

Looking up at those lovely riverside houses it occurred to me that what I needed for this river discovery project was a beachside house somewhere in Mosman Park from which I could launch my boat, though I don't suppose the owners of any of them would want to house swap with my Fremantle heritage tea-chest-with-cat-flap-at-either-end.

From The Coombe, for a kilometre or two to the north, the

steep banks are natural bushland. There was mallee in bloom with their intensely yellow flowers and big red flower buds. (Perhaps they're not mallee. Anyway, it's some sort of eucalypt.) Again, you can really enjoy this part of the river best by rowing slowly along right underneath the escarpment — unless there is a strong easterly wind in which case you and your boat will end up splintered and grated to pink gore on the jagged limestone boulders jumbled along the shore.

At the northern end of the high bush-clad bank, just before you get to the Swan Canoe Club, there are a number of pilings in the water, capped with metal fittings like the castles of a giant chess set. On some of the pilings the fittings support cross-arms like those of a rotary washing line, from which hang bits of broken plastic conduit. I supposed it must be a conceptual art installation, though the piles and caps looked too well engineered. Later I asked someone at the canoe club about them and learned that they are used for practising canoe slalom. No artistic statement was intended.

Just beyond the canoe club a restaurant, Meads on Mosman Bay, is built out over the water with an exclusive marina jetty in front. I was tempted to row in under the restaurant and beg for scraps from the beautiful people dining on the balcony but I'm told servings there are very small. Beyond Meads the road comes down to the river and there are houses on the inland side of the road which as investments are all about location, location, location. The architectural style ranges from fairly ordinary to very ordinary with a bit of tasteless thrown in to enliven it.

To continue north along the Peppermint Grove shore one has to head out around the marina of the Royal Freshwater Bay Yacht Club, arguably the most prestigious yacht club on the Swan and at times, it seems to me, the only one with the arrogance to actually obstruct navigation of the river.

The clubhouse is a beautiful building, beautifully situated except that it and the knoll it sits on are largely hidden from the river by the club's marina jetties and the hulking great motorboats berthed there — boats that seemingly never get used.

Because the jetties project into the river, they constrict the passage between the knoll, or hump, and the end of the Point Walter sandspit. This has always been the most dangerous passage of the river. There were numerous capsizes and even drownings there in the first decade of the Swan River Colony. If a strong south-westerly sea breeze is blowing, a sailing boat has to work dead to windward against a nasty chop to get around the end of the sand spit. Room for beating to windward (zigzagging or tacking) has been reduced by the jetties. This is no problem at all for modern yachts but it can be awkward for traditional boats that don't tack reliably, especially if the tide is against you. If the jetties weren't there you could make longer tacks and rely on going about (changing tack) in the sheltered water under the shore, but that's not possible and I've had one or two nasty moments tacking through there.

Butler's Hump
and the Royal Freshwater Bay Yacht Club

Aubrey Sherwood, grandson of Thomas Sherwood the founder of the Swan Brewery, founded Freshwater Bay Yacht Club in 1896 (at the age of thirty-six). The annual fee was £1 with founder members paying no joining fee. The escalation of fees at RFBYC has significantly exceeded inflation during the hundred years since the club's foundation. The clubhouse was built near a small headland that was called Minderup by the Nyungar Aboriginal people. By the non-indigenous people in 1896 it was called Butler's Hump, which sounds like a senior servant's perk. It was actually named after a Mr Butler who arrived in the Swan River Colony in January 1830, ran an unsuccessful hostelry, tried to sue almost everyone he had dealings with, and owned all the land in the area now called Peppermint Grove. The headland is now called Keane's Point after Sherwood's elderly and un-nautical co-founder of the yacht club who owned Butler's Hump when the club was formed. Until 1936 the club's boatshed and a modest clubhouse were at the northern end of Peppermint Grove beach where the Scotch College boatshed is today, not on Butler's Hump.

To atone for their river obstructing sins, the club is host to the Swan River fleet of couta boats — gaff-rigged racing boats of designs based on fast traditional fishing boats. The hulls' lines are elegant. They are much the prettiest fleet on the river, partly because they are not all painted white. The couta boats have strong colours: chrome yellow, royal blue, aqua, red; their big quadrilateral gaff sails filling with a stiff breeze create more interesting shapes than the tall lean triangles of modern yachts.

Anyway, having rounded the marina jetties without loss of life, I ate a sandwich and had a slurp of wine on the beach to the north of the yacht club. It is a popular picnic spot with a sandy beach, soft grass and plenty of shade provided by a big ficus tree and the peppermint gums that give Peppermint Grove its name. Lunch finished, I set the sail to head back to Blackwall Reach and on to North Fremantle where I intended to padlock the boat to a tree. I sailed out around the RFBYC jetties and cleared Point Walter spit again without trauma. Halfway along the spit I tacked and stood in under the Mosman shore. Reasonably close under, I dropped the sail and rowed again, about one hundred and fifty metres offshore. At this distance the scenery was attractive but nothing like so pretty as what you see when you hug the shore. The Mosman scarp is crowded with grand architect-designed houses all shouting 'look at me', 'look at me'. It is only strikingly lovely if you row slowly along the very edge of the river.

I tucked in close under Chidley Point where there are low limestone cliffs and, clinging to them, a few pines, bonsai-ed by the river eroding their roots — you can actually see the bonsai process at work when a large motorboat rumbles past kicking up a short sharp wash.

Rowing round Chidley Point I met the sea breeze that funnels down Blackwall Reach. I rowed against it for twenty or thirty minutes, making ground against the wind very slowly, again very close in under the steep shore, telling myself that I was enjoying the view and could set the sail if rowing became too tedious. In truth it was pretty tedious: in fifteen knots or more of headwind, rowing is nearly useless. After I had grounded on a sharp rock because I was tucking in too close to the shore to avoid the wind, I did set sail and tacked up through the Reach. When the wind gusted I had to spill wind from the sail and my little boat tended to sag away from the course I wanted to make. I could have reefed the sail but I suspected that if I did so she would sail sluggishly. It seemed that making progress against any stiff sea breeze was going to be a problem. Also, it was clear that tacking into a stiff breeze and a chop I was getting regularly doused with dollops of spray.

By the time I'd tacked around Preston Point the day was waning and the breeze was becoming fitful, so I downed sail again and rowed the last few hundred metres round to Prawn Bay where I dragged the boat out of the water, locked all its bits of gear to the thwarts and padlocked it to a tree. Borrowing the words of one of Australia's living national treasures, Barry Hicks, a traditional sailorman originally from the Thames estuary, I had a 'wet shirt and a happy heart'.

Chapter 2

Fremantle Harbour and the Mouth of the Swan

The next day I got up before seven, though it was a Sunday and St Patrick's day withal. Before eight I was back down at the boat, which I was pleased to find had not been vandalised during the night. Early on a Sunday morning the river is almost bustling with rowers and canoeists all getting in some quality time before the motorboat traffic chops up the water and spoils the quiet. Early on any autumn day, before human activity interferes, the cormorants and seagulls cruise together in large black and white convoys along the sandy North Fremantle shore. It's a lovely time of day and the best time for seeing the bird life.

Just downstream from where I launched the boat a very strange trimaran was anchored in the shallows. It hadn't been there the previous evening. The hulls weren't so very strange, though they looked a bit homemade, but there was a great big white fibreglass pod the shape of a gun turret, about eight feet (2.44m) high, covering the whole width of the trimaran. Straddling it was an impractical looking bipod mast. I rowed over intending to ask about the conception behind the design, or the accidents that had married a funny trimaran, a large fibreglass pod and a pair of flagpoles. On board were half-a-dozen sleepy-eyed young people crawling out from under blankets and scratching matted hair. Although I was sitting in a fairly eccentric looking boat myself they seemed rather hermetic and defensive so I kept my questions to myself and continued downstream to the harbour at the river's mouth.

It was my intention to investigate the river clockwise, looking at the right bank going upstream and the left bank while returning downstream, at least for the purpose of narrative structure. By convention, the right bank is the bank on the right hand side when looking downstream. That's simple enough, so let me confuse things by adding that the right bank is the bank to the left when looking upstream as you do when rowing downstream because when rowing you are always looking backwards. When looking upstream you can't call the bank on your right the right bank but, by another convention, you should call that bank the 'starboard hand bank' no matter which way you are looking. Although starboard means right hand side looking forward, the right bank and the starboard hand bank are opposite banks of the river. Going clockwise — right bank upstream, left bank downstream — does not fit with the international rule of the road for watercraft which is the equivalent of driving on the right, but my boat is small enough to tuck in under the bank when necessary to keep out of the way of larger vessels.

An unintended result of my clockwise itinerary and narrative is an apparent bias to the right bank which I investigated and describe first. Overall impressions of stretches of the river, and features such as bridges that really belong equally to both banks if they are to be useful, tend to get described when I first encountered them, following the right bank upstream. And so it turns out that the right bank chapters tend to be longer, giving the unfortunate, potentially invidious and incorrect impression that I prefer the right bank or that it is the more interesting bank. Since many Perth people identify quite strongly as 'north of the river' or 'south of the river' people I want to make it clear that I really enjoy both banks equally and to offer some means of redress. To some extent, south of the river readers might be able to remedy the structural imbalance by reading the book backwards. If that is too difficult, pages describing bridges and general features of the river can be cut out of the upstream chapters and sticky-taped into appropriate places in the downstream chapters.

I was not sure about including Fremantle Harbour at the mouth of the Swan in my clockwise exploration. It certainly is part of the river, and pleasure craft are allowed to transit the harbour on the way to and from the sea. Once a year there is even a yacht race inside the harbour, held as a spectator event; but normally one is not encouraged to linger in a harbour where large ships manoeuvre with the aid of tugs in very confined waters. The harbour pilots are understandably nervous about small craft sailing into the large blind spot under the bows of a ship piled to bridge level with hundreds of shipping containers. But since I wasn't quite ready to set off on a protracted voyage upriver I decided to row down to the harbour. I had phoned the Port Authority to check that there were no shipping movements scheduled for that morning.

Fremantle is very much a port town and has been since it was first conceived. Perth is Australia's only state capital that did not develop as a port accessible to ocean-going ships. Even Fremantle was a very unsatisfactory port when it was first developed. Until the end of the nineteenth century, when the rock bar blocking the mouth of the Swan to laden, ocean-going ships was removed, Fremantle was a port with no sheltered harbour.

With characteristically unjustified optimism, Captain James Stirling had proclaimed that Cockburn Sound and Gage Roads would provide extensive, safe and sheltered anchorage for the Swan River Colony. In truth, the only sheltered anchorage was the southern end of Cockburn Sound in the lee of Garden Island, much too far from the mouth of the Swan for convenient use as a port. Also, the entrance to Cockburn Sound was difficult and dangerous.

HMS *Challenger* and the chartered merchantman *Parmelia*, the first ships to arrive in 1829, both went aground trying to get into the sound. Within a year both the *Marquis of Anglesea* and *Rockingham* had been wrecked, blown ashore by westerly gales in Gage Roads and Cockburn Sound respectively.

(This is probably an appropriate place to explain to anyone who spots mistakes in the history I offer that not all the factual errors in my historical observations are simply the result of carelessness. As with any topic of research, the outline of the historical facts seemed simple enough when I started, but by the time I had read half-a-dozen respected historians and looked at some primary contemporary sources, I had collected six or seven conflicting, mutually negating, accounts of almost every episode. I have tried to impartially choose the versions of history that fit my notions of poetic justice and heap greatest discredit on revered figures of authority.)

Even in good weather unloading a cargo from a ship anchored out in Gage Roads and getting it to Perth was a laborious business. Cargoes had to be off-loaded into lighters. At the right state of the tide if there was not a sea running, lighters could cross the bar into the river, but this was not permitted by customs regulations unless the lighter operators paid large bonds on the goods. Usually cargoes were taken ashore to South Jetty south of the river mouth and unloaded there, then ported across the sand track to North Jetty in the river where they were loaded into another lighter or barge for the voyage up the river, to be off-loaded again at Perth.

Cargo being unloaded from Sea Ripple *to lighters*
Courtesy Ross Shardlow

In 1832, when the North and South jetties had been built, the per ton cost of moving bulk cargo such as wheat from the anchorage to Perth was as great as the freight from London to Fremantle. In winter, unloading could be delayed for many days by heavy weather. Because of the risk of dragging anchor or parting the anchor cables, ships were obliged to weigh or slip anchor and head back out to sea to ride out storms, sometimes more than once during their loading and unloading.

In the 1830s Nathaniel Ogle proposed cutting a channel from Leighton Beach to Rocky Bay to get ships into the Swan and calculated that eight hundred thousand cubic yards (612,000 m³) of limestone would have to be removed.

A harbour in the river was the more obvious answer but the engineering and the cost were insuperable problems for a small, struggling colony.

In 1856 the assistant surveyor, W Phelps, proposed cutting through the bar at the mouth of the river. In the following years there was some dredging of the sand from the rock bar so that deep-laden barges and unladen coastal schooners could more easily get in and out of the river. Thomas Browne, a civil engineer who had come to Western Australia as a convict, developed a detailed proposal for a river-mouth harbour in the 1870s. However, a far more eminent civil engineer, Sir John Coode (who had not visited Western Australia), advised that the longshore movement of sand would make it troublesome or impossible to keep a channel clear at the mouth of the river. He proposed building a harbour behind a long, curving seawall extending from Arthur Head on the south side of the river mouth. In 1886 he accepted an invitation to visit the colony and elaborated his proposal with the idea of a 2500 foot (762 m) long viaduct seawall which would carry a canal connected to the river.

Meanwhile, in 1872 a severe winter gale swept several ships ashore and that year construction of Ocean Jetty, usually called 'the Long Jetty', was commenced to replace South Jetty which was little more than a landing place for boats. The intention was to build a jetty out into deep water so that ocean-going ships could go alongside and off-load direct to road transport without using lighters. Originally it could take vessels up to twelve-foot (366 cm) draft if there was not a significant swell running. Larger vessels still had to discharge to lighters in the roadstead.

Ocean Jetty was later extended to 3,800 foot (1,160 m) in length, allowing vessels with up to twenty-foot (6 m) draft to lie alongside, but ships could only lie alongside in good weather. As soon as a strong wind blew up, or a big swell rolled in, they had to haul off. Ships were still sometimes delayed for weeks and even months in winter and were often damaged as they surged with the swell at the Long Jetty.

By the time the final extension to Ocean Jetty was completed in 1893, work had begun to create a large harbour in the mouth of the Swan River. The granting of 'responsible government' to the

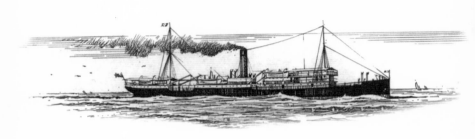

S S Sultan — *among the first ships to enter Fremantle Harbour*
Courtesy Ross Shardlow

colony in 1890 allowed the government to raise loans for capital works where previously all such loans had to be requested from the colonial office.

The Western Australian gold rush was attracting a great number of immigrants and the economy was booming. Premier John Forrest appointed an Irish engineer, C Y O'Connor, as Engineer-in-Chief to the Government of Western Australia in May 1891, to look after 'harbours, railways, everything'. The harbour was to be his first major project. Forrest himself was still persuaded by Sir John Coode's evidence that a river-mouth harbour was a bad idea. Nevertheless, O'Connor's ambitious Inner Harbour scheme, which involved massive use of explosives to remove the bar from the mouth of the Swan River, was endorsed by parliament in March 1892, despite Forrest's opposition.

Work started in November. The first phase was the construction of the north mole to provide shelter for the blasting work on the bar. Approximately 1.5 million cubic metres of rock had to be blasted away to create the harbour.

In April 1897 two sailing ships unloaded in the Inner Harbour, and on 4 May 1897, SS *Sultan* was taken through a narrow cut in the rock bar to enter the harbour. The first British mail steamer, RMS *Ormuz*, entered on 13 August 1900. Previously the Royal Mail steamers had gone to Albany because Fremantle was not considered a safe port.

The Perverse Greatness of Sir John Forrest

Sir John Forrest was a great premier of Western Australia who achieved much that he was opposed to. Not only was he opposed to creating a harbour in the mouth of the Swan River, he was philosophically opposed to female suffrage and to federation of the Australian states. Sir John's principal objection to giving women the vote was that taking an interest in politics might impinge on woman's attention to domestic duties — it would not be nice for a man to come home and find that his wife had gone out to a political meeting, he reasoned. But in 1899 he had a sudden conversion on the road to the federation referendum and he rapidly introduced legislation to give the vote to all the women of Western Australia, a wonderfully progressive innovation preceded only in New Zealand, four states of the USA and South Africa. Sir John knew that he'd failed to persuade the male population to vote against federation and hoped for more success with the women. And so it was that Western Australia introduced female suffrage and a majority of the entire adult population were able to vote in favour of the federation that Sir John Forrest didn't want.

It can be argued that most politicians demonstrate the same kind of perverse volition, accomplishing the opposite of their stated intention. Nearly all politicians, from both sides of politics (if there is still a left side of politics), make very clear their urgent desire to work and act for good of all, for the benefit of all Australians, and yet they almost unfailingly produce benefits for the few and for big business. Perhaps one should vote for the party espousing the most manifestly malevolent intentions in the hope that they will achieve the opposite. Perhaps most people do vote on that basis?

All major harbour works were completed by 1903 at a cost of about £1,500,000 which, by major civil engineering standards, was remarkably close to the original estimate of £800,000 made more than a decade earlier. Some features including a planned dry dock had been dropped from the scheme. O'Connor had gone on to work on railways and an especially challenging scheme to pipe water hundreds of miles across country to Kalgoorlie in the Goldfields. He had also committed suicide, apparently driven to a nervous breakdown by attacks in the press and almost constant interruptions to his work when called to give evidence to hostile parliamentary committees of enquiry.

Some members of his family believed that he had been 'sung' to his death by Nyungar people who regarded his engineering alterations to their landscapes as desecration of the Dreamtime creations. It is said that fording the rock bar at the mouth of the Swan was an important rite of passage for young men. It was also a right of passage to all Nyungar men; Nyungar women were obliged to cross the river at the shallows around Heirisson Island.

There may be some basis to the family belief, but Nyungars of both sexes were crossing the river on ferries right back in the 1830s and the first deepening of the river mouth, which must have disrupted the ford, took place more than two decades before C Y O'Connor came to Western Australia. It was Surveyor General John Septimus Roe, appointed chairman of a newly formed Fremantle Harbour Board in 1865, who was responsible for the first project to blast and dredge the river mouth rock bar.

The harbour which O'Connor created has served Fremantle remarkably well. Because he chose to build simple linear wharves, rather than finger jetties sticking out into the water, the basic design has needed no significant change during a century when the average size of ships has increased vastly and cargo handling techniques have shifted from ninety percent muscle and grunt to ninety-nine percent capital leverage. Bulk cargo handling has now moved to Fremantle's so-called Outer Harbour in Cockburn Sound but container shipping, car carriers, livestock carriers and passenger cruise ships still call at Fremantle.

There is a tension between a modern container port requiring acres of flat open space for stacking and handling containers, and an historic port integrated into a community sensitive to its architectural heritage. The Fremantle Harbour Trust, formed in 1903, renamed Fremantle Port Authority in the 1960s and more recently corporatised as Fremantle Port, is now exalted by the new creed of triple bottom lines and striving to earn a place as a well-liked corporate member of the community. But this wasn't always the case. The Harbour Trust would have torn down Fremantle's oldest building, the Round House, and levelled the headland it stands on had community opposition not been fierce and sustained.

As it was, they still removed a substantial chunk of Arthur Head to provide fill for wharf extensions made possible when the old railway bridge was removed in the 1960s. These days, all the old port sheds and the western end of Victoria Quay are heritage listed. Those wharf-side sheds have long been rendered obsolete for cargo handling and storage by the 'container revolution'.

When the harbour first opened, shipping movements were controlled by the harbourmaster and cargo handling was administered by the Railways Department. That arrangement was not a great success.

When the Fremantle Harbour Trust was initially formed it was not keen to be involved in cargo handling, preferring to leave that responsibility in the hands of private enterprise and the free market, which, as we all know, always does a much better and more competitive job of everything. But in those days, things were viewed differently. Having private stevedoring companies operating on a publicly funded wharf was seen as 'allowing development of private monopolies [we now have a duopoly] at public expense.'

Fremantle Chamber of Commerce members were so keen to get their cargoes out of the hands of rapaciously entrepreneurial stevedores that they declared themselves prepared to pay extra to have the Trust take over the responsibility. Curiously, the chairman of the Harbour Trust, Captain Laurie, was also the entrepreneur running the main stevedoring company.

Nevertheless, in 1904, the Trust acceded to commercial pressure and took up wharf-side cargo handling. They later

Victoria Quay, Fremantle Harbour, late 1890s
Courtesy Ross Shardlow

provided warehousing and delivery services, and even the division of consignments and delivery of parcels to multiple customers. They did not handle cargoes on board ships except for the stateships. During most of the twentieth century, stevedoring helped the Trust to run the harbour at a respectable profit and at times it was the only profitable arm of their operations.

The Trust's profits went into the state's consolidated revenue. From time to time there were ideologically driven moves to take stevedoring from the Trust and give it back to private enterprise, but the arrangement stood until the early 1990s. Fremantle was considered a relatively progressive port, albeit in the context that everywhere in Australia modernisation and mechanisation of the handling of general cargo was slow — ships could often off-load to the wharf, using their own cargo handling gear, faster than the cargo could be cleared from the dockside.

Passenger facilities were not very good. The Passenger Terminal, a building with all the architectural distinction of the average airport terminal, was built in time for the 1962 Commonwealth Games held in Perth. It is now preserved as part of the heritage of the many people who came to Fremantle as migrants, but the truth is that by 1962 Boeing 707s were already carrying passengers at close to the speed of sound and the number of people using air travel was increasing rapidly. By the end of the 1960s the first 747s were in the air and the long-distance passenger ships were all becoming cruise liners or converted to sheep ships.

During most of the post-Second World War immigration boom there was no passenger terminal building. Luggage was simply off-loaded to a patch of wharf and passengers queued for Customs and Immigration formalities under the blazing sun or in the rain. Then they could clamber over a poorly designed footbridge to cross the railway lines to Fremantle town wondering, 'What have we come to?' A bronze sculpture, a piece of 'public art' at the end of E-Shed, commemorates a migrant's rain-lashed, baggage encumbered arrival.

Across the road a bronze statue of Charles Yelverton O'Connor stands high on a stone plinth, staring far-sighted and looking rather like I K Brunel, oblivious to the weather and the pigeon shit.

These days Fremantle is primarily a container port and the locus of cargo handling has shifted from Victoria Quay on the left bank to the North Fremantle side where half-a-dozen huge container cranes operate. With the gantry raised, they are the tallest structures in Fremantle, visible above the horizon from miles inland when the rest of Fremantle is still hidden behind the limestone ridge that runs along the coast.

There has been considerable criticism of Australian wharfies and their level of productivity in terms of containers handled per hour. Efficiency is now high by international standards but it was not so good a decade back. Efficient handling of containers is not always possible, no matter how conscientious and well trained the wharfies. Picking up a container is not always a quick and easy operation, as I noticed while rowing slowly down the harbour. I watched an operator trying time after time to get the lifting gear to hook onto a recalcitrant forty-foot (12.2 m) container, trying first gentleness, then dropping the heavy spreader onto the container at different angles of approach. The flippers that position the spreader squarely on the container were flipping up and down until finally achieving a proper grip on all four corners. Perhaps the container's lugs were bent or damaged in some other way.

The quays or wharves in Fremantle Harbour were originally built, like the Swan River bridges, supported by hundreds and hundreds of timber pilings. Very few of those jarrah piles remain — only No. 1 berth on North Quay is still supported by timber piles — but viewed from underneath Victoria Quay is all a jumble of cracking concrete piles, timber chocks and rusting iron patches supporting the timber structure that still underlies the macadam and concrete wharf top.

The relatively small workforce who now operate the container terminal are reasonably well paid and work in reasonable conditions, but wharfies, who have a reputation for militancy and restrictive work practices, were not well treated during much of the twentieth century. There were no toilets or washing facilities for them on Victoria Quay. They were expected to climb down under the wharf and squat on a beam between the piles. Manhandling cargoes such as wheat in two-hundred-pound (90kg) sacks at a rate fast enough to ensure continued employment in the casual labour system was physically destructive. Men broke down after a few years and some of the restrictive practices were devised to provide work for the older men.

I rowed right down to the very seaward end of Victoria Quay where once a low ridge of limestone ended at Whiting Point and extended under the water where the rock bar blocked the harbour, where more recently was Lady Forrest Landing. Now it is the site of the brand new Maritime Museum building, which was still under construction when I rowed in underneath it.

The new museum was being erected primarily to house the 12-metre class yacht *Australia II* that won the America's Cup at Rhode Island back in 1983. *Australia II* was used as a trial horse against newer 12-metre yachts in preparations for the Australian defence of the cup in Fremantle in 1987 (an event that is often blamed for the yuppification of Fremantle, destroying its hard-bitten seaport character). After the Americans had regained the cup, *Australia II* was retired and found a home in B-shed, one of the Victoria Quay wharf-side sheds where a Historic Boats Museum had been opened during the America's Cup defence tizzying-up of Fremantle. B-shed was a less-than-ideal building for any museum displays and particularly unsuitable for a yacht that had a mast over thirty metres tall. The roof truss beams were actually too low to accommodate *Australia II*, even without her mast, so the floor had to be excavated to take the famous winged keel. She sat cramped like a swan stuffed into a small chicken coop, forlorn and dusty without her mast and sails for a year or two, and then went off to a nice new home in Sydney, in a gallery of the new Australian National Maritime Museum specially designed to accommodate her mast.

Some Western Australians were outraged by this appropriation of Western Australia's heritage and history by 'them Easterners' and 'them Federal Politicians over in Canberra'. Among the truly outraged was the leader of the opposition in the Western Australian parliament, Richard Court, himself a keen yachtsman. His outrage was not assuaged by his party's election victory in 1993 and his elevation to the position of premier. In fact, state premiers are more sensitive to the affronts perpetrated by Canberra politicians and bureaucrats than almost anyone in Australia. He maintained the rage and raised the sorry matter from time to time, but probably never entertained any serious expectation of getting his boat back.

If he was able to contain his anger and animosity for long enough to sit through Prime Minister Paul Keating's 'Creative Nation: Commonwealth Cultural Policy' statement in 1994, I imagine he would have listened to Mr Keating talking about 'conserving objects in their original place' and a 'sense of regional identity attached to objects' thinking, 'Good God! What's that fool going to give back to the Aborigines now?' I like to imagine that the offer to return *Australia II* to the community of Fremantle was a carefully calculated surprise and embarrassment devised for Richard Court by a prime minster who was known for a somewhat malicious sense of humour.

Clearly the Crown Jewel of 'Wessss Turn' (as Richard Court liked to enunciate it) — the Crown Jewel of Wesss Turn Australia's Yachting Heritage could not be shorn of her mast and shoved back in a dusty shed again. A building tall enough to display her flying, her soaring rig would be necessary — in Fremantle, where there is a height restriction on buildings to preserve the character of the old gold rush boomtown port; a town full of loony left-wingers furthermore, where there was considerable antipathy towards the razzamatazz of the America's Cup and towards *Australia II*'s original owner, the accident-prone and forgetful entrepreneur Alan Bond. The wail of protest started before Richard Court signalled his acceptance of *Australia II* on behalf of the good citizens of Fremantle. It was obvious that an *Australia II* museum would be very unpopular with the unquiet minority, but the premier had a vision of something more, a vision of a world-class maritime museum facility within a world-class maritime precinct.

Fremantle Council proved to be unimpressed by the offer to declare the wesss turn end of Fremantle a 'Maritime Heritage Precinct'. I naively thought it might be welcomed as a funding opportunity but the Council's Heritage experts explained that the only useful form of precinct for Fremantle would be a precinct without boundaries, reaching out, if I remember correctly, to Bombay where there was a church rather like Fremantle's St John's and to London where the archives of the East India Company have some tenuous connection to the founding of Fremantle. Being very literal minded I tend to think that precincts are defined by their boundaries and at the time I suggested that the heritage professionals were trying to say, 'No, we don't want a precinct' in a manner of such sophistry as to prove that only experts could even try to take part in the discussion.

A committee of experts and 'stakeholders' was established to decide the most appropriate site for the new world-class Maritime Museum in Fremantle. Sadly, after rigorous and sometimes acrimonious deliberations, they came up with the wrong decision and the committee had to be disbanded. A new committee was formed in the hope of identifying a preferred site more in accord with the premier's vision, and I was invited to be a member, wearing the hat of the president of the Maritime Heritage Association. We had meetings, about every month as I remember it, taking up the whole of Tuesday mornings. We were to come up with a preferred site, in a report to be presented to the premier by the end of 1995 so that the museum could be ready for the return of *Australia II* in 1997–98. To guide us towards an appropriate decision, seven of the ten suggested sites were removed from consideration because they were deemed not suitable for various reasons, some more persuasive than others. Some of the stipulated criteria defining a suitable site, such as access to marina facilities and jetties for small craft, turned out to be misleading and were excluded from final assessment criteria, and a system of 'weighted rankings' of the remaining criteria was devised to help channel our thinking.

I was away when the final assessment was formally finalised and I'm not sure that the committee voted as it was supposed to, but the museum has ended up where it was meant to go, albeit four years after *Australia II*'s return and at forty percent greater cost than originally calculated. The site was chosen to be a prominent landmark site, the building an 'entry statement' for Fremantle harbour.

Internally the building provides very exciting spaces, not wholly appropriate for museum displays from the technical, conservation of artefacts point of view, but … nothing will last for ever anyway. Externally the building is interesting rather than inspiring. The curved white shape projecting into a harbour is too obviously reminiscent of Sydney's Opera House for many people.

Architecture seems to have got itself into a bind where designs for large public buildings are either like that Opera House, or boxy and uninspired, or grotesque. The Maritime Museum building is supposed to resemble a capsized sailing skiff (really, I'm not making it up), and I have met someone who actually saw that resemblance without having it pointed out. Others have said it looks like something with a monstrous carapace crawling out of the ground. It depends where you look at it from. Up close, viewed from a small rowing boat, it is spectacular, but not as spectacular as the big new livestock carrier ship *Becrux* that was in Fremantle harbour the day I rowed back down to look at the finished museum from the water.

The designs of car carriers and livestock carriers seem to get more radical, and more astonishing as sculpture every year. At the waterline they are now sharper than any dainty tea clipper or slaver ever was and yet their topsides and superstructure are contrived to flare out to a huge bulging form like an over-inflated zeppelin floating over the water.

Livestock carriers or 'sheep ships' are not widely liked in Fremantle. I can make myself the object of universal loathing at any dinner party by speaking in favour of sheep ships. (I know several other ways of making myself deeply unpopular.) The shipping of live sheep to the Middle East is regarded as inhumane. Only a few years ago the majority of the sheep ships were converted freighters that should have gone to the breakers decades before. Sheep mortality rates were disgracefully high even on voyages when the ships didn't sink or catch fire and incinerate the whole cargo. The latest sheep ships are mostly converted car carriers rather than custom-built ships but they are greatly improved. It's my contention that shipping sheep overseas is no more or less humane than trucking them across country to abattoirs.

What people in Fremantle really object to is seeing the dozens of road trains carrying sheep to the ships, and they also object to the acrid stench of sheep shit and piss from the trucks and the ships. It seems to me that those aspects of the sheep trade are objectionable, but we soft, urban members of the chattering classes (most of whom eat meat) have no right to campaign for the abolition of a trade that provides livelihood to many hard-working farmers and truckers. Nearly four and a half million head of sheep, worth $196 million, sailed from Fremantle in accounting year 2001–02. And anyway, I like the look of the sheep ships.

There is an argument that the sheep ships are bad for Fremantle's tourist trade, especially when the luxury cruise liner *Crystal Rhapsody* ties up immediately astern of the redolent *Al Fahkawi* and the passengers find themselves sitting in a coach returning from a day tour of Perth and the wineries, staring out at road trains full of woolly, shit-smeared passengers on their way to a similar shuffle up the gangway to a very similar shaped ship. It has been suggested that the sheep ship loading should be removed to the Outer Harbour at Kwinana, but a survey of the people of Kwinana shows that they don't share my enthusiasm for sheep ships and think Fremantle should keep them.

Fremantle Port's first concern is the running of an efficient modern port, but, as previously noted, they are also anxious to be seen as good corporate citizens of Fremantle. They serve quite decent wine and finger food at the meetings of the Inner Harbour Community Liaison Committee. Of more general benefit to the community is the accommodation of two traditional boatbuilding businesses in old port buildings on Victoria Quay. Both pay commercial rental but they might have been squeezed out were it not for the goodwill of the Port Authority.

My friend Tup Lahiff has been running Wooden Boat Works since I first moved to Fremantle in 1992. He's genial in a very gruff and direct way and you can be quite direct with him. When I started planning a Swan River exploration I went to see Tup.

'Are you going to give me a boat for this project?' I asked.

'Oh yeah. We'll see what we can do,' he said.

They build some lovely boats at Wooden Boat Works. My problem with borrowing such a boat is that I would be dragging it up and down beaches and around a weir or two which would soon spoil the finish. My own approach to boatbuilding is very different from the Wooden Boat Works ethos. I built the boat, which I now seem to be calling *Earnest*, when I first moved to Fremantle.

(The difficulty with calling the boat Earnest is which pronoun applies? Boats and ships are traditionally feminine in English although all other sexless things have lost their gender. As far as I'm concerned boats can be feminine or they can be masculine, as they are in German; they just shouldn't be 'it'.)

Earnest is a dory-type boat — flat-bottomed with flaring flat sides — the simplest of designs to make from three or four sheets of ply, using the 'stitch and glue' technique of construction. I slapped house paint and paving paint on the plywood. The mast is a Swan River cypress sapling (not taken from the river bank) and it is none-too-straight, but *Earnest* rows and sails adequately.

For a few years I kept *Earnest* padlocked to a fence beside the river so that I could drag him/her down to the water and get under sail in ten minutes whenever I felt the urge. During a time when I was too busy or preoccupied to go for a sail for several months someone must have decided they'd found an unwanted boat — so they cut the padlock and stole her. I thought *Earnest*, who didn't have that name at the time, was lost forever, but many months later a friend told me that she was tied to a mooring, almost completely submerged with the stern smashed. We recovered the wreck and it had sat forsaken and derelict in the back garden for a year or three. I started repairs just before Christmas 2001 thinking that a patched wreck might be the ideal boat for parts of my Swan exploration in the same way that a beaten up old car can be seen as the ideal vehicle for bush-bashing if you can't afford to hire something smarter from Avis.

Chapter 3

THE LOWER SWAN

Back to the river, but not in *Earnest*.

There was no point in using a boat to investigate the river within easy walking distance of Fremantle where I live. It would be senseless to launch the boat, jump in and row a couple of hundred yards, just to drag it back up the beach and see what was there.

So I set off to the nearest stretch of the river on foot. The reach lying between Fremantle's two road traffic bridges — Fremantle Traffic Bridge and Stirling Bridge — was formerly known as Port Irwin (named for Frederick Chidley Irwin, one of the first settlers and commandant of the detachment of the 63rd regiment sent to the Swan River Colony.)

I walked down the grandiose Plympton Steps from Canning Highway which look as if they have been imported from a decrepit Roman villa and once led to the pub of football player Jack Sheedy, the Plympton Hotel. The steps take you down through the tiny

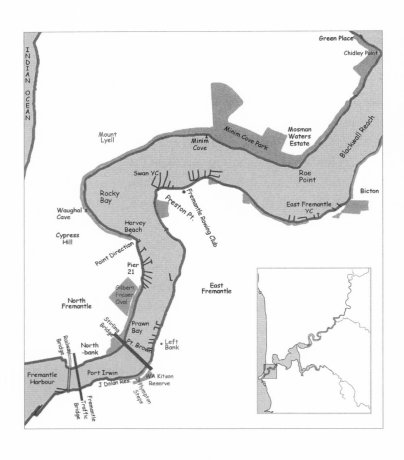

The Lower Swan: Fremantle Harbour to Blackwall Reach

W A Kitson Park to the river and there I turned downstream towards East Street Jetty where ferries embark and disembark passengers for Rottnest Island, whale spotting, and upstream to Perth.

It was my intention to find out the stories behind the naming of the various parks and reserves along the river's banks. W A Kitson Park and J Dolan Park, the two parks that run along the southern bank downstream of Stirling Bridge, are divided by Riverside Road. In fact J Dolan Park is only the narrow strip of grass between the river and Riverside Road. Both parks are named for deceased East Fremantle-based parliamentarians who were devoted to football, though to be fair, Jerry Dolan is also remembered as a much-loved teacher at Beaconsfield primary school.

There used to be commuter ferries to and from Perth which provided much the cheapest way to cruise the river, or to carry you with your bicycle from Fremantle to Perth during the rush hour, but they were under used and the services at hours when commuters would use them have now been withdrawn, though a shuttle service does still run through the middle of the day at an increased fare.

A large sign on the wall of the sheltered passenger waiting area reads:

TRAVELLING TO ROTTNEST
BICYCLE HELMETS
ARE COMPULSORY

Yet another ridiculous imposition one might think, but of course one can travel to Rottnest Island on the ferry without a bicycle helmet, it's just that you are required to wear one if you are riding a bicycle on Rottnest. I don't much like being obliged to wear a bicycle helmet but I suppose the opportunity to impose silly, fluorescent-coloured, new-age fruit bowls on the heads of respectable middle-aged people like me must be a pleasing compensation for long-lunch politicians grown too fat and sedentary to ride a bicycle.

There are actually two East Street jetties. Just downstream of the ferry jetty is a smaller public jetty where private vessels may go alongside to embark or disembark for a period of no more than fifteen minutes. From there it is a few steps to the Fremantle Traffic Bridge.

With convict labour employed on building the raised abutments, the first pile of the old Fremantle Traffic Bridge was driven in 1864 and it was completed in October 1867. It was originally 'camel-backed' so that sailing barges could get under it. Later it was cut down to be a flat-topped bridge for the trams to run over it. I wondered whether any of the original structure remains. There seemed to be evidence of three phases of construction. The three central spans are relatively wide (though only just wide enough for the largest ferries) and their structure is mainly steel. On either side of those central spans there are narrower spans with piers that are a mix of steel joists and timber

The construction of Fremantle Traffic Bridge

beams; then towards each bank are spans with mainly timber structure — I thought they must be the oldest part of the bridge and that perhaps some of the jarrah logs had been there since the nineteenth century.

The Swan River Trust website (a scholarly and detailed resource) describes the bridge as 'Federation style' but the bridge hasn't got the bullnosed verandah roof that the term 'Federation' usually implies in real-estate speak. In truth, the whole thing is as messy and utilitarian a structure as you could devise given a load of gnarly jarrah logs, big bolts and heavy steel brackets, but I was wrong in surmising that three phases of construction and modification are represented by the different constructions. A plaque on the Fremantle side shows that the current bridge was opened by Premier J C Willcock on 15 December 1939.

It certainly wasn't a high-tech bridge in 1939 but it is an impressive monument to the strength and durability of jarrah and other Western Australian timbers. The roadway is laid on top of jarrah planks which are supported by squared timber baulks, and they in turn are supported by jarrah logs that are chained down to steel girders at the top of the massive timber pilings that carry the whole structure. Those piles appear to be a mix of jarrah and other hardwood logs, probably wandoo or tuart, with their swirling grain. There are two hundred and forty timber piles if I counted and calculated correctly — eleven piers each made up of seven piles on the southern side and thirteen more sets of seven on the northern side, plus four central piers each made up of eighteen piles. Most of the piles have roman numerals carefully inscribed, but they aren't sequential numbers: several of the piles are numbered XLVIII. Many of the bolts in the structure have square heads and nuts (rather than the more modern hexagonal heads) and the steel-girder structure of the central spans is riveted together, not welded, showing that it is original.

The fender structures built around the piers of the central spans to protect the piles from damage by collision are popular fishing platforms, especially on weekends. There are plank gangways below the roadway that allow you to walk out from either north or south banks, clambering under diagonal timber braces. Some anglers prefer to climb down to the central piers from the roadway, perhaps because the piers accessible by gangways are a bit redolent with discarded bait and fish guts. Or perhaps because as anglers they are seeking a bit of peace and seclusion. Certainly the gentleman quietly fishing from the central pier was polite but not inclined to have a long chat with me about his choice of pier or what he was hoping to catch.

Climbing out along the gangway I kept expecting to see signs saying DANGER KEEP OFF but the only warnings are about ferries, about the minimum sizes for fish and a bag limit of eight tailer or tailor (*Pomatomus saltatrix*). Fishing from the Fremantle Traffic Bridge is a remnant of the old Swan River experience that so many people who grew up in Perth (or read Tim Winton's

Cloudstreet) remember. Almost everyone who grew up here has reminiscences about fishing,

> … prawning, crabbing and spearing cobblers by torchlight while dolphins blew as they passed you heading up to fish at the Causeway. As kids we did all that and also chased schools of mullet and smelt with tin boomerangs (called kylies and adopted from the NW Aboriginals who fished with wooden and then later, iron boomerangs). We made canoes of corrugated iron with prow and stern folded and beaten flat. My grandmother, who taught me fishing, would take us to Peppermint Grove jetty, the ferry used to pull up there, to catch flathead with green crayfish tail bait.
>
> (Kim Akerman: personal email message)

It was great fun, and slightly secret since there were dangers that parents would not approve of, and today would absolutely forbid if the authorities didn't. But you can still clamber out to the Fremantle bridge piers as long as you allow no fishing gear or part of your body to project when ferries are passing.

On the northern bank, in the shallows on the upstream side of the bridge, you can see the remains of an older bridge or a jetty, and as I went out to the northern pier there were large grey dolphins frolicking or fishing under the bridge.

Many Bridges to Cross

The first Fremantle Road Bridge was started in 1864 and opened without ceremony in October 1867. Before the construction of the bridge, the river was crossed by ferry. The earliest regular ferry operated from a point approximately where the Fremantle Port Authority building now stands. There was another ferry about a kilometre upstream, approximately where Burt Street now is, crossing to a little bay sometimes called Crab Bay which is now buried under container-ship berths 10 and 11 and the container storage area behind the berths. For those travelling overland by horse to Perth or further inland, a horse ferry crossed from Preston Point to Minim Cove another kilometre and a half upstream, avoiding the North Fremantle part of the Perth Road because it twisted through deep sand dunes full of dangerous tree stumps and roots.

Originally the Fremantle Road Bridge was forty-two feet (12.8 m) high above the river at its central spans to allow sailing barges to pass underneath without lowering their masts. It was a structure of several hundred jarrah logs and was sometimes known punningly as the 'Bridge of Styx'.

The first Railway Bridge, which crossed the river from a point close to James Street, was completed in 1880. It too was a timber structure but it was lower than the road bridge and obstructed sailing vessels.

In 1898 a second road bridge was built on the downstream side of the first road bridge. It too had a 'camel-backed' shape but was much lower. In the early twentieth century a new bridge to carry tram lines to North Fremantle was proposed. The low-level bridge was not suitable and it was assumed that the old bridge, which was only being used for pedestrian traffic, was too dilapidated. However, the old bridge was surveyed and found to be still sound; only six of the 319 piles were rotted. So in 1907–9, the old bridge was cut down in height to give it a widened flat roadway for trams. When the work was completed, the low-level bridge, which was already decayed though only a decade old, was removed, leaving part of its North Fremantle end as a landing stage.

The railway bridge collapsed on the North Fremantle side during floods in July 1926, and for the several months it was under repair the trams carried rail passengers to and from North Fremantle.

The current Fremantle Traffic Bridge was opened in December 1939. It has a similar plan to the first road bridge with the four central piers relatively widely spaced to allow river traffic through

and surrounded by protective timber fender structures. It was built downstream of the old bridge, converging with the old bridge towards the North Fremantle bank. Western Australian politicians argued for a more modern steel bridge but a timber bridge was all that the Federal Loans Department would finance. The old bridge was not demolished until 1947 when it was eighty years old. The remains of some of its piles can still be seen beside the Traffic Bridge on the North Fremantle shore.

The new steel railway bridge was built in 1964, just downstream from the Traffic Bridge. This necessitated the realignment of the railway line further to the east through North Fremantle and that realignment allowed expansion of the Port facilities and effectively amputated the south-western part of North Fremantle's residential settlement.

The Traffic Bridge underwent some repair after the Stirling Bridge was opened in 1973 and a more substantial repair in 1991–92. The Stirling Road Bridge is a pre-stressed concrete structure. Whether it's an elegant sweeping creation or an 'isolated and dominant structure over the river' creating 'a 'visual and physical barrier' as the Swan River Trust website says, is a matter of taste. It is a strong contrast to the Fremantle Traffic Bridge. Though it crosses the river at a wider point, it has only four piers in the river. Each pier has only a pair of columns and they are of an interesting geometric shape. Like the Traffic Bridge it is higher on the southern bank than the northern bank. In the case of the Traffic Bridge the difference in height has been achieved by the simple, old fashioned device of varying the height of the piers. The designers of the Stirling Bridge eschewed such a simple expedient, rather as modernist architects avoided simple pitched roofs that water could run off in favour of flat roofs that water runs through. The Stirling Bridge appears to have a fairly simple structure but each of the several moulded concrete sections that join together to form the bridge is tapered in shape, and no two are the same. The section at the southern bank is the deepest, giving the extra elevation at that end of the bridge.

It can be observed that there are surprisingly few bridges, municipal buildings, geographical features, etc. named as memorials to Western Australia's founder and founding Governor, James Stirling. Apart from the Stirling Bridge carrying the Stirling Highway, there is a silted up channel upstream of Garden Hill in Guildford which on old maps is called 'Lt. Gov's ditch'.

Immediately adjacent to the traffic bridge on the northern side the beach and the land behind the beach are scruffy wasteland, fragrant with wild fennel in early autumn. Kwong Alley runs between the embankment that carries the road to the traffic bridge and a disused industrial shed, and at the river end there is a dusty vacant block used as a car park.

Kwong or Quong Alley was originally an informal name for the area between the bridges that was used, until after the Second World War, by the Chinese population for market gardening. Today most of that land is filled by the glitz of the Northbank Estate.

The Northbank development is visually interesting. The postmodern architecture has a sense of fun. The buildings that front the river mix various decorative elements and some contextually appropriate industrial styling. Up close the fun isn't so obvious. The buildings have got names such as Belgravia, York and The Brighton that have stuffy Anglo connotations.

Apartments were marketed as an opportunity to become part of a 'self-contained urban village'. Sadly, things have not developed that way. There seem to be no shops, cafe or any other focus of community. The two retail leases on the north-west side of the riverfront buildings are both real estate agents' offices and neither of them attracted a single visitor while I was mooching around there. On the south-west corner there is an area intended for a restaurant/cafe. It has some river frontage, but rather more car park frontage, and is exposed more to the prevailing south-westerly than to the sun. (Anyone doubting the strength of the south-west wind could look at the windvane on the top of Belgravia Terrace — it wasn't indicating current wind direction, rather it was pointing almost straight upwards, having been bent about 60° askew by a south-westerly gale.)

If the restaurant lease remains vacant, the pleasant sandstone terrace in front provides a lovely spot for a riverside picnic with the possibility of shade or protection from the sea breeze.

Investment in the Northbank project has not gone entirely as projected. Somehow, the developers managed to obtain a waiver on the regulation that would have left a thirty-metre strip along the river to create a riverside reserve. That misguided or foolish waiver was apparently granted on the basis that facilities such as a

Stirling Bridge from the Old Signal Station

public jetty would be provided. Unfortunately, after putting up the buildings, the developers managed to go broke before putting in the infrastructure of community which was to have included the public jetty. There are four concrete boat ramps which predate the development, but they now have no road access.

Fremantle Council, who approved the development, have been obliged to take care of the foreshore which was left scruffy and eroding. I had thought that going broke must have involved some degree of personal tragedy for the developers, but the local newspaper published a letter, apparently without fear of libel action, describing the principal developer as 'laughing all the way to the bank'. It's difficult to summon much sympathy for the developers, and in the circumstances the powers of the Council seem inadequate — if I had dictatorial powers, the Council would have been able to seize the buildings, sell them to raise the cost of the required infrastructure and then disburse the surplus profits as generous grants to rabidly anti-development community groups and ecologically concerned loonies.

Prawn Bay is on the north bank just upstream of Stirling Bridge. Point Brown, where the bridge is built, separates Prawn and Crab bays, though some old maps show Crab Bay a little further downstream. Point Brown is probably named for Peter Brown (Browne or Broun) who was colonial secretary and acting treasurer in the first days of the colony.

The foreshore on the upstream side of Northbank is now very neat and includes a twee-oriental bridge over a token creekette. Currently that part of the shore is remarkably unused compared to the beach and foreshore just the other side of Stirling Bridge — on both upstream and downstream sides of the bridge there are pleasant white sand beaches. Even on a cool blustery weekday morning when I wandered there with my notebook, Prawn Bay was alive with people exercising small lively dogs and launching some of the many dinghies that are kept padlocked to stakes and trees along the foreshore.

Behind the narrow foreshore nature reserve there is a football/cricket oval with a fine grandstand (built in 1900). There were schoolboys in whites playing cricket as I wandered past: a cricket match played on a local green always gives a comfortable feeling of cultural continuity.

John Street, which runs parallel to the river on the other side of the oval, is a lovely street of cottage gardens and attractive old houses, mostly built about the same time as the grandstand. There are also some new houses that integrate well.

I recommend beaching one's boat in the shade under Stirling Bridge and walking through to John Street on the wooded pathway under the abutment that carries the Stirling Highway to the bridge. The pathway brings you to the western end of John Street where numbers 45 and 44, and the large house called Benningfield are outstanding. You can walk along John Street and peek into Passmore Lane and then walk back along the beach.

The boats moored off Prawn Bay are arguably among the most interesting selections of traditional wooden boats on the river. I talked to the owner of *Buffalo*, an auxiliary sailing fishing boat, now fifty years old and built locally. He was going out to wet down her wandoo planked decks, something that has to be done twice a day in hot weather to prevent the decks opening up and leaking.

'Some people play golf or walk the dog for exercise, but I row out to my boat and wet the decks,' he said.

At the upstream end of Prawn Bay I found a little timber jetty that I'd never noticed before. It stands only two or three feet above the water and even at the end, where just one pen provides a berth for a pretty little traditional motor-sailer yacht, the water is less than six feet 183 cm) deep. There is no gate preventing access and no sign saying KEEP OFF, though someone has painted that warning on the deck where it is rotted at the end of the jetty.

The little jetty is almost surrounded by the much larger jetties of the Pier 21 Marina which all do have large signs that read:

WARNING
PRIVATE JETTY
TRESPASSERS WILL
BE PROSECUTED

If the Prawn Bay fleet is an interesting collection, Pier 21 Marina offers as dull a homogeneity of white plastic powerboats as you could wish to ignore.

Pier 21 is built on the site of A E Brown's shipyard where Swan River paddlewheel ferries, Rottnest ferries, schooners and many pearling luggers were built. While access to the Pier 21 jetties is forbidden, there appears to be a public right of way along the foreshore and along a boardwalk in front of the Pier 21 and adjacent buildings.

At the time of writing that right of way was nearly blocked on the upstream side by a building site. Big, boxy, glass buildings were going up to take advantage of the river views. A large hoarding out on the street front side advertising apartments for sale quoted W Somerset Maugham to the effect that, 'It's a funny thing about life; if you refuse to accept anything but the very best, that's what you very often get.' And the buildings illustrate the point. No matter how petulantly anyone refuses to accept them, they will always look anything but the very best.

Next door in Direction Way there is some cheerfully and decorative postmodern and Tuscan-pastiche architecture in a small housing development. The local stone is light honey-coloured limestone and anywhere that honey-coloured limestone is used, the architecture is almost sure to be attractive. It's a large part of the secret of the villages of the Cotswolds in England and parts of Umbria and Tuscany in Italy.

Things get buried and things get dug up. Buried under the Pier 21 development was a property called Buxton. Out in the river, in front of Buxton, where the Pier 21 jetties now stand, a shallow bank with the wonderful name Paddy's Blunder has been removed. The story that led to the naming also seems to be lost along with the original direction in Direction Way that is named for Direction Point which is now somewhere underneath the Water Police offices. Buried with Direction Point was a jetty with the wreck of a timber-hulled river barge, *Eva*, close by.

Tucked in behind the Water Police and under the steep limestone bluff of Cypress Hill is a tiny hidden beach — Harvey Beach — where the patch of white sand is now retained by a stone wall. There is a short jetty and a couple of shaded huts with picnic tables. The shore is steep-to with deep water coming almost right to the retaining wall. It is a lovely secluded spot if there aren't too many kids shiacking and chucking each other off the jetty.

An overgrown path leads along the shore from Harvey Beach and then angles up the scarp of Cypress Hill. A little vertical rock climbing and scrambling up a scree are necessary to get to the top. You arrive right at the very crest of the hill, next to a bench shaded by a curiously pruned tree, and beside the tree is a smart brass plaque on a robust black steel pedestal.

The plaque tells a cautionary tale about the tree.

MOONAH

(*Melaleuca lanceolata*)

Rottnest Island Tea Tree

The Moonah is a hardy coastal species, abundant on Garden and Rottnest Islands, however very few specimens grow on the mainland.

This tree has unfortunately been vandalised, if anyone has information regarding this matter please contact City of Fremantle on 9432 9814.

People damaging trees face prosecution under Local Government by-laws.

Council will consider replacing trees that have been significantly vandalised or poisoned with steel replica trees covered with black netting material until replacement trees grow to a sufficient height.

It is widely believed that people vandalise trees that block the view from their house of the river or the sea. That belief must have been particularly embarrassing for the owners of the brand new house that looks over the pruned moonah tree to the river. It is part of a new housing development and when I was there it stood on its own with no neighbours at whom a finger of blame could be pointed, no matter how innocent of tree vandalism the owners of the house actually were. A good deal of ingenuity and stealth is employed in the war against view-spoiling trees. I was recently at a house-warming party in View Terrace on the opposite side of the river in East Fremantle. View Terrace is too high and steep for trees in public places to be much of an obstruction to its celebrated views over the river to the sea. We were sitting on the balcony some time after midnight, looking down over the less-elevated streets lying between us and the river, when a tree on Preston Point Road suddenly burst into flames, the flames running right up the tree as if petrol or some other volatile fuel had been ignited.

Melaleuca

Readers who are reasonably proficient at identifying native flora will enjoy a scornful sense of superiority when reading my botanical observations. Visitors to Western Australia and those who, like me, know almost nothing can usually get away with identifying most riverside native bushes and trees as melaleuca. There are many melaleuca species with a great range of size, leaf shape, bark colour and bark texture. Some melaleuca have papery bark and anything with papery bark can be confidently identified as such. Flowers similar to those of the bottlebrush are a likely indicator: most bottlebrushy-things are melaleuca species though the most common-or-the-garden red bottlebrush is *Callistemon*.

From the bench beside the moonah tree on the crest of Cypress Hill there is a fine view of Rocky Bay and across to Buckland Hill and Minim Cove. The ridge behind Minim Cove was being terraced and readied for (yet another) housing development. Perhaps this seems perverse, but it struck me as an example of a view that was being improved by a housing development.

Buckland Hill to the west was originally one of seven hills, known to the early English-speaking settlers first as Buckland Downs and then as the Seven Sisters, but the other six hills have been quarried for building stone since the early days of the Swan River Colony.

The really large-scale quarrying was started in the 1890s to provide material for the north and south moles at the mouth of Fremantle harbour. A branch of the railway line was laid to carry the stone to Rous Head (which was itself levelled). Before quarrying, the cliffs between Rocky Bay and Minim Cove had been over a hundred feet (30m) high. After the harbour was completed, stone from the quarries was used for building, most notably for the University of Western Australia's beautiful Crawley campus.

Once the hills were levelled, the area, complete with its branch railway line, was taken up for industrial use. There were the large industrial sheds of the Mount Lyell Mining and Railway Company which later became the Cuming-Smith British Phosphate industrial site. When the area was cleared in the 1960s it became a municipal rubbish dump and when that was recognised as an environmentally insensitive use of the river's banks it was left as a despoiled wasteland with no soil and almost no vegetation. In dry windy weather, scouring clouds of gritty dust blew from it.

Part of the recent improvement to the view of that desolation had been wrought by the facile means of spraying the dust and sand with a rubbery green emulsion, but that was a temporary expedient and limestone terraces were being built and trees transplanted.

One of the Seven Sisters, originally called Ratcliff Hill, has been partially resurrected by creating a small round hill with a lookout gazebo like a nipple on the top. The new hill has been cleverly named Mount Lyell for Sir Charles Lyell, whose seminal three-volume *Principles of Geology* (1830–33) propounding uniformitarian theories ultimately displaced the diluvial geology that William Buckland had supported and popularised, but the name is also a nod to the Mount Lyell Railway and Mining Company whose sheds were built where the hill now stands.

Buckland's diluvial geology was based on the idea that all the world's sedimentary rocks had been laid down during a great flood and that the processes of rock formation had long ago ceased. Geomorphology was therefore the study of erosion. Lyell's uniformitarian geology proposed that the processes of laying down geological layers and their uplifting to form hills and mountains, continued now much as it had done through the past.

The uplifting of Mount Lyell is probably not a good example

Is it a knob or a nipple that forms a steeple to Mount Lyell?

of what he had in mind, but the view from the top is good: you can see the whole of Cockburn Sound from Garden Island to the southern end of Rottnest Island, and the river from Stirling Bridge to Blackwall Reach. To the north there is Buckland Hill and hazy blue in the distance, the scarp of the Darling Ranges.

Buckland, Monument and Mosman

The name Buckland Downs first appears on an 1833 map by J S Roe. Roe was honouring William Buckland, FRS, the first reader of Geology at Oxford, a pious man who went on to become Dean of Westminster. Later the name Buckland Hill was applied to the largest remnant hill of the Buckland Downs and also used to name the whole surrounding area to the north of North Fremantle until the name Mosman Park was gazetted in 1933. By that time the hill's name, in popular toponymy, had become Monument Hill. An obelisk on the top of the hill marking a trigonometric point for cartographic survey was known as 'the monument' though it was really just a trig point.

Changes of name from Buckland Hill to Mosman Park and other various names were proposed a number of times in the decades before Mosman Park was finally accepted, but the relevance of the name Mosman is obscure. R J Yeldon, a local government notable of the early twentieth century, was born in Mosman, Sydney, and he seems to have called the part of the river previously known as Minderup, Samson Bay or Quarryman's Bay, 'Mosman Bay' in memory of his birthplace.

The obelisk/monument remains on the top of Buckland Hill but the monument and the top of the hill have both been moved. A reservoir was built on the hill beside the obelisk in 1924 and a decade later extended so that the obelisk then stood in the middle of the reservoir. More recently, when the reservoir was roofed over in 1983–84, the obelisk was moved forty-eight metres to the south so that it stands clear of the reservoir.

North Fremantle could have been an island. Under the cliffs on the western shore of Rocky Bay (formerly Rocky Cove) the river is only about six hundred metres from the sea. From the top of the cliffs one can see to the beach between the houses. During the nineteenth century, before the limestone bar blocking the mouth of the Swan River was blasted away, there was serious discussion of cutting a channel through to the sea from Rocky Bay and dredging the bay to create a harbour. There is deep water under the cliffs and another dredged channel under the Preston Point shore, but much of the bay is approximately waist deep.

Until recently, upstream-bound ferries followed the channel that runs close under the cliffs of Rocky Bay. The passing ferries set up a wash that broke heavily on the beach. Now that the ferries use the channel that runs close to Preston Point it is possible for boats to anchor on the edge of the other channel, sheltered from the sea breeze, right under the cliffs at Rocky Bay with a mooring line made fast to one of the boulders on the rocky shore. It is quickly becoming a popular spot on weekends and, thanks to the acoustics of the natural amphitheatre of the cliffs, it can sound quite riotous on a sunny Sunday afternoon.

Above the cliffs of Rocky Bay stands the old Soap Factory, now modishly converted to luxury apartments with views of both river and sea. Immediately below the Soap Factory in the limestone cliffs is a reasonably commodious cave whose inhabitants enjoy views of only the river. The lingering smell of wood-fire smoke shows that Garrungup caves have been very recently inhabited. According to Aboriginal history of the river, Waugal (Warrgal, Warrgle, Waakal, Wagyl, Waugyl, Wakyl, etc.) rested in the caves during the process of creating the river. Waugal equates with the rainbow serpent of other Aboriginal peoples' traditions about the creation of the world but is not always envisaged as having a snake-like form.

Most of the shore from Rocky Bay round past Minim Cove is rocky. A new jetty has been built at Minim Cove. Minim Cove is the name of the minuscule sandy cove between Rocky Bay and Roe Point but it is now also the name of a residential land development where there is nothing minimal about the land prices and architecture. Currently there are only a few houses nearing completion, but by the time I've finished bashing the whole story of the river voyages into my orange iMac's keyboard there will be a maze of sandstone terraces and mansions with streets named after local Anglo-Celtic notables winding back and forth between the terraces. It's being done with considerable expense and some taste. The stone mansion nearest to me as I scribbled my notes was being roofed with real slate. The slightly different tones of the hundreds of slates creates an attractive visual texture and lends the building a prestige that ceramic tiles couldn't compete with.

Minim Cove Estate will soon join up with Rocky Bay Estate but to the east it is separated from the next new estate, Mosman Waters (which is very similar in style), by Minim Cove Park. The park is partly natural bushland, once part of Billy Goat Farm, and it provides habitat for bird species including rainbow bee-eaters which have only recently spread to the Perth area.

On the Mosman Waters side there are tended lawns, duck ponds, an adventure playground, a drinking fountain, coin-operated barbecues, benches and tables, and an amazing space-age, TARDIS-like, EXELOO. 'EXELOO facilities are designed for your comfort and safety' the sign says, but reading the list of warnings and instructions left me a little doubtful.

Cleaning Cycle	When unoccupied this toilet is programmed to self clean.
Safety	Small children should be accompanied by an adult. Keep clear of door.
Loiter Alarm	After 10 minutes door will open automatically and alarm will sound (1 minute warning).

| Power Failure | Door can be opened manually. |
| Caution | Floor may be wet after wash cycle. |

From outside the EXELOO doesn't look large enough for anyone on the inside to keep clear of the door, but when you pluck up the courage to press the green button to open the door, you find that just like Dr Who's TARDIS, it is much more spacious internally, and much higher tech than an aircraft loo. There is even an automatic hand washer in case you're too lazy to wash your own hands or don't know how it's done.

Mosman Waters Estate stands on the hill above Roe Point, originally called Berreegup which is thought to mean black water, and named for John Septimus Roe. The hill used to be crowned by the CSR (Colonial Sugar Refineries) sugar refinery, a tall, unashamedly industrial brick building that managed to look dignified and even to enhance the landscape, like a castle perched on a hill hanging over the Rhine. The main thoroughfare of the new estate is called Colonial Gardens but that is the only acknowledgement of the previous history of the land and it will probably be read as a tribute to the architectural style rather than Colonial Sugar Refineries.

From Roe Point to Chidley Point the river runs straight and relatively narrow between steep limestone hills. This is Blackwall Reach, named after the reach of the Thames that it does not resemble in any way. Chidley Point, at the upstream end of the reach, where there is a pleasant sandy beach and a reserve, is named for Captain (later Major and Acting-Governor) Frederick Chidley Irwin, and was originally called Irwin Point.

Just around Chidley Point, looking out over Melville Water, is Green Place Park. The original Green Place was a fine house built by Lawrence Stirling Elliot in 1894. It was named after his family's ancestral home in Sussex, England. The elegant house which ended its days as a mental hospital for women has been demolished and replaced by a private home of some opulence, but the beach and the strip of land behind the beach are a tiny and delightful public park with a small wooden jetty. The park is well watered, carefully tended, and shaded. It is popular for picnics and weddings.

From Green Place, if you don't mind walking up a steep hill, you can gaze on some of the most conspicuously affluent real estate in Perth, including the hugely ostentatious Prix d'amour that the mining magnate (anyone who gets rich from mining is for some reason a magnate, not a baron, mogul or tycoon) the late Lang Hancock built for his wonderfully impenitent Filipino bride, Rose. Rumour has it that she intends to have it demolished and replaced soon which seems a touch prodigal. If she's bored with it, it might be worth trying a change of colour scheme first.

On a Monday morning I bought some of the items on the list of things I would need before setting off in earnest — a thin foam camping mat, a torch, a map showing the Middle and Upper Swan

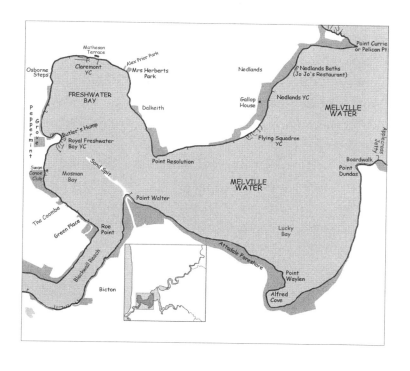

Lower Swan: Blackwall Reach, Freshwater Bay, Melville Water to Point Dundas and Pelican Point

(actually a cycling map), some black pumpernickel bread of the sort that keeps almost indefinitely (though I would never be far from shops).

It wasn't my intention to set off on a try-out overnight voyage until later in the week. I had an appointment in Fremantle for Wednesday morning, so spending Tuesday night away wasn't an option, but having bought the camping gear I thought, 'What's to stop you going now?' and I couldn't think of a convincing reason why not, so I stuffed a few spare clothes (long sleeves and long trousers), a sarong, toothbrush and toothpaste and a few other bits and pieces into a pack, grabbed my little tent and the new sleeping mat and within half an hour I was out on the river running under sail before a pleasant sea breeze.

The shores of Rocky Bay are well worth exploring by boat, rowing very close to the steep, rocky beaches. That way you see only the natural vegetation and the crumbly, honeycombed limestone which in places seems to be melting and dripping. If you are more than a few metres off the shore the whole effect is spoiled by the ribbon of houses that have been built along the top of the cliffs.

Having drifted under those strange cliffs I decided to get going. I set the sail and, keeping out in the middle of the stream to take advantage of the flooding tide, headed upstream to Blackwall Reach. Once through the Reach, I sailed on a beam-reach over towards Claremont, losing the wind under the lee of the shore and rowing gently towards Freshwater Bay.

Almost anywhere along the Swan, in sunny weather, you can see various species of shags (also called darters and cormorants), standing on beaches, on pilings, or on half-tide rocks, drying their wings. The darters particularly hold their wings up to the sun like a black shirt draped over a clothes hanger. Unlike other seabirds and waterfowl they don't exude oil to waterproof their feathers. The wetted feathers enable them to dive and stay under water better than most waterbirds but they're not so good for flying. Up close, darters are strange-looking birds with small pointy heads on the end of long, relatively thick, snake-like necks. They have often been seen as sinister birds.

The name cormorant is said by some to be derived from the Gaelic meaning 'old black (clad) woman', though dictionaries give the derivation as *Corvus marinus* — the Latin for sea raven.

WASHING DAY
by Rita Summers

The cormorants
hang their feathers
out to dry —
black velvet rags
showing threadbare
in the wind.
Like old women

living in the past,
they tend their
tattered finery
with talon fingers
and black
remembering eyes.

The cormorant, like the 'Ancient Mariner's' albatross, has
been a bird of ill omen in literature, and also on the Swan River.
In *Paradise Lost*, Milton sees Satan perched on the Tree of Life
in the form of a cormorant. Perhaps the most widely
remembered cormorants are the those on W W Gibson's
'Flannan Isle'.

And as into the tiny creek
We stole beneath the hanging crag,
We saw three queer, black, ugly birds —
Too big, by far, in my belief,
For cormorant or shag —
Like seamen sitting bolt-upright
Upon a half-tide reef:
But, as we neared, they plunged from sight,
Without a sound, or spurt of white.

Cormorants

There are five types of darter, cormorant or shag to be seen on the Swan:

Darter — *Anhinga melanogaster*
Great Cormorant — *Phalacrocorax carbo*
Pied Cormorant — *Phalacrocorax varius*
Little Pied Cormorant — *Phalacrocorax melanoleucos*
Little Black Cormorant — *Phalacrocorax sulcirostris*

Because they have different colouration in different life phases there seem to be more than five species.

Early in the twentieth century, Douglas Roe, a grandson of John Septimus Roe (first surveyor general of the Swan River Colony) was shooting shags from his parents' launch *Chirritta,* moored off the Peppermint Grove Esplanade, when he accidentally shot his mother Mary, wounding her fatally. Roe Buoy, off the Scotch College Boat Sheds, which is used as a rounding mark for yacht races, commemorates that tragedy and also marks the place where Douglas Roe's ashes were scattered in 1977 after a long and accomplished life.

Another tragedy occurred in the Peppermint Grove corner of Freshwater Bay in the 1920s when Charles Torquil Robinson, aged thirteen, was taken by a shark. His death is the only known shark attack fatality in the river and sharks have not been reported in the river in recent years. Dolphins and seals and, probably on rare occasions, sharks still swim in the river, the dolphins sometimes going many kilometres upstream beyond the city.

Freshwater Bay does not contain fresh water: like all of the Lower Swan it is just about as salty as the sea by the end of a dry summer. One of the explanations of the name that has been offered is that brumbies used to paw (or hoof) holes in the beach sand to find drinkable water. In fact the bay was already known as Fresh Water Bay before any brumbies were there and James Stirling noted the freshwater springs along the northern shores of the bay in 1827.

From Peppermint Grove round to Claremont the steep limestone banks are natural vegetation with an attractive mix of eucalypts and the native conifers (Swan River cypress: *Callitris preissii*), and on that sunny morning the trees were full of parrots squawking to each other and flitting from tree to tree in flashes of colour. There are big weathered boulders along the water's edge, some with stunted trees clinging to them. Though many of the trees and bushes are small they are luxuriant and perhaps the prettiest vegetation on the Lower Swan if you go close enough to enjoy it. That corner of Freshwater Bay is designated a waterski area but it's not on the way to anywhere for river traffic and it is often quiet.

It seems that the land along the shore towards Claremont is all privately owned. Tucked right in a tiny bay, under the sheer cliff, hidden by the bamboo-like reeds that grow all along the banks, there is a little boatshed. Makeshift steps lead down the precipice to it from a house perched a hundred feet above. Launching and retrieving a boat on the rocky beach would not be easy.

A little further along the shore the vegetation on the water's edge was all dusted with something white. Lime? Shag shit? Cement powder? Probably not unrelated to the white powdering, a four-inch water pipe goes up the cliff to a house on the ridge. Presumably it sends up water from a spring. It seemed likely that fine alluvial clay slurry had been sprayed around when a pipe burst. I didn't investigate closely because there were two large signs reading:

PRIVATE PROPERTY
THIS PROPERTY EXTENDS TO HIGH WATER MARK

PLEASE
KEEP OUT
CAMERA SURVEILLANCE

I wonder what they're up to. Camera surveillance for a precipitous patch of rocky scrub seems extravagant and unnecessary. The psychotically suspicious might decide that there must be a secret submarine base or a narcotics factory hidden there.

As you get closer to Claremont, where the banks are a little less steep and the beach a little wider, there are fences just behind the beach to keep out people like me.

J K Jerome, the noted nineteenth-century commentator on riparian (river bank) activities, noted:

The selfishness of the riparian proprietor grows with every year. If those men had their way they would close the … river altogether … They drive posts … and nail huge notice-boards on every tree.

While Jerome's reproach remains valid today, the current 'War on Terror' makes the murder of complete families and wholesale destruction of riverside housing advocated in *Three Men in a Boat* a risky strategy likely to be mistaken for nothing short of terrorism.

Claremont Yacht Club is not quite as ritzy as the Royal Freshwater but it too has plenty of big white plastic motorboats that fortunately hardly ever get used. This is part of the paradox of modern life — mass tourism inevitably spoils the unspoiled places tourists set out to enjoy. If half the powerboats went out on the same day the whole river would be motorboat soup, the state's supply of fuel would be all used up and the erosion of the river banks would become a crisis, but luckily cruising up and down in a powerboat soon becomes too boring to be worth the trouble of throwing off the mooring lines.

They are arrogantly ugly things, those big fat modern powerboats, all power and no subtlety, designed like fat stubby fingers, or some other blokish appendage, jabbing into the river, the sea, or Rottnest Island with maximum intrusive insolence. I do enjoy checking the names of the big motorboats though: they're so original and unassuming: *Key Largo*, *Raconteur*, *The Entertainer*, *Celebrity*, *Ruthless*, *Bloodsport*, *Thrill Seeker*, *Adrenalin Sprint*, *Testosterone Spurt*.

The Claremont shore is nothing special and most of the land behind the beach is private so I sailed down into the corner of Freshwater Bay where Mrs Herberts Park is located. Mrs Herberts (there is no apostrophe: apparently there is a convention that apostrophes are not used in place names) is a very small park, but well appointed with benches, tables, drinking fountain, public loos, adventure playground and barbecues. The turf is soft and well watered and there is plenty of shade from big old peppermint gums and other eucalypts. It's a lovely corner of Freshwater Bay to slip quietly into on a bright weekday morning.

The shallows of the bay are weed beds with thousands of little fish flitting in and out of the clumps of weed, but the weeds also hide rocks so it is best to slip very slowly into the shallows. There was a pair of black swans cruising in the weed beds. For several decades black swans have not bred on the river that was named for them but they are starting to return, a sign that environmental protection and remediation programs are working.

There are two houses that seem to be built with river frontage right inside Mrs Herberts Park — pleasant-looking houses with attractive gardens, but they are definitely private property, walled and fenced about. Claremont local government seems to have had a particularly laissez faire approach to private acquisition and use of river bank land.

It might also seem that they also couldn't care less about public access to the river's banks and deserve a special discredit for their approach to cycle tracks. One could cycle to Perth from Fremantle and back again around the river banks north and south of the river were it not for a disgraceful break in the generally excellent cycleways in Claremont where one is forced onto the main highway or the footpath beside it. Claremont actually appears to celebrate the lost public access to the river. At the end of Osborne Parade, high above the river, there is a little lookout offering a very fine view, and one can read a small brass plaque put there during the 1988 bicentennial celebrations declaring that it is the site of the Osborne Steps that 'gave access to the river'.

Part of the problem is that Claremont is a relatively old settlement and the riverside blocks were created a long time before the district of Claremont had been thought of, when most of the river's banks were completely undeveloped. It is a problem that has been obvious to the people of Claremont for a long time too. Bay View Terrace in Claremont was named for the splendid view of the river at the end of the street but that view has been completely blocked by Matheson's Terrace (now called Bay View Mansions) since the 1890s.

The residential blocks that prompted this diatribe actually

divide a park in two, creating two parks — little Mrs Herberts Park and tiny Alan Prior Park, only half the size. Should you be wondering who Mrs Herbert was, a visit to Claremont Museum, housed in an old school building within Mrs H's Park, is recommended, but it's open only on weekday afternoons. The Freshwater Bay school was the first school opened after the initial three at Fremantle, Perth and Guildford.

There was a community of Pensioner Guards at Freshwater Bay started in the 1850s. Pensioner Guards were recruited from soldiers invalided, recently retired or close to retirement from the army. In Britain their role was similar to that of the National Guard in the United States, maintaining order and preventing mass insurrection. They were also recruited to act as guards or warders on ships carrying convicts out to Australia.

Once they reached the Swan River Colony, usually with their family, they were allocated ten acres of land and a cottage built by convict labour. Typically there was a small riverside block with the cottage on it and the balance of the ten acres (4.05 ha) was some distance away where land was less valuable. (A Pensioner Guard residential block that has not yet been subdivided — April 2002 — can be seen running between John Street and Harvest Street in North Fremantle.) At Freshwater Bay the Pensioner Guards were allocated half acre (.2 ha) blocks along the shore of the bay and nine and a half acre (3.84 ha) lots around Butler's Swamp to the north. The swamp is now Lake Claremont.

The Freshwater Bay community was regarded as very isolated in the 1850s and it seems that the Pensioner Guards sent there were not the most enterprising or lucky. In general they were old soldiers who had remained as privates in the ranks through their long service and some of them were understandably dispirited when the Fremantle Pensioner Guards Staff Officer, Captain Christopher Vaughan Foss, embezzled and lost the life savings they had entrusted to him.

Many of them scraped a living by cutting firewood which sold in Fremantle for fourteen to sixteen shillings per cord. (A cord was supposed to be 128 cubic feet, nearly 3.5 cubic metres. It was usually a cylindrical bundle about five feet diameter and five feet long.) Unfortunately most of the profit went to the owners of the two rival fleets of flats (sailing barges) that carried the firewood to Fremantle. They were ticket-of-leave men — convicts allowed to live and work outside of gaol if they conformed with the conditions of their probation.

One of them, Samuel Brake, employed a significant number of ticket-of-leave men, including three carpenters and a boatbuilder, at Freshwater Bay in 1851. He went on to contract boatbuilding work from the government, and in 1856 built a fairly large and sharp-lined schooner for the coastal trade in Fremantle. The following year he was convicted for the theft of five blocks (pulleys) and a deadeye (a disc of wood with three holes in it) despite evidence that he had been framed. After a year's imprisonment with hard labour he resumed the operation of a successful shipping business.

Because most of the profits from firewood cutting were going to the flat owners, Captain John Bruce, commander of the Pensioner Guards, put up £30 to buy a flat for three Pensioner Guards to operate in partnership. Rather than carrying firewood cut by their comrades, they built up a business carrying limestone from a quarry on Point Resolution. Their main charterer was a Fremantle innkeeper and they used to stop for a few drinks at his inn after each delivery. One of the men negotiated an arrangement whereby he seemed to be buying most of the drinks for the three of them, but the drinks were actually charged against the freights earned by the flat. When his partners understood what had been going on the partnership disintegrated and the flat fell into disuse.

Another Pensioner Guard, John Day, bought a flat to carry his own firewood, but drowned along with his crew, a ticket-of-leave convict called Honeychurch, in 1852 when the flat swamped in stormy weather.

Almost next door to Mrs Herbert's old schoolhouse there is a house that was built for a colourful entrepreneur named Alan Bond in 1977. It is very much grander than the schoolhouse or the tea-chest-with-cat-flaps-at-either-end that I call my Fremantle Heritage Cottage, but that's not saying much at all. In fact Mr Bond's old house is nothing particularly spectacular to look at in that affluent riverside suburb. If you want to identify it you will need to buy a copy of the Captain Cook Cruises Souvenir Guide 'The Scenic Swan River from Perth to Fremantle' that gloatingly lists most of the celebrity-millionaires' residences to be seen from the river and provides photographs and a map for identification. I never cruise the river without my copy.

Rowing slowly under the Dalkeith shore from Mrs Herberts Park to Point Resolution one can inspect the styles of architecture chosen by those who can choose location, location, location. Some of it is pleasing, some less than pleasing. There are one or two modest 1960s brick bungalows still standing; there is a very striking example of sculptured late-modernist, and there are still one or two vacant blocks towards Point Resolution Reserve.

The Reserve is mostly native vegetation when seen from the river and very lovely it is too. One could walk along the beach from Claremont around Point Resolution and eastwards to Beaton Park, and in fact walk all the way round to Matilda Bay, either on the beach or in foreshore parks (skirting a couple of yacht clubs) were it not for one property at the western end of Jutland Parade (called 'Millionaires Row' in the Captain Cook Guide) which projects a lawn on reclaimed ground, fenced with cyclone wire topped with barbed wire, into the river. According to the Captain Cook Guide, the property was originally built for Michael Edgely, who is apparently 'a well known Australian entrepreneur', and it has had several owners since Mr Edgely moved to Sydney.

Presumably Jutland Parade was named for the Battle of Jutland (the biggest naval battle of the First World War) but its original name, Hardman Road, might still be appropriate.

Halfway along the Millionaires Row of glittering Jutland Parade properties built over the river on the low limestone cliffs is a heart-meltingly lovely Italianate mansion with pastel green shutters and terraced gardens: a piece of elegance and perfection in my eye. I'd love to go to a party there to munch canapés and slurp tureen-size glasses of crisp cold chablis. I had assumed the house was built by an established family of particularly good taste at least a century ago, but if your eyes are good and you are sailing close to the shore, you will be able to read the date of construction on a badge centred high on the front of the house — it was built in 1990.

The shore from Point Resolution to Point Currie is not easily investigated by boat. Part of it is a lee shore in both a south-westerly and a south-easterly breeze — the predominant wind directions — and much of the shore is concrete and stone embankments with no beach. Furthermore there are extensive shallows to the west of the Perth Flying Squadron Yacht Club and to the south of Nedlands jetty. The foreshore along the long Dalkeith shore is manicured lawn with plenty of trees and bushes in most places.

The Perth Flying Squadron Yacht Club is so named because early in the twentieth century the club, like the Sydney Flying Squadron, raced the 18-foot skiffs that carried a huge press of sail and almost flew over the water. In the days when the club was primarily a sailing boat club, they had an attractive timber clubhouse at the foot of William Street in Perth. In 1962 they moved to the current site on the Dalkeith shore near Armstrong Spit. The club has been expanding, adding more marina pens, mostly for large, white, plastic motorboats with flying bridges. The most recently added jetties are much the ugliest, and if the club is allowed to expand any more it will constitute a significant visual blight on the Dalkeith-Nedlands shore.

While the Flying Squadron is growing into an ugly monster, Nedlands Yacht Club is surprisingly small and has only a few pens berthing small yachts.

The nice old building up behind Nedlands Yacht Club is Gallop House. James Gallop took over part of the property first selected by Adam Armstrong, who had been manager of the Earl of Dalkeith's estate in Scotland, and named the selection after his former employer. James Gallop ran a notably successful business growing fruit and vegetables.

A bit further north is Nedlands Jetty and the former Nedlands Baths, now Jo Jo's Café and Restaurant, built on piles over the water. There are plenty of marina pens in front of Jo Jo's, few of them used. As I rowed past, a hooded tern, three shags and two big pelicans were preening themselves and looking dignified and proprietorial, standing on the tall timber piles that separate the pens at the southern end of the little marina.

In one of the pens was my favorite Swan River traditional sailing boat, *Mafalda*. She was built as a sailing fishing boat in the 1920s by Robin Gourley of East Fremantle. Along with seven or eight sisters built by Gourley she has a unique shape and structure to her stern, sometimes called a 'cartwheel transom'. Technically it's a very sharp form of round tuck stern, and very elegant indeed.

The Nedlands shore is a concrete embankment and a broad, flat lawn with not a tree to spoil the river views of Nedlands' residents. Obviously it would not be worth trying to grow trees since Nedlands residents could easily afford to have them vandalised while they lie innocently in their opulently appointed boudoirs.

After the carefully manicured shores of Dalkeith and the short but singularly dull Nedlands shore, Matilda Bay Reserve on Pelican Point is a welcome patch of natural vegetation. The Point has long been known as Pelican Point (and longer known as Bootanup) but was also called Point Currie, while the bank of sand that extends from Pelican Point was called Currie's Spit.

The long shallow Currie's Spit should be given a wide berth, particularly in windy weather. It was there that I very nearly swamped the three-man wherry we used in 1997 for a re-enactment on the three-hundredth anniversary of de Vlamingh's expedition up the Swan.

Capt. Mark John Currie

First Harbourmaster of the Swan River Colony, Currie, had sailed in Australian waters as commander of HM Sloop *Satellite* during 1822–23 when Philip Parker King and J S Roe were completing their surveys. No doubt Currie was a fine officer who served his country well, but I have only been able to find unfortunate and whimsical details of his career at Swan River. When *Parmelia*, carrying the first settlers, arrived in Gage Roads on 2 June 1829, the intended harbourmaster of the new colony went ahead in a boat to survey the passage into Cockburn Sound. Unfortunately he didn't locate a dangerous bank and *Parmelia* went aground. She remained aground for eighteen hours at considerable risk and sustained significant damage. Most of the passengers were trans-shipped to HMS *Challenger* and some to Carnac Island.

Then on 25 June, Captain Currie led an expedition up the Swan River intending to investigate the Canning River, but unfortunately, on the first day, one of his party shot him in the head, curtailing the expedition. Currie's injuries were not fatal. The next day Lt. James Henry led a different party on a more successful outing to find the source of the Canning.

Currie was harbourmaster for only a few months. He was appointed Commissioner of Counsel and Audit, and Captain Daniel Scott was appointed assistant harbourmaster and took over the harbourmaster's duties.

The Currie's property, Redcliffe, included the area now known as the Redcliffe Industrial Estate and the northern part of Perth Airport. George Fletcher Moore used to stop there for convivial parties on Friday nights when he was walking home to the Swan

Valley after a week presiding in court in Perth, but that was probably after the Curries had left the colony.

Like Stirling and a number of other settlers, Currie remained a naval officer on half-pay while living in Western Australia. He returned to an active-service naval career and ended it as an admiral. Were the Curries a bit obtuse? The ship *Cleopatra* brought news of George IV's death in November 1830, yet Mrs Jane Currie's diary for 5th March 1831 records, 'Ship *Eliza* ... brought news of King George's death ...' She was a good watercolourist.

Around the other side of Currie Point, in Matilda Bay, are the Matilda Bay Sailing Club and the Royal Perth Yacht Club, the club that once won the America's Cup. A few years ago I was taken to an excellent lunch at the RPYC. I could probably get a regular crew position on a RPYC boat if I wanted, but it's rather a long way from Fremantle, I'd have difficulty keeping clean the spotless white shirt and shorts that crew must wear, and I probably wouldn't fit in.

From the yacht club all the way round to Mounts Bay Road the beach is sandy and the foreshore is grassy and shaded. It is very popular with families and with students from the nearby University of Western Australia for picnics. It is the archetypal Swan River family picnic location evoked in Tim Winton's wonderful *Cloudstreet*, a novel in which the river is the central character and the source of redemption:

On the long grassy bank beneath the peppermint trees and the cavernous roots of the Moreton Bay figs, they lay blankets and white tablecloths which break up in the filtered sunlight and they sprawl …

The university clock chimes and a rowing team slides past with the sun in its eyes. A formation of pelicans rises bigbodied from the water, the sweet coppery water where the jellyfish float and the blowfish bloat …

But here, here by the river, the beautiful, the beautiful the river …

Beyond that grassy picnic shore, where Mounts Bay Road runs along the foreshore to the Narrows, it is not much fun for boating. Apart from the constant noise of the traffic (which is far more annoying in a boat than it is on a bicycle), the stone embankments don't encourage landing, and there's a lot of chop and wash from river traffic heading to and from the Narrows that leads to Perth Water. It's a shore that is better viewed from the cyclepath, or better still, I would imagine, sweeping smoothly around the curves of Mounts Bay Road in an open-top vintage Rolls Royce, but I haven't got one.

The only building along the shore under Mount Eliza and Kings Park is the former Swan Brewery. The Swan Brewery Development has a jetty and landing place that could be used to visit the restaurants and cafes, but you'd need good fenders to

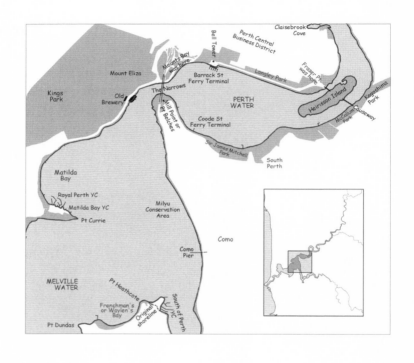

*Lower Swan: Melville Water above Point Dundas
and Perth Water*

protect the varnished rails of your opulently appointed motor yacht. The development has preserved the style of the old brewery building but it's no longer possible to determine which parts are based on the original structure and which bits are new. The brewery was built on the site of a spring which has sacred significance for the Swan River Nyungar people and is still accessible on the northern side of the road. There has been considerable debate and anger about the extension of the old brewery building as a residential development on that sacred site. Perhaps that is why the building seems to have been expunged from Perth UBD road maps.

Noongar, Nyoongar, Nyungar

The Aboriginal people of the Swan and Canning River areas identify themselves as Noongar, Nyoongar, Nyungar or Nungar. There are also variant spellings with an 'ah' ending. All the spellings are accepted and Yoongar has also been used. Sometimes more than one spelling is used in a single document, presumably in support of Mark Twain's dictum that anyone who can only think of one way to spell a word lacks imagination.

Nyungar and cognates is the word meaning 'person' or 'human being' in the closely related languages that were spoken throughout south-western Australia. The peoples of that language group can be called the Bibulmun Nation or Bibulmun linguistic group, or called Nyungar. Anthropologically the Nyungar can be distinguished from neighbouring peoples by the non-practice of circumcision as well as their language.

The Whadjug or Whadjuk Nyungar are the people of the land south of the Swan River, while the Juet Nyungar are the people whose land is to the north. Other ethnic and clan divisions are recognised. At the time of white settlement the Morro or Mooro Nyungar were the people of the Upper Swan area and to the north of Perth; the Beelu Nyungar were the people of the land between the Canning River and Helena River; and the Beeliar Nyungar were from the Canning River to the sea. Swan River Nyungar people can be called Darbalyung Nyungar — Derbal Naran being the Nyungar name of the Middle and Upper Swan River, Derbal Yerigan or Yarragan is the Lower Swan.

Upstream from the Narrows, where two huge road bridges carry the Kwinana Freeway over the river and into the city, Mounts Bay Road follows the shore of Mounts Bay, but Mounts Bay isn't there any more, it has been reclaimed. (Why do we describe land created by filling in a river or the sea as 'reclaimed', as if the water had stolen it from us? It's like forestry industries 'recovering' timber from the trees they cut down.) Anyway, Mounts Bay is now a pleasant expanse of parkland ornamented by ponds and patches of wetland habitat with freeways swirling through it and flyovers flying over it.

During the last sitting days before the long Christmas recess in December 1963, the Brand Liberal government rushed through the bill to allow the reclamation of the nineteen acres (7.7 ha) that were Mounts Bay for the Mitchell Freeway and the Kwinana Freeway to meet each other and a tangle of other roads to loop around them. There were many voices raised in dissent. Big, overflowing protest meetings were held and motions condemning and demanding were carried unanimously, but the government, as always, knew what was in the best interest of Western Australians and courageously favoured progress over silly sentiment.

Among the community groups that had organised opposition to the loss of Mounts Bay and the high-handed process that had decreed it was the Women's Services Guilds of Western Australia, an organisation that had included among its many worthy causes the conservation of the Swan River since the 1940s and Kings Park since Sir John Forrest had been a pro-development chairman of the Kings Park Board.

On a cold and showery 20 April 1964, the first truckload of sand was dumped in the river and the eighty-nine year old life vice-president of the Women's Services Guilds, Bessie Rischbieth, waded into the river to stand in front of the bulldozers. Her protest attracted plenty of attention: a photograph appeared on the front page of the *Daily News*, but nothing could save Mounts Bay. Four days later another photograph showed the river apparently covered with icefloes, actually a scum of limestone dust from the massive reclamation works.

Bessie Rischbieth, who was eminently accompanied by R M Forrest and C P Lefroy in her protest, was herself a widely revered and charismatic woman who had been a prominent member of Perth society since the beginning of the twentieth century. Her manner was usually poised and composed but she was genuinely angry in 1964:

> There are women on the warpath
> And we mean to make it plain,
> That dictatorial parties
> Won't get our votes again!

Three years later, in one of the many obituary pieces *in memoriam*, Mary Ferber observed 'She was the nearest thing to a resident queen that WA would ever know.' Premier Brand remembered Bessie Rischbieth as 'forthright' and echoing two of Voltaire's aphorisms upheld her right to express her views (on the understanding that she was dead).

Bessie Rischbieth, grand lady of the Swan

Bessie Rischbieth came to Western Australia with her husband Henry Wills Rischbieth in 1898, and for much of the next seventy-one years her home was Unala, a fine house looking over the Swan from View Street in Peppermint Grove. She was beautiful, elegant and wealthy, persuasive and energetic, a paradigm of femininity and a resolute leader of the feminist struggle for equality. She campaigned not only against inequality of sexes but for equality and justice for all humankind, for citizenship and equality for Aborigines, against all racial discrimination, for the interests of children, and, among other things, against compulsory physical examination of sex workers. She believed devoutly in the value of international organisations — the League of Nations and its successor the United Nations — and was scrupulously non-partisan in her approach to politics.

She was motivated, at least in part, by theosophist beliefs. Theosophists espoused religious and spiritual beliefs without affiliation to one particular religion and looked to the improvement of all humankind through enlightenment and elevation to higher planes of existence. The theosophist believed that the truest knowledge came not through reason or the senses, but through a direct communion of the soul with divine reality. They'd be a very successful branch of New Ageism had they not thought indulgence in sex coarsened the spirit and identified the spiritual master and next World Teacher who would lead us to the Coming Age and the seeding of the Sixth Root Race in a ten-year-old Indian boy, Krishnamurti Jiddhu. Krishnamurti grew up to repudiate all the theosophist claims made on his behalf in 1931.

Bessie Rischbieth and Edith Cowan were both influenced by theosophy in the early twentieth century. In 1909 when Bessie returned from a visit to England (where she had met leading suffragettes) she and Edith Cowan both became foundation vice-presidents of the Women's Services Guild, a body affiliated with other women's organisations and promoting theosophist ideals including service to humankind. The Guild (later 'Guilds', representing several branches) for more than half a century promoted feminist interests and actively pursued a range of humanitarian causes. Bessie Rischbieth served for many years as President of the WSG and also as President of the Australian Federation of Women's Societies, a role that brought her into conflict with Edith Cowan, who had defected and become president of a rival National Council of Women (WA). It was a spiteful and one-sided conflict or feud that reflected no credit on Edith Cowan. In 1924 there were some attempts to broker a reconciliation, probably because the argy-bargy was likely to harm Edith Cowan's chances of re-election to her West Perth seat in the Western Australian parliament. She did indeed lose her seat but she was tough and unprincipled enough for party politics and went on to become the first woman to represent Western Australia in federal parliament.

Out on Perth Water the view back to Mount Eliza has always struck me as unattractive, but it was only after sailing Perth Water several times that I realised what was wrong. I'm sorry to say that, for me, Mount Eliza is wrecked by the big brutal plinth and obelisk of the Cenotaph Memorial to the Western Australian men and women who fell in the First World War. I certainly don't intend any disrespect towards those men and women who obviously weren't consulted about the location or design of their memorial. Nor any dishonour to those who attend ceremonies of remembrance there, but because of the square bulk of the plinth it is an ugly monument seen from below, and it violently disrupts the rounded, irregular shape of the wooded hill.

The conical campanile standing erect on the Perth foreshore

None of the Perth shore is really suitable for exploration by small boat. The dredged channel where the ferries run is close to the shore and Langley Park is just a wide expanse of flat lawn, more like an airfield than a park. I always keep well away, out in the middle or towards the left bank when traversing Perth Water. But Perth's history is very much built on the river. The site for the Swan River Colony's capital city was selected from a number of possible riverside locations as being the one closest to midway between Fremantle on the coast and the agriculturally promising Upper Swan land around Guildford. There would have been no colony had the river not allowed Captain James Stirling to explore the hinterland and provided a highway for bringing in settlers and their equipment.

There have been boats ferrying people to and from the vicinity of the current Barrack Street jetties since Perth was established in 1829. For a reason I have not been able to discover, Barrack Street Jetty was popularly known as King Cole's Jetty in the mid-nineteenth century. The first substantial Perth jetty, South Jetty, was built in 1854 but the water at the end was not deep enough for the steam ferry *Les Trois Amis*. At that time the foreshore was still where the Esplanade now runs. The road called the Esplanade was earlier called Bazaar Street and then Bazaar Terrace. There was a market there with produce mostly brought in by boat. Reclamation of the foreshore started in the 1880s.

River ferries have declined in importance since the railway was opened in 1880, but they are enjoying a resurgence and the Ferry Terminus at Barrack Street has been smartened up at significant expense in recent years, most notably by the construction of the copper and glass belltower, a sculpturesque needle that houses a set of bells presented in 1987 by the City of London to the City of Perth to commemorate Australia's bicentenary of first settlement by the British.

The bells languished with no home for more than a decade until the last term of Richard Court's government when an ambitious erection was planned. In Jakarta, the tall, somewhat phallic, Independence Monument put up just before President Sukarno was overthrown is known as 'Sukarno's last erection'. If the belltower becomes known as Court's terminal tumescence the surrounding ornamental ponds should always be associated with the drug squad officer who, returning from a Christmas Party on a Rottnest Island ferry, perhaps confused by the new layout of the precinct, mistook a pond for a toilet.

Although the Perth shore is not very inviting for boating, there is a pleasant and popular walking and cycling track all along the foreshore. As I've noted, there are parts of the right bank in the smart suburbs of Mosman Park, Peppermint Grove, Dalkeith and especially Claremont where private property keeps pedestrians and cyclists from the river. But from Beaton Park in Dalkeith one can walk the right bank all the way round Point Currie, Matilda Bay, past the city and then on around East Perth and Claisebrook. There is a short break in river access in Mount Lawley but from Bardon Park you can walk (but not cycle) right around the Maylands Peninsula on the edge of the golf course and all the way to Ashfield without interruption.

I had sailed *Earnest* all the way from Claremont with a fine breeze, not stopping to put ashore anywhere. Around the inland side of the Burswood peninsula we were becalmed under the lee of the river bank and teased by puffs from all directions so I rowed for a while, then sailed again down Belmont or Rivervale Reach. Off Maylands slipway I furled the sail and stowed the mast.

The afternoon was growing late when I passed under the Garratt Road Bridge. It is a nice old bridge, actually a pair of bridges, constructed almost entirely of rough finished jarrah logs. The structure is all about practicality with no pretension to styling and would have been considered low-tech in China two thousand years ago, but the big-scale chunky carpentry is interesting. Several other Swan bridges have the same structure.

Above the Garratt Road Bridge is the part of the river most used by rowers and canoeists. Speeding up and down the river, in comparison to my rate of progress, were coxless fours, individual and double sculls, and various types of racing canoe. I couldn't help noticing that more than fifty percent of the rowers were attractive and friendly young women, many of whom smiled and said hello. (Is rowing good for firming breasts?) Solo male canoeists tend to be more competitive, paddling fast and breathing hard through gritted teeth as they slash past.

Ron Courtney Island, on a sharp bend in the river between the suburbs of Ashfield to the north and Ascot to the south, was my main objective on my first overnight outing. It is an artificial island, created in 1968 when a channel was cut to reduce erosion where the river turns sharply against the low cliffs on the Ashfield side.

I was pleased to find that the island is not swampy and has flat grassy spaces where one might discreetly pitch a small tent after dark and slip away at dawn with little risk of exciting any trouble from the authorities. One could easily camp overnight in many places along the banks of the Swan above Perth — the Peninsula Golf Course has particularly soft-looking green turf — but on an island, no drunk, no fugitive homicide, no stray-dog-looking-for-something-to-piss-on, or courting couple from the Police Academy is likely to happen upon you.

I didn't stop at the island but rowed on past, glad to follow the river turning to the north and escape the glare of the setting sun burning in my eyes. I rowed on into the approaching dusk. It was growing dark as I passed the mouth of the Helena River and almost completely dark when I sighted the West Swan Road Bridge from Guildford Reach. It was my intention that I would not investigate the river above the bridge, which I had decided was the start of the Upper Swan, until I had done the northern banks of the lower and middle river fairly thoroughly.

I sat quietly in the middle of the river for a few minutes, looking through the trees to the lights of Guildford, and then turned around and rowed gently against the fading breeze back to Point Reserve, which is not on any point but is in Bassendean on the western bank of the river opposite Kings Meadow Oval and the confluence of the Helena River.

Point Reserve is well appointed with powerful floodlights, good benches and tables, soft turf, public lavatories and a sandy beach between two jetties. Sitting at a well-lit table I ate a late dinner of ryebread, cheese and tomatoes while writing notes and slurping wine from a plastic bottle. Later I read for a while, and then at about 9.30 I got back in the boat and rowed back downstream to Ron C. Island. There I pitched the inner tent as a mosquito net, not bothering with the fly since it was an entirely cloudless night after a cloudless afternoon. I was pleasantly surprised not to have needed to apply any mosquito repellent at sunset; I hadn't been troubled by mosquitoes at all.

Everything was quiet on the island. There was silence in Garvey Park on the Ascot shore and on the Ashfield shore too, but Ron Courtney Island is only about a kilometre from the Great Eastern Highway, the Tonkin Highway and Guildford Road, and only a couple of kilometres from the domestic airport where maintenance engineers like to rev aircraft engines at night. On a still night the traffic noise carries loud and clear.

Nevertheless, I slept reasonably well until about one o'clock when I woke absolutely freezing. I was amazed at how cold it was. I got the outer fly of the tent and wrapped myself in it and pulled it over my head. Fortunately it has a reflective silver coating which traps heat (and condensation) very effectively so I survived the night which turned out to be the coldest March night since the glaciers retreated. A thin foam mat does not provide much comfort. I woke needing to roll over every half-hour and thought I was hardly sleeping at all, but it was already light when an easterly wind rustling the tent woke me.

Early morning canoeists were already puffing past as I rolled up the tent and brushed my teeth. (On later voyages I learned that the keenest canoeists take to the water well before the first glimmer of dawn on fine autumn and winter mornings.)

Just after six o'clock I was under way again, and I passed Maylands slip about an hour later by which time there were lots of rowers and canoeists on the river, many of them friendly and handsome.

On the wide part of the river between Belmont and the southeast corner of the Maylands peninsula, I met several eights and some coxless fours from Trinity College, out for an early morning practice. I tried to join in by calling to a passing crew 'Right boys, take your time from me.' They laughed and offered me a race.

Early morning exercise on the river for schoolboys is laudable, but if I lived in one of the houses or blocks of flats overlooking that reach of the river, and I owned a rifle, I'd be very tempted to take pot shots at their coaches who hoon up and down the river bellowing through megaphones over the roar of their outboard motors. One of them, probably a prefect rather than a teacher, was swearing and screaming almost hysterically: 'Keeps your heads up. Up. Headsupoarsclosetothewater, close to the, not that much Mark, Mark, fuck's sake Mark, not so much …'

Coaches weren't always so irritating. When I rowed for Cambridge before The War, our coach followed us along the muddy bank on a bicycle shouting against the freezing wind through his speaking trumpet when he thought he had got within range. We could seldom hear a word he said but we rowed like men possessed in the knowledge that if we went fast enough we were likely to see him and his bike swerve from the slippery mud into the icy waters.

It seems to me that these days sporting coaches are almost exclusively red-faced balding men with no talent for anything other than shouting. If I go bald I might be able to take it up myself.

By the time I'd reached the other end of the Belmont Reach in my shambling, uncoached rowing style, the proper rowers and their apoplectic coaches had disappeared. I saw a man launch a small motorboat, park his car and then set off downstream at a very sensible speed, only slowly gaining on me even when he was steering in a straight line rather than rooting around in the bow and letting the boat steer itself in wide circles. As he drew alongside he was obviously keen to say hello and have a chat.

'Good exercise?' he asked.

He had only recently bought his second-hand aluminium dinghy which was jauntily painted red and white. There was a pair of oars painted blue. He stopped the elderly Johnson outboard motor and tried rowing but he obviously hadn't done it before and his oars had those silly rubber sleeves that fit into the rowlocks so that you can't manipulate them properly. We didn't row very far in company. With the motor idling he kept pace with me.

'How far you going?' he asked.

'Fremantle.'

'Fremantle!?'

'Insha'allah,' I added, partly out of fatalism — I subscribe to Alan Villiers' view that no vessel is ever bound for anywhere until it actually gets there — and partly fishing for a response.

'What you say?'

'Insha'allah.'

'You are a Muslim? I'm a Muslim.'

Umar was from Jakarta and was probably a little surprised to find a man rowing a scruffy sampan down an Australian river who spoke reasonably fluent Indonesian. We chatted for a while and then he went ahead, intending to visit his uncle who lived near the river in Dalkeith, he said. I hope he gets a lot of enjoyment from his boat, which he handled in a gentle and respectful way.

After Umar had motored ahead I stopped for breakfast opposite Maylands Yacht Club then rowed on to pass Heirisson Island, three hours from Ron Courtney Island. By that time I felt I deserved a rest so I stepped the mast, shipped the rudder and set sail, although there was scarcely enough breeze to ruffle the water.

It took nearly an hour to drift down Perth Water. I rowed through the Narrows and out towards Pelican Point against a slowly strengthening sea breeze. At about eleven I set sail again and stood southwards. I tacked off Point Dundas, tacked back again off Nedlands Yacht Club, again off Point Waylen, Attadale, and weathered Point Resolution thanks to a wind shift, then tacked back towards the Point Walter sandspit for the portage across the lowest point of the spit.

Point Walter spit is a full kilometre long so it's well worth going over it rather than right around it when tacking to windward or rowing. Back in the 1830s and 40s there was a canal cut through the landward end of the spit to shorten the voyage between Fremantle and Perth. Alas, any sign of the canal has long disappeared.

I tacked up Blackwall Reach and beached the boat under the shelter of a big old peppermint gum, where I ate a bit of ryebread and sweaty cheese and enjoyed the last slurp of red wine from the plastic Coca-Cola bottle I decant cask wine into for boating outings or space shuttle flights.

Then I got under way again and sailed the rest of the way back to North Fremantle. Actually I dropped the sail and rowed the last half kilometre. A small powerboatful of beery louts jeered at me as they went past.

'Yerr. Rowin'. Get some technology mate.'

Why are they so anxious to convert everyone to motorboating? You'd think they invented the internal combustion engine themselves. People in motorboats can be very unkind towards those in rowing boats or in homemade sailing boats, especially children who like to call out, 'Hello Mr Tablecloth Sail' just because my sail happens to be a blue gingham pattern.

The plywood centreboard had swollen and was jamming in the centreboard case, and the centreboard case was leaking slightly because of my application of brute force to the problem, but overall it had been a satisfying and successful outing. I'd found that Ron Courtney Island would make a good base for the Middle Swan. My little boat, that I was beginning to think of calling 'Earnest' so that I could set off in Earnest, had proved capable of tacking all the way up Melville Water and to Fremantle against the sea breeze. I'd averaged more than four kilometres per hour while rowing. I was definitely going to need a sleeping-bag but, all in all, although my Swan River voyaging might be a silly idea, it wasn't completely daft.

Ferries on the Swan and Canning Rivers

The Swan River was the main highway from Fremantle to the inland settlements around Perth and Guildford in the early days of the Swan River Colony. James C Smith was the Government Boatbuilder who came to the colony with the first settlers on the *Parmelia*. W H Edwards, another boatbuilder, arrived a few months later in October 1829.

Probably the most renowned Swan River boatbuilding dynasty was started by the arrival of Thomas William Mews on the ship *Rockingham* early in 1830.

James Stirling, governor of the colony, estimated there were already forty boats owned in the colony in 1830. Some of them were not particularly fine craft. Dr T B Wilson, RN, who was at the colony in its first year recorded meeting a gentleman, a former army officer, building a flat-bottomed punt who admitted to being 'completely out of his element'. (My own flat-bottomed boat might be a replica of that gentleman's boat.) Mary Friend, who as the wife of Captain Matthew Friend of the ship *Wanstead* is certain to have known about boats, described the river boats in her diary: '... they have made some flat-bottomed boats something like half a packing case.' Stirling himself had an official galley, painted white, with red and white awning and manned by four seamen in naval uniform.

The first cross-river ferry was near the mouth of the river at Fremantle, run by Robert Thompson who had come from Kent and later lived on Rottnest Island.

Ownership of a shallow draft cargo boat on the river was one of the surest ways of gaining wealth, though there were several drownings and loss of goods through capsizes and other accidents.

In a sense, river drownings were the equivalent of today's road death toll. In the first years, 1829 to 1831, freight rates on the river were very high. Moving a family's possessions from Fremantle to Perth could cost £20.

In 1833 cargoes were transported up the Swan for thirty shillings per ton in Lionel Lukin's weekly ferry, and boats were hired for 'several guineas' per day. Ten years later the rate was only half of that, but in 1840 a trip out to a ship in Gage Roads, returning with a passenger and baggage, could still cost £4.

Some of the early river boats were fairly large. Lionel Lukin's *Fanny* carried ten tons.

There were a number of fast whaleboats as well as the larger vessels running weekly ferry services between Fremantle and Perth, but in adverse conditions the voyage could take all day. In summer it could be very hot work for the oarsmen and unpleasant enough for the passengers since there would be no shade in a whaleboat. For those reasons many people preferred to take a horse across the river at the Preston Point horse ferry and ride to Perth. The horse ferry at Preston Point started in 1833 and was operated by John Weavell, who at that time was granted exclusive rights to run all ferries, cross-river or along-river, between Fremantle and the Narrows. But there was not enough traffic for Weavell to prosper and he left for Van Diemen's Land in 1835.

In the absence of Weavell, the ferry returned from Preston Point to Fremantle, crossing from a point below Cantonment Hill. It was supposed to be operated by John Hole Duffield, but it was often left to children to run it. (John H Duffield and his son John Duffield were busy since they were, amongst other things, brewers.)

In 1836 the government paid Mews and Cox £100 to build a new horse ferry for the Preston Point crossing. In 1839 Duffield gave up the right to operate the Fremantle ferry and no one else wanted it, so the only regular cross-river ferry service was the Preston Point horse ferry. The tariff was 9d per person, 1s 6d for horse and rider, 9s for a heavy wagon, and 10s for sixty sheep.

Nathaniel Ogle in his *The Colony of Western Australia: a manual for Emigrants,* 1839, reported that 'Passage-boats regularly ply between Freemantle and Perth, performing the distance in about two hours.' It was the easiest way to travel from Fremantle to Perth, but the cost of three to four shillings was considered high and the crews who rowed the whaleboats were regarded as drunken scoundrels. Mrs Thomas Brown wrote in a letter:

The boatmen all bear a very bad character — there is said to be not one honest and sober man of that calling who plies the river. We ran aground full twenty times in coming up to Mr Tanner's and coming up the Swan did really appear to me the most dangerous part of the voyage.

By 1839 a canal had been cut through the flats at Burswood so that boats could navigate to Guildford in the summer, though it was still very shallow around Heirisson Islands. In the 1840s whaleboats were hired out on the river for five shillings per day, fifteen shillings per week, and it was in that decade that several daily ferry services started. In 1843, Henry Gray's *Bridegroom* operated the first daily ferry service, which ran from Perth to Fremantle in the morning and returned in the afternoon. But because freight rates had declined, in 1845 there were only eight vessels licensed to carry goods and passengers on the river.

Henry Gray operated the biggest fleet, including the whaleboat *Bride,* which made the run all the way from Fremantle to Guildford and back each two days. Gray was not only in the river transport business but was also a trader, exchanging imported goods for farm and bush produce. George Glyde and James Stokes were also river traders, and competition between those three gentlemen was sometimes rather Wild West in character.

During the 1840s there were a number of proposals for a steamer to operate on the run between Fremantle and Perth. The Swan River Steam Navigation Company was formed by subscription in July 1847, but by June of 1853 still didn't have a vessel operating, and the company was dissolved.

In 1850 there had been a misguided attempt to introduce a paddlewheel-propelled vessel — a whaleboat with hand-cranked paddlewheels. It was unable to make any headway against a sea breeze and 'the labour of working the paddles is stated to be so severe as to preclude any chance of the scheme ever becoming successful.'

Following the demise of the Steam Navigation Company in January 1854, a new company was formed to take up a steamer already under construction by Thomas William Mews. The vessel was launched 14 April 1854, minus the engine that was being built by Solomon Cook. *Speculator* made her first trial run in December 1854 but with a very homemade engine it was little faster than the hand-cranked paddlewheeler had been. The engine had a square-sectioned cylinder and a square piston which leaked most of the steam pressure. *Speculator* was sold by auction a couple of weeks after her trial.

In March 1855 a small schooner-rigged auxiliary steamer *Les Trois Amis* arrived in Fremantle where she was derigged and unballasted to operate as a steam ferry on the Swan. The capital investment was considerable and the possibilities for a reasonable rate of return were not certain, particularly since *Les Trois Amis* was too deep to go alongside the jetties at Perth and Fremantle. To offset the operating costs her owner, William Hinton Campbell, applied for, and was granted, a 'free license for the sale of spirits, arrack and beer' on board the ferry. The first voyage was made on 29 March 1855 sailing from Perth to Fremantle in two hours and returning in one and a half hours.

On 4 April, W H Campbell advertised for tenders to supply one and a half to two cords of cleft firewood per day, to be delivered to *Les Trois Amis* 'out of flats [barges] or boats.' Things seemed to be going well and later in April, Campbell sent an order to England for a more shallow-drafted steamer. However, the truth was that dredging at the Fremantle and Perth jetties was not going well, so passengers still had to be shuttled to and from *Les Trois Amis* by boat. Campbell was making a loss, but he continued to run the service until November 1855 when he drowned, apparently by accident, in Perth Water. *Les Trois Amis* was then laid up.

Speculator, in the meantime, had been renamed *Lively* and her machinery was modified. Trials in January 1856 showed that her performance had improved but was still not really good enough. Again she was sold by auction. At the end of the year *Les Trois Amis* was bought by George Shenton and returned to service. She had been passed in at an auction where the last offer was £860. At that time the parts of a new prefabricated steamer, ordered by a Mr Homfray, had arrived in Fremantle. She was to be named *Lady*

Stirling. The intention was that when *Lady Stirling* entered service, *Les Trois Amis* would be rerigged and ballasted, her engine would be removed and she would work as a sailing vessel in the coasting trade.

By this time there were twenty-three vessels registered at Fremantle as ferries.

Lady Stirling was assembled at Fremantle in 1857 and made her first voyage to Perth on 16 May of that year. In July *Les Trois Amis* sailed for Geraldton with her machinery still in place, operating as an auxiliary schooner.

Steam engines had been used for nearly a century but their development continued to be a dangerous experiment. *Lady Stirling's* boiler blew up in 1860, killing her engineer by scalding. *Speculator/Lively* was damaged by fire and converted to a sailing lighter, and Solomon Cook started construction of machinery for another steamer, to be called *Pioneer*, for the Perth–Guildford run. She made her first successful run up to Guildford in January 1857 but at Guildford there was a dangerous escape of steam and a small fire on board. Some dredging and clearing of the river was necessary to facilitate her navigation. Another voyage was made in early February with Governor Kennedy on board.

Solomon Cook, who built the engines for *Speculator* and *Pioneer*, also built the first Canning Bridge (for £400). He was obviously a resourceful man.

Chapter 4

THE MIDDLE SWAN, RIGHT BANK

With the knowledge that my boat was adequate and that rowing and sailing on the river was pleasant and satisfying, I did nothing for the next week or two, though the autumn weather was absolutely ideal. I am basically a hardworking, responsible, sober and enterprising person so it surprises me that I often seem to be a layabout and so practised at procrastination. I have a number of theories about this masked enterprise, responsibility and diligence syndrome (MERDS).

Many people have observed that time seems to be passing faster and faster. The year is scarcely started when Easter comes around and before you know it, it's Christmas again. Most of us find it harder and harder to fit all the tasks required of us into a day. Only procrastination seems easier and easier.

This is often dismissed as a purely perceptual phenomenon, entirely the result of changing, subjective, perceptions. One explanation is that, as you get older, your metabolism slows while time and the speed of light remain constant, but you and your slowing metabolism perceive time as speeding up because it is leaving you behind. Another approach is to argue that with each passing day, week, month or year, any given unit of time becomes a smaller fraction of your elapsed lifetime — the time span that you have experienced and perceived. When you're eight years old, it is about one percent of your elapsed lifetime; when you're forty, a month is only about 0.2 percent — a month is only about a fifth of what it once was.

No doubt there is something in this. Perception of time does change with age, but my experience as a maritime archaeologist has suggested that something of more cosmological significance is going on. The quality of time may be changing.

I was involved in recent years in the *Duyfken* Replica Project, building a replica of the small Dutch ship *Duyfken*, which in 1606 made the first historically recorded voyage to Australia. In trying to reconstruct the design of such a ship, we looked at various types of evidence, including contemporary contracts for the construction of similar vessels. One of the most interesting contracts was not actually for construction, but for the rebuilding, from the waterline up, of a vessel similar in size to *Duyfken*. It was a *jacht* intended for one of Willem Barentszoon's voyages of arctic exploration. The contract specified the number of men who were to undertake the work and the time in which it was to be completed, including the planing — the final finishing and smoothing. Sixteen men were to do the job, including planing, in ten weeks. It is not clear whether they first had to demolish the existing structure before starting the rebuild, but it is clear that they got the job done on time because the ship was able to sail away, as planned, at the right time of year for arctic exploration.

The *Duyfken* replica was built by a similar number of people, mostly men, over a period of two years up to launching and another six months with a smaller team employed up to readiness for the first sailing trials.

Obviously there are differences between the ways shipwrights work now and what was done four hundred years ago. Most of the *Duyfken* shipwrights worked a less than forty-hour week, and I believe all of them were completely sober much of the time. They used an array of power tools and much of the timber was delivered to the shipyard already rough sawn to the required sizes. None of these things would have been true four hundred years ago. Some of those differences in conditions would theoretically speed the modern shipwrights' progress and others might slow it.

The curious fact is that our highly skilled and motivated team of late twentieth-century shipwrights would not have been able to effect that rebuild from the waterline up in anything less than about fifty weeks — that's five times as long as it took at the end of the sixteenth century. I can't formulate any combination of factors that would fully explain that huge time difference.

I am told that the Egyptian pyramids' construction raises a similar problem. The various steps necessary for building pyramids with the available technology can be seen as difficult, but not impossible. However, actually getting the several very large pyramids completed in a few decades, given the theorised population and infrastructure supporting the workers then available, more or less defies explanation. (In recent years some archaeologists have attempted to demonstrate that building the pyramids was not such a difficult undertaking but none of them have actually built a pyramid to prove their point.)

Evolution is too gradual a process to supply the explanation. The intervening centuries are just not enough time for so great a change in average human stamina and strength as would be needed to supply the explanation. An evolutionary biologist with whom I discussed this denied that it could even be a factor. It seems as if the actual quality of time is measurably changing through historical time. As if a unit of time such as a day is now able to contain less of any activity … other than procrastination.

While I should have been doing something else, I speculated that perhaps this had something to do with the red shift — with the expansion of the universe. As the universe increases in space/volume, the time within the time-space continuum gets stretched or attenuated and therefore it can contain less.

A refinement of that idea posits that the sum total of the time and space in the universe is constant. So, as the amount of infinite space encompassed by the universe increases, the amount of time encompassed must reciprocally decrease.

This very simple model will present considerable difficulties for cosmological theoreticians and will probably be opposed. If it is correct, physicists can stop their search for the dark matter that they thought was required to stop the ever accelerating expansion of the universe. With no extra mass for gravity to act on, the universe will stop expanding when there is no time left for it to expand into. Obviously this is not a good thing for people employed in the dark matter industry, an industry that has seen tremendous growth in recent years and has created a wonderful array of undetectable particles.

On the other hand, there are exciting opportunities for the integration of physics and the soft sciences or humanities.

Since the changing of the quality of time is so easily detectable through historical research, and even our own perceptions, it would seem that we are already close to the point where time runs out. A relatively small residuum of time is already stretched very thinly in a huge universe, and the end of this time is close at hand. But just how close urgently requires historical research.

The outline of the history of the universe is clear enough. At the big bang the universe encompassed almost zero space but time was extremely capacious, allowing a very great deal to occur in the first few nanoseconds. Since then the universe has been expanding and time has been diminishing in capacity. (This hypothesis draws attention to the dual nature of time: it is linear, moving from the past to the future, and it has volume, making it capable of containing events, whereas a line has no volume or ability to contain anything other than dimensionless points. But time is not proceeding from past to future without losing something — it loses capacity.)

My mathematical modelling of the progression from Big Bang to Time Zero is currently an area of unsophisticated speculation, as I will demonstrate. Imagine a graph with the capacity of time as the vertical axis and the passage of time on the horizontal axis. We start at somewhere a long way off the floor on the extreme left of the graph (big bang) and we are proceeding to somewhere on the floor at the far right margin of the graph (time zero), but are we travelling in a straight line or on an exponential curve that goes into a nose dive as we approach time zero?

The mathematically more adventurous might prefer a three-dimensional graph with the space volume of the universe as the extra axis along the right hand wall. Again, is the plot of the graph travelling in a straight line from the top corner opposite us to the point at our feet, or is it now hanging almost right over our heads having first swerved out to the left near the ceiling? It certainly feels like an exponential curve, and one that is approaching free fall even now.

But did it feel any different to the Cro-Magnon people or the pharaohs? Careful historical and sociological research may shed light on the way the times are a-changing.

However, it may be a more complex question than it appears at first glance. Dr Willem de Winter, at the University of Western Australia, suggested that there may be local or micro implications of my theory which will be relatively easily investigated, but will complicate any attempt at a universal measurement of change in time's capacity.

Willem's insight is based on the empirical observation that time seems to pass at different rates in different places and that this seems to be related to the amount of space available locally. Things seem to happen relatively slowly in, for example, Tennant Creek where there is lots of space, by comparison with, say, Hong Kong, where there is rather less space. Furthermore, he proposes that per capita rates of production may be different in Tennant Creek as compared to Hong Kong, in line with the way that the effective rates of wooden shipbuilding have slowed as the space in the universe has increased.

The two big questions are: 'How close are we to time zero?' and 'What happens after time zero?'

Before the red shift turned blue, my next outing on the river started with the discovery that *Earnest* had been tagged. Early in the day I walked down to the North Fremantle river bank where my little boat lies chained to a tree when not in use and found her beautiful paving-paint grey topsides highlighted with an angry orange scrawl. Since *Earnest* was lying upside down when tagged, the tagger's signature appears upside down when she's afloat, but I can't read it either way up. It looks a bit like *ARAS*.

Not particularly bothered by a little graffito I set off for the Middle Swan, tacking all the way up Melville Water and Perth Water against a gusty easterly breeze with the sail reefed at times. My earlier suspicion that *Earnest* would sail sluggishly under reefed sail proved quite unfounded.

For my purposes Heirisson Island and the Causeway divide the Middle Swan from the Lower Swan. The Lower Swan is very much a *ria*, a drowned river valley created by the rise of sea-level in the global warming since the last ice age. The broad expanses of Melville Water and Perth Water are really arms of the sea. In fact the Middle Swan is also tidal and salt water except during the winter rains, but it meanders from side to side of its flood plain like a real river rather than filling the whole valley.

The Narrows and Mount Eliza mark the inland edge of the coastal limestone ridges which are calcified or fossilised sand dunes. In preparation for the construction of the Narrows Bridge, exploratory bores were taken in the Narrows which found peaty deposits twenty-one metres below current sea level. This represents the level of the river at about ten thousand years ago before the sea level started rising rapidly. At that time the river ran in a narrow gully with the cliffs of Mount Eliza, King's Park, twice as high above it as they now are. The river met the sea somewhere north-west of where Rottnest Island now lies. By five thousand years ago sea level had reached approximately current levels. George Fletcher Moore (a pioneer settler) recorded Aboriginal knowledge that Garden Island, Carnac island and Rottnest had once formed part of the mainland.

Heirisson Island, Matagarup to the Nyungar people, was originally Iles de Heirisson (Heirisson's Islands), named by Captain Hamelin of *Naturaliste* for Midshipman Heirisson who, with Midshipman Bailly, led the French expedition up the river in 1801. They got stuck in the shallows near the islands and spent a very anxious night there having heard the loud roaring of an animal which they thought must have been a large and aggressive quadruped. It is suspected that they heard some kind of frog.

The island that we see today is artificial. Heirisson found a number of smaller islands in an area of swamp where the river divided into several shallow channels. Probably the first bridge over the Swan was the 1842 bridge built from Fraser Point over a dredged channel on the Perth side of the shallows or flats. The rest of the shallows and islands were crossed by a causeway which is why the bridges on either side of Heirisson Island are called the Causeway. Prior to 1839 the dredged channel was on the southern side of the islands. In 1862 Lt. Oliver, fiancé of Governor Kennedy's daughter, drowned while trying to cross the causeway

The little inlet on Heirisson Island where I often stopped
to stretch my legs

during a flood. After the flood subsided the causeway was raised higher and a new bridge was built.

All the bridges over the Swan provide shade that attracts both fish and fishers in sunny weather. The Causeway bridges are the lowest, and even my boat's short mast has to be unstepped to get under either of them. As I rowed under the bridge on my second visit to the Middle Swan in *Earnest*, a Vietnamese couple were anchored under the bridge earnestly fishing, he from the stern, she from the bow of their little half-cabin boat. They were catching small mullet or bream which I can imagine fried until their fins and skin are crispy, served with rice and a chilli and lemongrass sauce.

The downstream part of the island is a fenced-off nature reserve but there are no signs asking you to keep out. The fence is apparently to keep the kangaroos off the road rather than keep people out and I have landed there (to take a pee in the she-oaks).

There is a tiny artificial cove upstream from the bridge on the northern side of the island where one can beach a boat protected from the wash of passing motorboats and ferries. The grass is mown and in places almost golf-course green, and there are benches and tables. I had stopped there with my friend Bill on my first expedition up the Swan in 1994 and had speculated inaccurately about the origins of the island's name, the wildlife, and several other subjects.

JOURNAL OF AN EXPEDITION TO INVESTIGATE
THE SWAN RIVER

(First published in the *Maritime Heritage Association Journal*, Vol. 5, No. 2)

28 FEBRUARY 1994

PROLOGUE TO AN EXPEDITION.

It is nearly 167 years, to the day, since Captain James Stirling launched his expedition to survey the Swan River and surrounding country. Today, Captain Bill Brown will lead a re-enactment voyage up the Swan in a traditional rowing boat.

Bill Brown is a tough Glaswegian seaman who first went to sea as a teenager on North Sea freighters. (Nowadays Bill, and Susanne his aristocratic Swiss wife, run Porthole Prints — a gallery of maritime art prints and paintings in East Fremantle.) The expedition's boat is a Penobscott Bay boat, built by Jay Lawrie; it is rather smaller than the cutter and launch used by Stirling.

Stirling's expedition in 1827 took nearly a week to reach the area now known as Guildford [that's not correct, they got up the river quite quickly and spent some days investigating the land]. *According to modern maps this equals an average rate of progress of only about five miles per day; although Stirling thought that he had travelled further. In fact there were many diversions and delays such as dragging the heavy boats over extensive sandbanks. Stirling had no prior knowledge of the course of the river and the position of the deep water channel. On the other hand, Bill and I are both reasonably familiar with the river between its mouth and Blackwall Reach, so we have decided to start our voyage from Point Walter where the real voyage of discovery will begin for us.*

We have chosen to start on 28th February (rather than the anniversary date of March 8th) because Bill has time off work, and also we intend to take advantage of the moon which has just passed full. It is our intention that we can use an afternoon sea breeze and sail on through the night until the easterly asserts itself, in order to make a relatively easy ascent of the river. But unfortunately, this morning dawned cool with a stiff and blustery easterly. There seems little likelihood of any sea breeze today. We will launch after midday when the easterly should have moderated a little.

Captain Stirling's party had to land each afternoon in time to set up camp, shoot local fauna, and make the fires to cook their dinner. But we shall not be doing that: today there is a total fire ban, and in any case, wallabies have been largely displaced by domestic dogs and cats which we should probably not eat. So, we shall take along some bread and cheese (plus various salamis and cold meats, pickles, olives, salads, a curry and rice, beer and half a crate of wine).

We actually launched from Deepwater Point on the Canning River at 1320hrs. The wind was moderate with some stronger gusts out of the east, or slightly south of east. We were able to set the spritsail to reach out of the Canning and northwards along the Como and South Perth shores of Melville Water, enjoying our first beers. Bill's boat Friend *is very stable and sails well on a reach or fetching to windward, despite a deplorably cut spritsail.*

Out on Melville Water it was easy to understand how Stirling's expedition could have spent so much time getting up the Swan — the Narrows would have been very difficult to find if one didn't already know it was there. However, we had no trouble finding the Narrows: we just sailed parallel to the traffic on the Kwinana Freeway. Sailing quietly in a traditional open boat, it doesn't take long to develop a sense of the surreality of modern urban social organisation. At 1430 on a Monday afternoon, the Kwinana Freeway is thick with traffic speeding in both directions. 'Where can they all be going?' Bill reasoned. The offices in the city are all crammed with workers; the shopping centres and city centre are all aflood with gently ambulating shoppers; yet this wide freeway is a torrent of speeding cars. It was a mystery to both of us, and the ecological implications of it all were too horrible to contemplate on a sunny afternoon. We sipped our beer and followed the traffic to the Narrows, where we turned eastwards and met the easterly wind funnelling in from Perth Water. We beached

Friend *in the shade under the Narrows Bridge and unstepped the mast in preparation for a long row to windward, up to Heirisson Island. With the mast and sprit stowed, we both rowed, taking one oar each and made fairly slow progress when the wind gusted against us. Our timing and co-ordination on the oars was good enough to make headway, but it was far from perfect as we slogged slowly past the city. Bill favours rowing in waltz-time — slow, slow, quick-quick, slow — while I have a random pattern which I insist is completely regular. On that bright and clear afternoon, with no haze to lend distance, the glass and chrome skyscrapers of the city looked curiously small, like a collection of models, and we had plenty of time to look at them.*

It was 1530 when we rowed into the little cove on the north-east side of Heirisson Island. There we stretched our legs and ate bread and cheese etc, washed down with a delicious can of beer. As we ate, we were watched by a squawking flock of black and white birds: quite probably they are called heirissons and the island is named after them. Bill tried to catch a heirisson for our dinner, but the sly creatures avoided his grasp.

At 1600, with the mast restepped and the sail set, we reached and then ran northwards from the island, under the Bunbury Railway Bridge and on to Bardon Park in Maylands. The river meanders eastwards there, and we again met a headwind. We tried tacking for a while, but Friend *does not like going hard to windward. We brailed-up the sail and rowed to windward for a* while, but it was slow work, so we unstepped the mast to reduce windage, and settled in to a long and slow row to windward. The wind tends to veer and follow the course of the river, constrained by the river's banks, so it is either a following wind or a headwind much of the time. We experienced a headwind as we rowed south, then east, around the Maylands meander. Eventually we were able to run under sail again, past Tranby House and Maylands Boatshed. But soon we had to unstep the mast as we rowed east, under the Garratt Road Bridge.

Just before the sun set, at 1830, we tied up at a jetty, not far from the Tonkin Highway Bridge. With the mast restepped and the sail furled to get it out of the way, we took our dinner on board. Our aperitif was a Minton Farm sauvignon blanc/colombard. Not a particularly promising blend, I thought, but it was dry with plenty of acid and enough fruit, and it proved to be invigorating and refreshing. Dinner was rice and a very good rendang curry, made for us by Susanne.

While we were taking dinner, the easterly breeze dropped away completely. This gave us much better conditions for rowing upstream. I took the oars, and Bill, whose fundament was rather worn and sore from a long afternoon on the rowing thwart, took the tiller, sitting uncomfortably in the stern sheets. I rowed gently into the night, towards Guildford, Friend gliding easily through the calm waters.

I'm not very familiar with the suburbs east of the city, and I had

Tranby House
Courtesy Ross Shardlow

only a vague idea where we had got to. Bill assured me that we were already close to Guildford. I knew that before we reached Guildford we should find the confluence of the Helena and Swan rivers. In the dark, before the moon rose, we peered into a couple of short creeks that might have been the Helena, but weren't. I felt less and less certain that Bill knew where we were, or alternatively that Bill might be exaggerating how far we had progressed in the hope of persuading me to turn round. On and on I rowed, at a very gentle pace. Bill kept predicting that we would see Guildford Road Bridge around every bend in the river, but we didn't. Eventually he asked two fishermen on the northern bank where the bridge was.

'It's up that way. Over the river: you can't miss it,' they replied helpfully.

And they were quite right: the bridge is built over the river. We found it a few hundred metres past the confluence of the Helena. There were also two railway bridges, and a little further upstream, a very fine cantilever suspension bridge carrying a water main. Here the river's banks are steep and high. With the moon still low in the sky the river was dark and mysterious.

When finally we entered the reach of the river that runs east past Guildford, at a little after 2130, I agreed to turn around.

Bill took the oars and, despite obvious discomfort, rowed vigorously downstream. We stopped at a riverside park provided with a jetty and street lighting to fortify ourselves with half a bottle of Taylor's 1988 cabernet sauvignon. By that time it was distinctly chilly and Bill was actually shivering with a recurrence of the ague he caught on one of his expeditions up the Limpopo river. Nevertheless, after a couple of glasses of red and a short lie-down, he rowed on downstream to where we had taken dinner. And there we finished the cab-sav.

I took over the rowing and Bill, somewhat addled by wine and the Limpopo ague, took the tiller to bounce us off the riverbanks and sandbanks before turning westwards into a dead-end arm of the river in Belmont. Eventually we unshipped the rudder and Friend kept sensibly to the middle of the river thereafter. From Rivervale to Maylands, Bill rowed again with a gradually increasing south-easterly breeze, while I took a snooze in the stern sheets. Then I rowed against the wind under the Bunbury Railway Bridge, and at 0300 reached the little cove on Heirisson Island (eleven hours since we had left it). We shipped the rudder again and prepared the sail for setting. I rowed out of the lee of the island and there we set the sail. Bill slept fitfully under a pile of sarongs and tarpaulins, balancing on the midship thwart, while Friend broad-reached sedately across in front of the glittering city. The breeze improved gradually as we sailed back through the Narrows. Out on Melville Water it was a little choppy and we had to sheet-in, in order to head south, clear of Point Currie. By dawn we were reaching along, half a mile off the Nedlands shore. As the sky grew lighter, and then the sun rose, we ran north-west to pass around the end of the Point Walter sandspit. We ran aground three times trying *to short-cut around the end of the spit, and then had to tack up to Chidley Point, using the oars to improve the windward performance. Bill gamely rowed up to Chidley Point. We found Blackwall Reach becalmed and I took the oars until a breeze returned and carried us round Roe Point to Rocky Bay.*

At 0750, on the morning of 1st March, we landed at East Fremantle boat ramp, rather cold, tired and blistered; but on the whole it had been an interesting and not-too-unpleasant trip.

I had rather expected to find that areas of the river bank, to the east of the city, would be blighted with scruffy light industry and dusty acres of prefabricated warehouses. I was pleasantly surprised to find that the banks are everywhere green, and there are considerable stretches that have probably changed very little in character since Stirling first passed by, blasting away at the waterfowl with muzzle-loaders.

YAGAN

At the western end of Heirisson Island there is a bronze statue representing the Beeliar Nyungar warrior Yagan. This is not an original observation on my part, but it is interesting to reflect on the respective locations of the statue commemorating Yagan, an Aboriginal warrior, and the State War Memorial. Yagan stands unobtrusively on a (white)man-made island while the War Memorial stands high above the opposite end of Perth Water on the most prominent natural feature.

Yagan himself was a man of impressive physical stature, not to be ignored, and was an important man in traditional Nyungar law. The colonial authorities identified him as a leader of the Beeliar Nyungar although Nyungar society was not structured with leaders or councils who could make binding decisions on behalf of a whole community.

Mrs Frances Lochee recalled that 'Yagan was a fine fellow and had always wanted to be friends with the white people.' But he was not submissive or acquiescent. Yagan was among the group that attacked settlers in retribution for the shooting of a Nyungar who had been taking potatoes from Archibald Butler's property in 1831, by a servant named Smedley. Enion (or Anyon) Entwhistle, another servant of Butler, was speared in the retribution.

In June 1832 a man named Gaze was killed by Nyungars on the Canning River. Yagan was named as one of the leaders responsible and declared an outlaw. He was captured later in 1832.

Yagan was probably saved from execution by a missionary settler, Robert Milne Lyon, who argued that Yagan should be treated as a prisoner of war rather than a criminal. Yagan and two companions were exiled to Carnac Island, where Lyon accompanied them. After six weeks on tiger-snake infested Carnac, Yagan and his Nyungar companions stole a small boat and escaped to the mainland. Curiously he was not rearrested although he visited Perth and Fremantle. During this time Lyon wrote several articles about Yagan and about Nyungar culture and language for publication in the local press, arguing vehemently against the attitude and actions of Stirling and the colonial establishment, and promoting an attempt to understand a Nyungar perspective. At a meeting in Guildford called to discuss the problems with the

Aborigines, Lyon concluded his address with this unequivocal warning to the settlers:

Reflect. You have seized upon a land that is not yours.

Beware, and do not, as a people, add to this the guilt of dipping your hands in the blood of those whom you have spoiled of their country.

Lyon hoped and believed that conversion to Christianity would eventually bring reconciliation of Nyungar and colonist objectives.

In 1833 Yagan, with his father Midgegooroo and Munday, who the authorities regarded as the leader of the Beeloo Nyungar, and about forty others, ambushed and killed two settlers, the Velvik brothers, in retribution for the shooting of Yagan's brother Domjum who had been trying to break into a store in Fremantle.

The three men were declared 'Wanted Dead or Alive' with a bounty of £30 on Yagan's head and £20 each on the others. At this time many settlers were in genuine fear of an organised uprising and probably a significant number of Nyungars were shot by settlers who believed the government was not acting aggressively enough. The previous year, Captain Fremantle on a short return visit to the colony, had observed that the persecution of the Aborigines, 'almost amounts to a war of extermination'.

Midgegooroo was captured and shot by a firing squad in Perth.

Yagan appeared with Munday, Weeip and several others at the homestead of George Fletcher Moore, one of the leading settlers who was known to sympathise with the Nyungars' situation, asking what had happened to Midgegooroo. Moore and Yagan had a lengthy, if not clearly understood, discussion or debate (Moore's account appears in the section on G F Moore in chapter 6, p 260). At the end Yagan said he would kill three white men to avenge the death of his father. Moore tried to warn him against such a course which he regarded as barbaric but admitted, 'There is something in his daring which one is forced to admire.'

Yagan remained at large for some time. Settlers such as Moore would not undertake the capture or killing of him, but he was eventually shot through the back of the head, while eating, by William Keats (Keating in some souces) an eighteen-year-old shepherd accompanied by his thirteen-year-old brother, James. William was speared by Yagan's companions but James escaped. The killing took place across the river from Moore's property on the Upper Swan in July 1833, not, as is widely believed, on Heirisson Island.

Following his death, Yagan's head was cut off, preserved by smoking, and sent to England to be exhibited. It lay for a century in Liverpool Museum and then was buried in 1964. In 1997 the skull was disinterred and returned to the Nyungar people for appropriate burial near the Swan River Nyoongar Community. During the campaign for the return of the skull, the head was sawn off the statue of Yagan on Heirisson Island by a person or persons with a loathsomely warped sense of what? Humour? Righteous indignation?

It was at Claise Brook, just upstream from Heirisson Island, that Stirling first encountered Nyungar people in 1827. They seemed hostile and angry. It is believed that they had recently been attacked and some women abducted by George Randell and his crew from the sealing vessel *Ann*. Stirling's expedition later met a group of about thirty Nyungars, probably in what is now Ascot. The women and children withdrew while the men followed Stirling's boats on the high banks of the river. When Stirling and his men landed further upstream the Nyungar men gathered around them and exchanged spears and woomeras for clothes and some black swans that Stirling's men had shot.

Following Captain James Stirling's glowing report on the prospects for a Swan River colony, the British government undertook in 1828 to proclaim possession of Western Australia (the colony of New South Wales at that time comprised the eastern two-thirds of the continent while the western third was unclaimed) but they insisted that the transport of the colonists and the establishment of the colony should entail no cost to the government. To an extent this was a political stance and did not mean that they would cover none of the costs, nor was that actually the case. Even the transporting of the colonists and supplies was partly undertaken by the Royal Navy.

Captain C H Fremantle was to sail to Western Australia in HMS *Challenger* to proclaim possession of the colony, and Stirling was to go out as commander of HM Bomb *Sulphur* taking the first settlers with him. (A 'bomb' was not just a clapped-out vehicle, though in a sense that is implicit. A bomb was a ship that had originally been built to mount a huge mortar for close-range bombardment of shore installations. Bombs were very heavily constructed and usually rather slow.) *Sulphur* was not large enough to transport all the first settlers and their belongings, so Stirling chartered the merchant ship *Parmelia* and sailed as a passenger with the other settlers on her. *Sulphur*, commanded by Captain Dance, carried, among many other things, the military contingent dispatched to the new colony, and was severely overloaded despite the charter of *Parmelia*. Some of the ten thousand bricks for Stirling to build a new home with were actually stowed on *Sulphur*'s weather deck at the start of the voyage! *Sulphur* got beaten up by heavy weather in the English Channel, driven past her rendezvous with *Parmelia* in Portsmouth, and limped into Plymouth where the deck-cargo bricks were put ashore. When she reached Cape Town she was leaking badly around the waterline and had to be partially recaulked before continuing. *Sulphur* remained attached to the fledgling colony for three years, surveying the coast and bringing in essential supplies.

Captain Fremantle anchored HMS *Challenger* off Garden Island on 25 April 1829. The following day Bradshaw, the sailing master, surveyed the entrance to Cockburn Sound by boat and buoyed the channel and rocks. Unfortunately he then misinterpreted his own buoying system and sailed *Challenger* straight onto a rock marked by a buoy, thinking it was the channel. No serious damage occurred but Captain Fremantle was understandably very angry.

Fremantle took formal possession of Western Australia for Britain on 2 May 1829. His instructions included the proviso that he 'ask the Aboriginals if they objected to his doing so.' There was no indication of what he was to do if the Aboriginal people said, 'Go away' but, as events show, he knew what he was expected to do. The day after the proclamation he launched a short expedition up the river, and at Blackwall Reach he 'saw & heard natives on both sides [of the river], who halloa'd to us very loud & appeard to cry out "Warra Warra" which I suppose to be "go away" I took no notice …' Warra means 'bad' so Fremantle correctly interpreted the sentiment.

He didn't go away but continued up the river, camping overnight at Point Heathcote, and met with another group of Aboriginal people with whom he and his crew were able to make contact. Fremantle gave his hat to an Aboriginal man and other gifts were exchanged. Amicable relations continued during the following days at Fremantle's encampment.

Relations deteriorated, however, during the early days of the colony. The causes of hostility can be debated and blame apportioned to either side but it is reasonable to suppose that the Nyungar people objected to not being allowed to take animals on their land and having their most productive land taken from them. Captain Fremantle perceived the situation very clearly when he made a return visit to the colony in 1832:

We take possession of their country, occupy the most fertile parts, where they are in the habit of resorting for nourishment, destroy their fishing and kangaroo, and almost drive them to starvation, and they naturally consider themselves entitled to our sheep and stock whenever they can get hold of them.

Some fought valiantly but of course they could not match the capacity for retribution and pre-emptive retaliation that firearms gave the invaders.

The settlers genuinely feared the Aboriginal tribes and it is widely accepted that they wrongly interpreted the annual firing of the land as deliberate hostility. That might be a disingenuous interpretation, though in some cases the settlers were right in the assessment that the fires were lit with hostile intent. The establishment of a settlement at Kelmscott on the Upper Canning River was almost abandoned after a year because of the appropriation of crops and stock and firing of farm buildings by Beeliar Nyungars. The settlers did understand something of the reason for burning off the land.

George Fletcher Moore observed in the 1830s that if pasture was not burned for several years, grasshoppers increased to such an extent that they did great damage. Mary Friend recorded in her diary in 1830, 'The natives had made a large fire to drive the kangaroos. It spread rapidly ... and reached the encampment of Mr Watson which was entirely burnt.' This not only shows that the reasons for firing were at least partly understood, it also suggests that the Nyungars had some thought of deliberately burning settlers' possessions.

The two cultures were hugely different and it can be argued that the colonists were blinded by preconceptions about 'primitive' cultures while the Nyungar were unequipped with conceptual models for understanding the colonists, but Nyungars were not unprepared to try for such an understanding. George Moore recorded in a letter the observation that 'they are quick of apprehension, and capable of reflecting on the difference between our manners and their own, in a degree you would scarcely expect.'

Following the right bank upstream from Heirisson Island you will probably run aground because there is a very shallow sandbank. Until it was dredged, the whole width of the river was very shallow around Heirisson's Islands and upstream to Claise Brook. It was usually necessary to get out of the boat and 'light it' (push and lift) through the mud. Having skirted the remnant mud bank where fishermen sometimes go to dig for worms, one comes to Claisebrook Cove, the mouth of the tributary brook named for Surgeon F R Clause who had sailed with Stirling on HMS *Success* when he first visited Western Australia and also with Fremantle on HMS *Challenger* when he first came. Clause pronounced his name Claise.

The UBD road map showed me that at the very mouth of the cove, in Victoria Gardens, there is something called 'Ngango Battas Mooditcher Path'. Ashore I found a gravel path that follows a row and circle of tall granite boulders standing on end like

The basin at Claisebrook

dolmens. I couldn't find any mention of Ngango Battas Mooditcher: the path is signed as the 'Illa Kuri Sacred Path' though a website tells me that it should be 'Ngango Batta's Path'. Subsequent research has revealed that 'ngango batta' means 'sun beam' in Nyungar. Nine of the boulders represent the nine lakes that have been filled in or reclaimed to build Perth city.

There is also a stone with a plaque explaining about the communities (once called tribes) of the Nyungar peoples of the Bibulmun Nation and their six skin groups (Ballarak, Drondarap, Dijikok, Nagonak, Ngotak, Waddarak). Skin group determines, most importantly, who one may marry. One cannot marry within one's own group and ideally will marry someone from the most distant skin group.

Claisebrook Cove is the site of several other pieces of public outdoor art, including a conceptually challenging bench, and also Janet Holmes à Court's Art Gallery.

You can row under Trafalgar Bridge and into the cove, which is actually more a basin or dock than a cove. According to an East Perth website,

The gentle curves of the harbour reflect the original wetlands and the history buried beneath the new urban landscape. This has been chartered through public art in and around the water's edge.

I wonder what 'chartered' means in that sentence; 'gentle curves' doesn't mean much at all.

The architecture that surrounds you is interesting. It's all new, all obviously expensive, very self-conscious and postmodern ironic, and for me the interesting thing is why some of it doesn't work. There's a house that has obviously been built with no expense spared; it incorporates decorative elements including neoclassical but it seems to exemplify what goes wrong if architecture ignores or mixes established rules about ratios of proportions. Quite simply, neoclassical doesn't work if the windows are disproportionately big. It loses most of its dignity, and even a building skilfully assembled from attractive stone can look cheap and gimmicky.

Of course, I don't mean that. What kind of philistine do you take me for? Contemporary architecture is exciting conceptual discourse, but it is like a book of poetry — you have to be able to read it to enjoy it and you must involve yourself. Contemporary architecture is dialogue and the process of the dialogue can produce, through the very nature of its dynamic, an interchange of ideas.

Let me take you on an architectural adventure. What is it that arrests our gaze on this small corner block? Certainly a place of stoppage — speaking a language of clean lines and distinct planes, grounded in street-corner sensibilities through simple bold statement of the concrete texture. In creating an unresolved dialogue of the spatial axes, in order to speak that corner theme, the architect has audaciously fronted the side street and with a stroke of spatial legerdemain backed the side to face the busy main-street front, with the open garage doors articulating an uninterrupted flow between internal and external space. Yet, it is the front door on the side street that defines the entry and hints at the volumes within.

Let's take a look inside … and notice how the view from and of the interior is quite different from the exterior views. It is the walls that create the difference and define the volumes, but it is the windows that have been used to make visually manifest that comparison of interior and exterior. Yes, internally this is micro-urbanism writ large. The floors, on three levels, break up the object-like form through a series of horizontally stratified planes, interconnected by pivotally located stairs, in alignment with voids that puncture those horizontal planes.

Perhaps I am getting a bit carried away here, but I delight in the way the builders have articulated the sense that the living/dining/karaoke space is an extension of the exterior courtyard space by tramping sand and mud through the double sliding glass portal to the clean and distinct plane of the polished concrete floor.

If you were to consider this house without the benefit of thought mediated through the sophisticated dialogue of contemporary architecture, you might see little more than an ill-designed concrete box fitted with doors, windows and awkwardly placed stairs.

Upstream of Claisebrook the river is crossed by the Goongoonup Bridge, which replaced the Bunbury Railway Bridge, and Windan

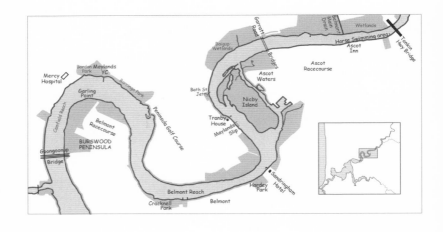

Middle Swan: Claisebrook, Burswood Peninsula, Maylands Peninsula, Ascot and Bayswater to Tonkin Highway Bridge

Bridge, which carries the new Graham Farmer northern city bypass. Windan is a fine bridge and Graham Farmer is, I understand, a retired footballer whose friends were encouraged to call him 'Polly'.

Immediately upstream there are derelict power station buildings waiting to be converted to luxury apartments, and then a short stretch of natural swampy river bank which you can only get to by boat because this short stretch of the river is under the local government control of the City of Vincent which, like Claremont, doesn't seem to care much about pedestrian and cyclist access to the river. A significant part of the river bank there appears to be the property of Mercy Hospital and if I were a cynic I might observe that it's not in the interest of a hospital to promote healthy activities like walking and cycling.

Terrestrial access to the river starts again as soon as you cross into the suburb of Maylands in the Bayswater local government area. Bardon Park has wondrously green lawns sweeping down to Chinaman Bay and to Camfield's Reach, a stretch of the river past Claisebrook called after the Camfields who owned the whole Burswood peninsula and land to the south. Bardon is not a large park but it merges into Berringa Park which in turn runs into the Peninsula Golf Course that takes up much of the western half of the Maylands Peninsula. The golf course is, of course, close-cropped, well-watered lawns and tidy stands of trees but the riverbanks are mostly fringed with wetland vegetation and melaleucas, and that is true of much of the Middle Swan.

Camfield Reach, with Perth in the background

Rowing around the south-eastern corner of the Maylands peninsula, looking back downstream (as one does when rowing upstream), I realised that the only building I could see was an old boatshed built over the water. It's not that there are no buildings along the banks of the Middle Swan, far from it, there is hardly anywhere that one bank or the other has no buildings, but the houses are mostly fairly well set back from the river and they are hidden by the trees if you look up or downstream along the river. If you look across at the adjacent bank then you can see the buildings.

Because the river meanders from side to side, in general, one bank or the other is close to the edge of the flood plain, and that bank is fairly steep and has houses on it above the flood level, while the other bank is low. Here the flood plain is broad and, because it is subject to flooding, has been left as natural swamp, wetland and heath. In places the melaleuca fringe is narrow; the edge of the Redcliffe Industrial Area in Ascot is only a hundred metres from the river, but unless you peer through the trees to see it, it doesn't impinge on the way one experiences the Middle Swan.

Round on the eastern side of Maylands peninsula is Maylands slipway. The guides providing commentary on the tourist cruises call it 'the boats' graveyard — where old boats go to die' and there certainly are plenty of old boat restoration projects that will never be finished. Some of them are not even keeping pace with deterioration. The boats are parked in rows, propped up by wooden shores and metal jacks (Acroprops). Some of the boats that seem to have gone there to die have actually never been in the water, they're still under construction and some of the more misguided projects will still be unfinished when their builders have gone somewhere else to die. I think of it as the white elephants' graveyard.

Some projects do get afloat. Freshly painted, stainless steel fittings all aglitter, they are launched. Then, when final fitting-out is finished, bearing a terrible burden of dreams, they motor down to the sea, masts lowered for passing under the bridges. The best and the luckiest of them are remembered occasionally when a postcard arrives at Maylands Slip from the Maldives or from tropical Far North Queensland. Others go out to sea for the first time and fill their owners with awful fear — a series of near disasters that they survive mostly thanks to God's protection of fools. And so they return to Maylands and re-slip the boat, not saying too much about the shakedown cruise but talking about making a few modifications to the galley and the engine controls. And the next two or three years are spent building in superfluous lockers and shelves until there's no room left to fit another shelf. Then the boat of dreams is put up for sale.

Building and cruising a sailing boat on a limited budget is largely the resort of the eccentric, autodidactic, anti-establishment type (I should know). Some do it very well; their boats are prodigies of invention, resourcefulness, self-sufficiency and craftsmanship (meaning craftspersonship if you prefer). Some are less skilled and tend to reinvent the wheel unsuccessfully for each problem they face.

While I was wandering around the boatyard looking at the boats and admiring some of them I nodded to someone behind sunglasses who looked familiar. He was an old friend from Wooden Boat Works, the traditional boatbuilding school and workshop that has been accommodated, at different times, in three different heritage sheds in the Victoria Quay area of the Port of Fremantle.

When Ray was at Wooden Boat Works he was building a curragh, a traditional design of rowing boat from the west coast of Ireland. Ray himself is from Ireland and has an attractive broad Irish brogue, a friendly smile and a great fondness for a chat. He's a thoroughly amiable man, good fun to talk with and somewhat eccentric.

Building a curragh could be seen as eccentric. The curragh was designed to be rowed out through the surf on open Atlantic beaches. It was also designed to be very cheap and to use minimal timber — they were built in an area where little timber was available. The timber frame of a curragh is covered with leather or tarred canvas. The flat-bottomed, round bilged shape with high rounded bow and cut-off flat stern is unstable without ballast or cargo and, while it would survive in the surf, it didn't row particularly well.

Ray was almost the only person who could keep his curragh the right way up and he told me that he managed that by using the heavy, clumsy, oars as balancing beams. Nevertheless he ended up building seven of them for display in various Irish pubs, clubs and other cultural centres.

Since then Ray has taken to building with fibreglass and other more modern materials such as forty-four gallon drums. I accepted his invitation for a cup of tea on board his catamaran/trimaran/raft *The Flying Paddy*. She is twenty-six feet (7.93 m) long, bright orange and pretty as an oil rig. Indeed she looks like a broken off bit of oil rig. In terms of cabin space she is remarkable. A big rounded orange dome covers much of the vessel and there is standing headroom through most of it. Two short, unstayed masts carry not-quite-right Chinese junk-type sails.

The Chinese junk rig has enjoyed tremendous vogue with non-conformist sailors and boatbuilders. It does have some considerable advantages if you make it from lightweight, strong, modern materials. It's a complex rig with lots of components that don't work the way they're supposed to if something is not quite right. Real junk rig is heavy, far from foolproof, and requires strength and skill to use successfully.

Ray is still looking for ways to improve the performance of *The Flying Paddy*.

His next project is a large raft made from rows of forty-four gallon drums. He will fix an old Holden station wagon in the middle of it for accommodation and the gearbox will connect to a propeller shaft for forward and reverse propulsion. Perhaps the steering wheel will be connected to the rudder too. There will also be a single mast with a lugsail like my little boat's. Ray plans to circumnavigate Australia single-handed in his sea-going Holden. I didn't ask how his partner and young son feel about that.

Next door to Maylands Slip is Tranby House, a National Trust property. At Tranby House you can feel closer to the first years of the Swan River Colony than just about anywhere else. Tranby was the name of a ship (not really a ship in the strict sense of being square-rigged on three masts but a snow-brig which is square-rigged on her two masts and has the gaff spanker set on a little jackmast just abaft the main lower mast). She was chartered to carry a group of Methodist settlers from Hull in north-east England to the Swan River Colony a few months after Stirling had sailed with the first settlers. It is usually said that the ship was chartered by a group of Methodists from Yorkshire which sounds like an especially dour and hardworking combination.

In fact, the Hardeys who built Tranby House were from Barton and Barrow in Lincolnshire, *acruss tuther sah doovt oomber* (across the other side of the river Humber). That northern part of Lincolnshire was the birthplace of the Reverend John Wesley who led the Evangelical Revival of the Church of England and eventually formed a Methodist Church separate from the Church of England. It was also the origin of the Scrooby Congregation of Puritans who sailed to North America on the *Mayflower* and established the Plymouth Colony.

Three Hardey brothers sailed on the *Tranby* in 1829: John Wall Hardey (born 1802), Joseph Hardey (born 1804), and William Hardey (born 1813). The two older brothers were accompanied by the wives they had married in the weeks before setting sail. John Wall's wife Elisabeth was just seventeen while Joseph's wife Ann was twenty-nine.

William Hardey died on the voyage out in mysterious circumstances. Joseph Hardey made no mention of the cause of death in his diary but a fellow passenger, George Johnson, recorded that William was found dead in his bunk, and that he

> had a silk handkerchief wrapped twice around his neck and tied on a hard knot ... his neck was black and had evident marks that the shirt or Handkerchief had been too tight during the night.

The ship's surgeon, Mr Brownell, confirmed that William had died of strangulation.

In Fremantle the *Tranby* migrants found many settlers waiting forlornly for land allocations in the scruffy encampment on the beach, many of the men consoling themselves with drink. Open-air preaching, both by the clergy and lay preachers, is an important duty for Methodists so Joseph took to preaching among the settlers and also to pressing the governor for a speedy allocation of land.

The Hardeys, along with fellow Methodists the Clarksons and

Brownells, with about forty servants and artisans, were allowed several small allocations of land on the Maylands peninsula while waiting for larger land allocations further inland. Governor Stirling had originally intended the flat peninsula east of Perth to be a horseracing course.

Joseph Hardey's farm on the Maylands peninsula was called Peninsula Farm and the Swan River Colony's first wheat crop was grown there.

The current Tranby House was built by Joseph Hardey in 1839 after his first and second, much simpler houses, built closer to river level, had been damaged by floods. For this reason it is usually said that the current Tranby House is the third Tranby House, but you could say it is the fourth because there was briefly a Tranby House at Fremantle. Mary Friend's diary records going to a church service at Tranby House in Fremantle in 1830. It was a prefabricated wooden house. The Hardeys left it in Fremantle when they moved to Maylands and for a few months received £1 10s a week rent from the people running a coffee house in it. Then in October 1830 John Wall Hardey swapped the first Tranby House for Phillip Dod's two thousand-acre (810 ha) land allocation across the river from the Maylands peninsula.

Around the current Tranby House there are oak trees and olive trees grown from seeds that were planted in the 1830s. The house was restored by the National Trust in the 1980s, its tin roof replaced with casuarina shingles. The house is well presented with plenty of appropriate furniture, utensils and tools, though none of them were actually owned by the Hardeys. I was particularly impressed by the cellar coolroom. Around the walls of the cellar there are troughs which would have contained water to keep wet the screens of hessian hung all around the room to create a passive evaporative airconditioning system. It is very ingenious and apparently it worked well enough that jellies would set even in summer.

What is not clear to me is when the coolroom was constructed — did the pioneer settlers sit down to a nice cool jelly after a day of clearing scrub and creating fields or do the jellies belong to better established late-Victorian times? Certainly the cluttered Victorian furnishings and decorations of some of the rooms seems more about sepia-toned bric-a-brac nostalgia than about how the West was won.

The green shaded gardens contribute to the conflict between the themes of pioneering hardship and nostalgia for a comfortable, genteel past. There are displays about shingle making and a few of the many other backbreaking tasks that would have been necessary, dawn until dusk, to turn virgin bush into a self-sufficient farm. But it is very, very difficult to imagine those pioneering days. The National Trust could provide logs for visitors to hand saw into planks and rows of potatoes to bank up. But since they don't, one can share another type of experience of the nineteenth century by taking a traditional and refreshing cup of tea at the pleasant Tranby House Tea House. They also do traditional farmers' fare: beef and ale pie, even bread and butter pudding, and there is traditional

Tranby House

1970s English pub food in the form of Ploughman's Lunch, but if you want the honest plain victoria sponge cake that epitomises the dull decorousness of nineteenth-century tea on the lawn you will have to order it in advance. Sandra Martin who runs the Tea House is from redoubtable pioneer and convict stock.

I was told that Tranby House is built of sun-dried mud bricks that the Hardeys made themselves: if that is the case they are remarkably durable and they look as good as well-fired bricks. The volunteer guides are friendly and helpful, happy to let you wander around undisturbed, but always ready to answer questions, even to the extent of making up history on the spot.

The Tranby House Hardeys

Joseph Hardey, who built Tranby House, was a hardworking and skilled farmer. He was widely regarded as a pious man of charitable works and was a pillar of Methodism in Western Australia. Reflecting his origins in dour Lincolnshire Methodist farming stock he was probably not the most light-hearted or openly affectionate of men. Hardey family tradition holds that he would not allow any of his six daughters to marry unless their spouse were a Methodist minister. Since the very few Methodist ministers who came to the colony were already married, and one was their uncle the Reverend Samuel Hardey, all but one of the Hardey girls remained unmarried. The second daughter, Mary Jane, managed to snare the widower Reverend William Lowe when she was forty. It seems only fair that Joseph's only son, Richard, was restricted to daughters of Methodist ministers in his search for a bride. He married Janie Wounder Lowe, the Reverend Lowe's daughter from his first marriage in 1876, a year after his father's death.

How good or bad, how altruistically virtuous or unreasonably harsh was Joseph Hardey? Much of what has been written about him reads as uncritical hagiography. He is said to have been deeply concerned for the spiritual and material welfare of the Aborigines, but his feeling for the Nyungar people was a stern love, and he publicly urged that more of them should gain the benefits that accrued from a term of imprisonment on Rottnest Island.

Undoubtedly he was a man capable of expressing impatience. He demanded the highest moral standards of himself and of others. His moral code was strict and enforced with zeal, but not entirely without flexibility and accommodation. As a Methodist he supported the aims of the Total Abstinence Society (the 'Teetotalers') but as a keen and successful viticulturist he was capable of understanding other aims. In 1863 he agitated for shopkeepers to be allowed to sell locally produced wine in bottles — shopkeepers could sell wine by the gallon but only publicans could retail it in bottles. Hardey was anxious that a working man should be able to drink a bottle of wine at home with his family rather than go down to the pub. If that were possible, 'one step towards a higher state of morals would be obtained,' Hardey wrote in a letter to the governor, the letter annexed by a petition whose wine-producing signatories included Dr Ferguson from Houghtons, Edward Hamersley and Alfred Waylen. The Legislative Assembly passed a bill to implement Hardey's liberal proposal with the complicating administrative innovation that shopkeepers wishing to retail wine (bottled or otherwise) would now need to apply for a licence and pay a fee of £1, a fee that they hiked to £5 a couple of years later.

In 1856, when he was twelve, Joseph and Ann Hardey sent their son Richard Watson Hardey, to Britain for education in Methodist schools. He was schooled for three years on the island of Jersey and then in Leeds, which was closer to relatives' homes. During summer holidays he helped his uncle Robinson, a farmer, with haymaking. A letter to his sister Sarah shows that he was genuinely interested in farming and he described the Yorkshire Agricultural Show with relish. When he had finished his schooling he went to work and study agriculture on the farm of Dr and Mrs Watson in the East Riding of Yorkshire. At the age of twenty-two he returned to take up the management of Peninsula Farm. Whether he was keen to return to his home and family in Western Australia is not clear. His uncle Robert Hardey, who he visited frequently, wrote to Joseph in 1865, 'He does not talk much, but seems more anxious to return to you at the "Swan".' The question is 'more anxious' than what? He retained the inclination to say little through his life and as a member of the Legislative Council seems to have made very little contribution to parliamentary debate.

It was ten years after his return to Peninsula Farm, recently appointed to the Legislative Council, that Richard married Janie Lowe. They had one child, Hubert Richard Lowe, born in 1882. Janie died four years later and Hubert was brought up by his grandfather and his aunt — the Reverend William Lowe and Mary Jane Lowe (née Hardey) — at York. According to Hubert's son, Strelley Hardey, Hubert 'hardly knew his father'.

In 1878 a Peninsula Farm wine won a gold medal in a Paris exhibition. During the 1880s Richard Hardey leased out Peninsula

Tranby House

Farm and put much of his energy into establishing a new property over the Darling Ranges in the area now called Glen Forrest. He planted a thirty-five-acre (13.77 ha) vineyard and Glen Hardey wines gained considerable prestige in the colony.

Richard Hardey married again in 1892, during a second term as an appointed member of the Legislative Council. His bride, Kathleen Emily Beurteaux, was twenty-two years his junior. They had two children, Joseph and Gretchen.

Much of Peninsula Farm was sold as subdivisions in 1903 but the Hardeys retained Tranby House and acquired some extra riverfront land to the north of the house. After Richard's death in 1913 his widow Kathleen sold the farm.

It's a pity that a new housing estate neighbours Tranby House; it was easier to imagine the early colonists' environment when the Tranby gardens were backed by arid scrub. But from the river you can't see the new houses as you follow the steep banks around to Bath Street jetty.

That jetty is less than three kilometres as the shag flies from Claisebrook in the city but, thanks to the meanders around the Burswood and Maylands peninsulas, one will have travelled considerably more than twice that following the river. For walkers there is a very short break in riverside access upstream of Bath Street, then the path cuts through the melaleuca and she-oak Baigup Wetland. The path is wide and the thick melaleuca stands are not close to it, but in a couple of places you can take a side track through them. The melaleuca stands are amazingly thick and dark. Like all swamps they have a primeval feel, even under the brightest midday sky. The dense, needle-leafed foliage of both the swamp *Melaleuca lanceolata* and the casuarina (she-oak) produces a soft but insistent susurration even from a light breeze; it seems to absorb all other sounds adding to the eeriness of a swamp even when you are only a few hundred yards from a main road. The path through the wetlands and the right bank of the river curve around a swampy and wooded shore towards the Garratt Road Bridge.

There are actually two Garratt Road Bridges built of rough-hewn jarrah logs, one carrying northbound traffic and the other southbound traffic, although Garratt Road is not a particularly important road. The two bridges are of similar structure but of different heights. Probably one of the bridges was the railway bridge, built there before the Second World War when a branch line from Bayswater took punters across the river to the Ascot racetrack.

Still only three and a half kilometres from Claisebrook on the eastern side of the city, a more rural way of life is evident. The parks and reserves closer to the city and downstream towards the sea are equipped with barbecue facilities which are really electric hotplates, but out here the barbecues are designed so that you can actually build a wood fire in them. Further out there is an even more bucolic style of barbecue made from old oil drums which you build a fire in; when the fire is going well you close the hotplate lid and cremate your sausages on it.

From Garratt Road to the Tonkin Highway Bridge the river runs straight for two kilometres, which is handy for the Rowing Club. The right bank is parkland in the form of A P Hinds Park, Bayswater Gardens and Riverside Park, which merge into each other and are followed by a wetlands reserve where the swampy flats are all pinks, reds and purple in autumn, tinted by the leaves of two or more species of samphire (a type of succulent) that grow there. Behind Riverside Park is a small lake that forms part of the Eric Singleton Bird Sanctuary.

The parks and sanctuary are fairly recently created — it used

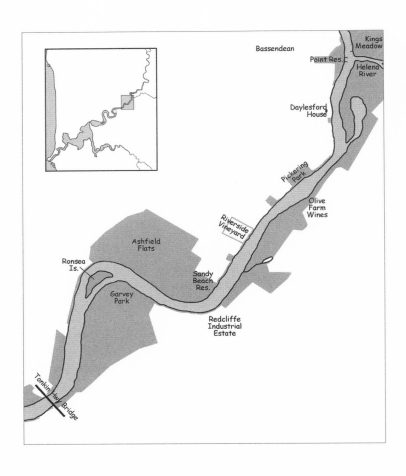

Middle Swan: Tonkin Highway Bridge
to confluence of the Helena River

to be Bayswater rubbish dump and the Bayswater main drain runs through the middle of it. Before that, Chinese-owned market gardens were there. Land in the Bayswater area was first selected by James Brook but his several attempts to sink a well found only brackish water.

In February 1830 Dr James Whatley and family took over the selection and a house that Brook had started. Their first attempt to sink a well produced good sweet water. They called the property Hone's Green after the family home in England. The house was inundated in the winter floods of 1830 and they had to rebuild on higher ground, but things seemed to be going well with farming and Dr Whatley was earning useful cash by treating settlers in the area for conditions including scurvy. Then the doctor went down to Fremantle to buy a cow and was drowned along with Captain Stryan while trying to ferry the beast across the river in too small a boat.

Bayswater is to be commended for the paths, reserves and parks created along the river bank, but around the Tonkin Highway Bridge, which is a popular fishing spot, partly because of the shade the bridge provides, there is more litter and broken glass than anywhere else on the river. The cause of the problem is clear — access by car is too easy — a slip-road leads down to a car park right under the bridge and Katanning Street runs right down to the river on the upstream side. The closer cars can get to the river the worse the littering. Back in 1970, George Seddon warned in his book *Swan River Landscapes* 'There is too little foreshore reserve to make car parks out of it.'

There is another equally cogent reason for keeping car parks away from the river's edge. As well as being horribly littered, the wetland scrub downstream of the bridge is all torn up by cars' wheels. It seems that anyone too lazy or too poorly socialised to take their rubbish away with them is also too lazy to walk more than ten or fifteen metres from their car to the river.

The Swan River Trust's field teams remove shocking volumes of rubbish from the river, beaches and foreshores. According to the Trust's statistics for the accounting year 2000/2001, they removed sixty-five tonnes of 'domestic rubbish', by which one would hope they mean non-industrial litter (that people should have taken to their domicile) rather than stuff people have collected in their homes and brought to dump on the beaches. However, the rubbish included eleven fridges and washing machines that obviously didn't fall out of anyone's pocket after they'd eaten the contents. The field teams also removed 494 tonnes of rotting weed from foreshores, ninety-nine tonnes of fallen logs and branches, six tonnes of rotting fish 'left by prawning parties', and 179 dead birds. Not only that: they salvaged two stolen vehicles and three derelict or abandoned boats from the river, and removed forty-three dead sheep and cattle, and ninety-one drowned shopping trolleys. The livestock were victims of winter floods but shopping trolleys are appallingly reckless in what they will do to get attention or make a statement. I've seen them dangling at the top of flagpoles, grazing playing fields like herds of buffalo and hanging around bikie headquarters, and it is only constant vigilance that keeps them from posing as the Monarch of the Glen at the summit of Uluru.

Of the four big concrete bridges over the Swan, the Tonkin Highway Bridge is the one I like best. Seen from underneath, the carriageway is an elegant structure and dwarfs its piers.

Upstream of the Tonkin Bridge the river is narrower, more thickly tree-lined and, in autumn, it seems to be the upper reach of the thick swarms of brown jellyfish, so I suppose it marks the point where the river's salinity decreases significantly.

Early in the morning and at the end of some days the river is cheerful and busy with canoeists and rowers, but for the rest of a weekday it is a place of solitude. There is almost no one on the river, only the tourist boats and they are hermetically sealed, airconditioned, tinted glass boxes that a few elderly tourists stare blankly out from. Along the banks there are stern, well-heeled women walking various types of pedigree dog. They say hello but they certainly don't stop for a chat. There are a few people fishing: usually divorcee fathers and their school-truant sons privately enjoying quality time together.

Tonkin Highway Bridge

Upstream of the bridge where the river curves north there is another nature reserve and then, where the river banks are higher with some cliffs, there are houses in amongst the trees. A single property runs its fences right down to the water and prevents walkers from following the river from the reserve to Ashfield Parade along the top of the cliffs. Then the river bank curves back to the south-east and the right bank is undeveloped flood plain again — the Ashfield Flats — round to the next bend and Sandy Beach Reserve.

Property along the river banks is obviously valuable and desirable. Upstream of Sandy Beach Reserve there are still a couple of modest old cottages with small plantings of citrus and other fruit trees around them, and a little further upstream Riverside Vineyard still produces grapes. The vineyard was planted in 1939 by Luigi Nicoletto growing mainly shiraz and grenache for wine making.

Presumably the close proximity of an industrial estate and the airport on the opposite bank have kept away the bourgeoisie until relatively recently, but along the rest of the right bank, northwards to Pickering Park and onwards all the way to Point Reserve and thence to Guildford Road Bridge and Success Hill, there are smarter and grander houses with tidy landscaped gardens. Most are of fairly recent construction. One exception is Daylesford House which stands on the highest part of the bank.

I put ashore at the end of a road nearby and walked up to Daylesford Road for a closer look, but from the land you can see nothing other than the garage and some trees in a very ordinary suburban street — another example of how much more special the river experience is. Daylesford was built at the end of the nineteenth century for Cyril Jackson, the inspector general of schools at that time. He stayed for only seven years in Australia.

Walking the river through that part of Bassendean (on the Heritage Trail opened by Bassendean's most famous son, Rolf Harris) is frustrating because the only access to the river is through a series of tiny riverside parks, each at the end of a dead-end street. Some private riverside properties bordering on the parks allow access to the river banks, fencing their gardens above the flood plain, but it only takes one fence run down to the water and a TRESPASSERS WILL BE PROSECUTED to block what ought to be a public right of way.

I have been told that when John Septimus Roe, the first surveyor general, divided up riverside lands he insisted on a thirty-foot (9.15 m) setback to fencing to allow access and right of way, partly for the Nyungar people. But I can find no evidence for that. The large blocks that run right down to the river from North Road are old, the first of them allocated in 1831, and one of them was acquired by John Septimus Roe.

The idea of a fence setback and a continuous riverside reserve was introduced in the 1960s but has not yet been completely implemented because of lack of political will and funding. When properties are subdivided the reserve automatically comes into effect. In some places the Swan River Trust effects acquisition of

Daylesford House peeping through the trees

the reserved riverside land, but old properties that have not been subdivided or developed retain the right to block river bank access. There is, however, a requirement that all fencing should be 'open-view' fencing and there is one property in Bassendean that still flouts that regulation.

Peter Brown, 'founder' of Bassendean

Peter Nicholas Brown, also Broun and Browne, was colonial secretary and acting treasurer in the first years of the colony. When he arrived at the colony he generally favoured the spelling B-R-O-W-N, but as time went by he used B-R-O-U-N more frequently and towards the end of his life only used that spelling. He was from Guernsey but his family had some aristocratic Scots connections like James Stirling's. He was also a naval officer. It was on the recommendation of Sir George Murray, a friend of his dad and also of Stirling's family, that he was appointed colonial secretary.

Broun left England to take up the post of secretary of the new Swan River Colony seriously in debt and he ran up more debts in the colony. He mortgaged his property Bassendean to the government for £1500 to pay off some of those debts and never repaid the loan. It was eventually recovered when the property was sold ten years after his death. He also failed to pay off creditors in England, one of whom wrote complaining to Stirling:

I understand he is living in princely manner, and that he has purchased 2000 acres of land from the Government, no doubt with the money he should have paid his creditors who are toiling and starving here, to pay the Taxes in order to pay him his salary.

He was fond of good living. Captain Fremantle noted:

Mr Brown has a nice cottage & beautifully situated; it might be made a pretty & enjoyable place, but I doubt whether Mrs B. or himself have much turn or taste for a settler's life or understand making the best of things.

Broun had certainly intended to make a go of being a gentleman farmer for included in his goods and chattels that loaded up the *Parmelia* were a bull and a cow, four pigs, two horses, a goat, two dogs, fowl, geese, turkeys and ducks. But Fremantle was, no doubt, correct in assessment and it was probably Broun as much as anyone that his neighbour James Henty had in mind when he wrote:

The farmers as they call themselves are a parcel of half pay captains and officers. If they could grow corn on the table where there is plenty of wine and brandy a throwing about, they might do very well then.

He and wife Caroline were parents to ten children, the first two born before they came to Australia.

Broun favoured taking harsh measures against the Aborigines and clashed with Robert Milne Lyon who felt differently and protected Yagan and others when he could.

Point Resolution in Dalkeith was also known as Point Brown and another Point Brown, which to this day has no other name, is right under the carriageway of Stirling Bridge on the north-western shore of Port Irwin, North Fremantle.

Broun has been regarded as the founder of Bassendean because he acquired from James Henty a largish selection in what is now southern Bassendean or Ashfield on which he built a homestead called, with his fondness for alternative spellings, Bassendene, Bassingdean or Bassendean. It was demolished in 1946, one hundred years after Broun had died at the age of forty-nine. The suburb of Bassendean was called West Guildford until 1912.

Broun had a larger selection in the Swan Valley that he called Coulston after the family seat in Berwickshire, Scotland.

The area that is now Bassendean was a distinctly unwanted area in the early days of the colony. It was first allocated to Captain Thomas Bannister but he didn't want it. It was then taken up by James Henty, though it was not the Hentys' first choice. Six months after taking up the selection of 1555 acres, Henty wrote to the governor saying that his stock were starving, he hadn't wanted the sandy selection that he'd been allocated, and he needed better land.

Eventually the Hentys — James, William and Stephen — left the Swan River Colony, hoping to exchange their Western Australian lands for a smaller selection in Van Diemen's Land where their father's family had decided to settle. That exchange was not allowed and free land grants in Van Diemen's Land had ended. The Hentys began looking at land across Bass Strait on the mainland and also continued trading in Fremantle and England.

Despite official discouragement they settled at Portland, Port Phillip Bay, in November 1834, creating the first white settlement in what became Victoria.

The Hentys' problems with the land available in Western Australia were far from unusual. Stirling and the botanist Fraser had been much too optimistic in their initial assessment of the quality of the soils in the Swan River catchment and the extent of tillable soils. The Swan River Colony was established on the basis of observations from a jolly picnic voyage on the rivers, much like my own survey one hundred and seventy-five years later, and, as I was learning, it is a very restricted view — the place one sees from down on the river is a much greener and pleasanter place than most of the dry coastal plain.

Mary Friend, a visitor to the Swan River Colony in 1830, sailing with her husband who was skipper of the ship *Wanstead*, reflected sardonically on Stirling's description: 'It is very true that the country is "beautiful, undulating and thinly wooded," but alas the soil is nothing but sand.' She also discussed the other problem for settlers looking for fertile land:

> The Governor has likewise given good grants to the officers of the different Men of War that have been at Port. They are gone away for three years and in the mean time the land lies idle, and numerous Settlers are waiting on the beach for their grants.

Captain Fremantle was an officer who didn't take up the offer of land and it doesn't take too much reading between the lines of his diary to see that he thought Stirling a bit of a prat on the subject of soil fertility right from first acquaintance.

Lionel Lukin, who arrived on *Egyptian* in February 1830, wrote to Lord Glenelg about land allocations:

> To my surprise, however, I find all the bank of the Swan and Canning rivers granted mostly to officers of the Army and Navy on full pay, who never brought a sixpence worth of property into the colony, and who had not the means of improving the land granted to them, having no servants.

In that comment he was not being entirely fair, because, as he was to discover, army and navy officers enjoyed a considerable advantage in improving their land since they could often employ army privates as labourers for one shilling and sixpence a day, while the going rate for servants and labourers was five shillings. Even if they didn't do that, there was another use to which they could put their free land grant — they could sell it to a better heeled settler.

Since the early days there had been a Guildford ferry approximately where the road and rail bridges connecting Bassendean and Guildford now stand. The first officially licensed ferry was operated from 1831 by a Dr Crowcher who owned a number of the Guildford Town Land Allocations adjacent to the market reserve.

The good doctor seems to have earned a very inadequate income from medical practice and from the ferry on which the charge was threepence per person or one shilling for someone with a horse, but no charge could be levied for officers, soldiers or any person in the civil service. Guildford seemingly did not have the population to support the Crowchers and with his children starving he returned to Fremantle to earn a living as a medical practitioner in 1833.

The first Guildford Road Bridge was built in 1885 by Benjamin Mason who also built the Fremantle Bridge. A second bridge was built in 1904 and that was replaced by a third, of very similar structure, in 1937. That bridge, with some addition and replacement, still stands today.

On the Bassendean bank upstream of the bridge the large and attractive house is called Earlsferry, not because there was a ferry there but named after a place in Scotland where Mr Short who had the house built came from. Or, according to another source, it was called Briarleigh until it became a home for mentally retarded girls in the 1960s.

On the river bank below Earlsferry there is a plaque that reads:

Dr R K Constable

1788–1988

This was particularly interesting to me because at a dinner function at which I had booked a table for a small group of friends we were joined by a Dr Constable and his wife. I thought his wife looked a bit younger and more cheerful than he, but it had never occurred to me that he could be over two hundred years old and had been dead since 1988. I'm still very dubious and have been told that Bassendean is in the habit of inscribing on plaques similarly hyperbolic claims of longevity on behalf of residents and former residents, including J S Roe.

John Septimus Roe: 1797–1878

Born 8 May 1797 in Barking, England, where his father was the curate. The family moved to the parish of St Nicholas, Newbury, Berkshire, when he was still very young.

Roe has been described as having an upper-class background and his philosophy as 'undemocratic'. But he was not born with a silver spoon in his mouth. Both his grandfathers were clergymen and his father was a minor clergyman who struggled to find the funds to send John Septimus, the seventh of ten children, to school.

At the age of ten he was sent to Christ's Hospital School to prepare for being a Royal Navy midshipman. He didn't want to go to sea but acceded to his parents' decision.

In May 1813 he was offered a berth on HMS *Rippon*, a seventy-four gun ship. He served a little more than a year on *Rippon* in the Channel fleet and saw action. During his brief service on the seventy-four he was quickly noted as a competent artist, mathematician and surveyor, but he fell ill and partially lost the sight in his right eye.

His next ship was the frigate HMS *Horatio*.

Still a midshipman and twenty years old he was selected to sail with Lieutenant Phillip Parker King to continue the Royal Navy's detailed survey of the Australian coast that had been started by Matthew Flinders, but aborted when Flinders felt that his ship *Investigator* was unsound. Roe sailed with King on all of his long surveying voyages aboard the cutter *Mermaid* and the brig *Bathurst*. Roe and another midshipman, Bedwell, served as King's officers. Roe was King's second-in-command and worked indefatigably on surveying and preparing superbly detailed charts despite his impaired eye.

After five years of exploring Australia's most remote coasts, King and his crew returned to England where Roe continued to work on Australian charts and sailing directions based on the survey work. The *Sailing Directions for Australian Waters*, which he prepared, were published by the Hydrographic Office in 1830 when Francis Beaufort (later Sir Francis) took over as hydrographer and elevated the office from a map repository to a department directing world-wide hydrographic surveys and publishing the results. Previously the results of a hydrographic survey were published by the officers who undertook the survey. (Elizabeth Cook, widow of James Cook, died a relatively wealthy woman thanks to the publication of her husband's charts, a pension and business acumen.)

In 1824 he joined HMS *Tamar* as lieutenant, sailing to Australia again. Captain James Bremer of HMS *Tamar* proclaimed formal possession of part of Australia's northern coast and set up the unsuccessful Fort Dundas settlement at Melville Island, ignoring instructions to locate the settlement at Port Essington further east. Roe surveyed Apsley Strait between Melville and Bathurst Island and later produced a detailed chart which was not superseded until the second half of the twentieth century.

He was back in England in 1827 and on 7 January 1829 he married Matilda Bennett.

Later in that year John Septimus Roe was appointed the Surveyor General of the Swan River Colony. He went on to serve forty-two years in that office. Initially he received £400 per annum as surveyor general; he remained on full pay as a naval officer for some time and then went to half pay, rising to the rank of commodore, which he applied for on a short visit to England in 1860.

As Surveyor General, Roe served in government as a member of the Legislative and Executive Assemblies. Like most of his cohorts, he did not get on with Stirling. Even before sailing to the Swan River Colony he bluntly stated, 'I must say I do not like the man,' in a letter to his father. Their professional relationship was not helped by Stirling frequently changing his mind about which lands he wanted to make up his hundred thousand acre land grant, nor by Stirling allowing the whole system of land titles to degenerate into an extra-legal chaos. Roe was scrupulous about not using his position for personal benefit while Stirling was seemingly unable to distinguish between public and personal property. Yet Roe called on Stirling when he visited England in 1860.

Roe was a hardworking and honest public servant; he was also a loyal husband and a committed farmer, but he does not seem to have been a very warm or sociable man. A relative, James Elphinstone Roe, an Oxford-educated minister of religion, came to Western Australia in 1862. He was transported having been convicted of forgery (his family always believed he was innocent). In time his large family came to Australia and both he and his wife worked as teachers. Like other educated convicts trying to improve their lot and gain professional employment, J E Roe found himself thwarted by government officials at times. Nevertheless, he made important, uncompromising and constructive recommendations about the development of Western Australia's education system and later, with two other former convicts, James Pearce and the Hon. William De La Poer Beresford, he co-edited the *Fremantle Herald*, a fearless and sometimes scurrilous critic of the administration. John Septimus Roe was always 'distant in manner as well as relationship' according to his distant cousin James Elphinstone Roe.

Roe belonged to the elite lineage of maritime surveyors who explored Australia's coasts — a lineage that can be traced running directly from James Cook, and it was Roe who began the serious (non-indigenous) exploration and survey of the interior.

He led sixteen expeditions to explore the inland. Later explorers, including Gregory, learned their navigation and survey techniques on expeditions with Roe. He collected biological and geological samples on his expeditions and was elected a member of the Linnean Society. He was also founding president of the Swan River Mechanics Institute (not a club for car mechanics) which was the basis of both the State Library and Museum.

A lineage of Australian Maritime Exploration

James Cook can be seen as beginning the hydrographic survey of Australia using accurate scientific techniques that had not been available to earlier Dutch explorers.

From Cook to Roe and beyond one can trace a lineage of navigators passing the task and the skills from one generation to the next.

William Bligh sailed with Cook as sailing master on HMS *Resolution*.

Matthew Flinders sailed with Bligh on HMS *Providence*.

Phillip Parker King first met Flinders as a boy in Australia. As a young naval officer he was recommended by Flinders to Sir Joseph Banks, who had sponsored Australian discovery since Cook, and to Thomas Hurd, head of the Royal Navy Hydrographic Office.

Bungaree, an Aboriginal leader from the Sydney area, sailed with both Flinders and King on voyages around Australia.

King, with Roe as his second-in-command, surveyed more of the Australian coastline, particularly the northern and western coasts, than either Flinders or Cook.

King went on to command HMS *Adventure* and HM Brig *Beagle* on two voyages of exploration. Then, between 1837 and 1843, *Beagle*, commanded first by J C Wickham and later by John Lort Stokes, was set to complete the basic survey of Australia's coasts, filling in the gaps left by P P King's survey. Wickham sailed to the Swan River Colony to consult with Roe before starting his surveying work.

The first railway bridge at Guildford was built in 1897 but the current pair of railway bridges is quite recent.

On the first expedition up the Swan, Bill and I had approached Success Hill in the night with the moon low in the sky. I had noted 'a very fine cantilever suspension bridge carrying a water main'. In daylight the cantilever suspension bridge is not quite so impressive, and it probably carries a sewage pipe. But Success Hill is still a delightful part of the river — the hill creates steep, high banks with trees hanging over the river. There are no buildings in sight on either bank.

The absence of buildings on the left bank, where Guildford lies, was a surprise and, in a way it was a disappointment too. I'd done some reading about the history of Guildford, a settlement as old as Fremantle and Perth. Guildford owes its existence to the river but you can't really see the town from the water. A little further upstream a few houses are visible through the trees, across the flood plain, none of them very grand and some of them obviously new.

But Guildford is on the left bank, so it belongs to another part of my narrative. On the right bank, above Success Hill the river bank changes character again. There are open agricultural paddocks and you can see traditional agricultural elements which have considerable historic significance, such as horses and cattle.

Success Hill is usually said to have been named by Stirling after his ship HMS *Success* and to reflect his expedition's success in

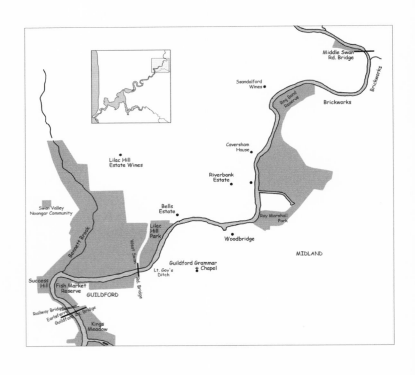

Middle and Upper Swan: Success Hill to the
Middle Swan Road Bridge

finding a freshwater spring which flows out from the side of the hill over the river, and from which they filled the ship's barrels. Stirling's journal does not lend support to that story. The hill might have been named by Lt. William Preston who owned adjacent land and had sailed on HMS *Success*. The spring and the hill were very significant to the Morro Nyungar people. It was a meeting place for major cultural processes and ceremonies — corroboree as we wadjella or whitefella like to say.

Unlike many other attractive riverside parks, Success Hill has never been used as a rubbish dump. There have been Chinese market gardens on the northern side, and the hill has been reduced by sand mining.

Just past Success Hill, Bennett Brook flows into the Swan. It was also known as Preston's Creek when William Preston owned the land it flows through. Below the confluence of the creek and the Swan, Waugal, the Dreamtime creator being, is said to live in a sub-riverine cavern.

A small boat can get into Bennett Brook, even at the end of a dry summer, but it is difficult to make much progress up the brook which is obstructed by fallen melaleuca trees. I turned back after a couple of hundred metres. In earlier times the brook was obviously more navigable because you can see the remains of small jetties and what looks like a weir.

Bennett Brook (Bennett's Brook when apostrophes were still

allowed in place names) was named for Matilda Roe whose maiden name was Bennett. Matilda Roe came to the Swan River Colony among the first settlers, newly married to John Septimus Roe. The Roes stayed in Western Australia and were parents to thirteen children.

I decided to walk beside the melaleuca swamp that encloses Bennett Brook on a path from Success Hill. After a few hundred metres the path leads up on to the ridge above the flood plain, and at a point just past a sign warning that snakes have been seen in the vicinity, another path branches back down to the flood plain and follows the edge of the melaleuca swamp again. It leads to a derelict bridge made from two large logs. Almost all the timber decking between the logs has gone, but if you teeter across balancing on one of the logs, there seems to be a path leading from the bridge across the flat paddocks to the West Swan Road.

Having looked across the paddocks, I chose to wobble back across the bridge again and continue following the brook's western bank through the open woodland on the edge of the swamp. That pleasant walk was increasingly marred by dead cars lying stripped and vandalised in the scrub. The first ones I saw had been there for some years and were rusting into the landscape, but others were newly wrecked and small, worthless personal items (broken sunglasses and hairclips) from the gutted glove boxes were scattered around them, among the broken glass.

Just past a savagely vandalised lawn mower sitting in the

middle of circular flood pan, looking as if it had taken a direct hit from a mortar, the track petered out. I could have battled my way through the scrub but I chose to follow a track up towards Lord Street which runs on the ridge parallel to the Brook.

At the top of the ridge I came to what was obviously a Nyungar community — the largest building was decorated with a Nyungar mural, the small buildings were all apparently identical single-storey cabins and there was loud country music coming from one of them. As I got closer I passed a pile of trashed bicycles, and then a terrible domestic argument broke out in the nearest cabin. I turned back for a moment, but then decided to walk past taking no obvious notice. Two fairly ugly dogs decided to take notice of me. They barked and snarled but didn't actually attack. Since they had come from behind they blocked any possibility of my turning back.

On the other side of the settlement I was quizzed, not unpleasantly, by an elderly man.

'Who you looking for?'

'No one, I'm just walking.'

'You know this is private property?'

'No. I was just following a track beside the brook. There are no signs.'

'Oh, so you come through the back door. If I come to your house, I come through the back door?'

I shrugged.

'I'm only telling you your law, not ours.'

'Sorry about that.' I said lamely.

Out on Lord Street it was only a short walk to Benara Road which crosses Bennett Brook. The UBD road map shows that the brook widens to a broad pond, but that pond's margins are actually the extent of the flood plain. Where Benara Road crosses, the brook is little more than a trickle completely covered by water plants in the summer. The brook is surrounded by natural flood plain vegetation and provides a good refuge for waterfowl and other wildlife.

Crossing to the left bank (eastern side) of the brook, one enters the Swan Valley wine-producing country. There are vineyards all around. I visited Lilac Hill Estate winery, formerly known as Valencia, before that part of the Santa Rosa winery, and established as Carlisle in 1890.

A tall, square brick building makes the winery easily spotted from the road: it was the distillery tower in the days when Valencia produced bulk wines and distilled alcohol for pharmaceutical use. It is sometimes said that the Swan Valley is best suited to the production of bulk wine. The summer climate is hot and the vineyards are irrigated because there is usually no significant rain in late spring and summer when the grapes develop (nor in autumn after the grapes are picked). A longer, cooler, less dry ripening season is generally reckoned to produce more intense and complex flavours but smaller volumes of fruit.

Many of the Swan River wineries produce good quality wine; at least they put it in bottles so it's not bulk wine. The larger wineries use grapes from other areas along with Swan Valley fruit to produce wines of consistent quality in significant volume.

Lilac Hill Estate produce varieties including chardonnay, semillon, verdelho (which doesn't mind hot conditions), cabernet sauvignon, merlot, shiraz and, unique in the Swan Valley, zinfandel. I thought the zinfandel very good. After a wine-tasting I purchased a glass of it to sip while I wrote a few notes in the shaded garden, and I'm seriously considering ordering a case of it now.

Lilacs and Lilac Hill

Lilac Hill Estate Winery is named after Lilac Hill and Lilac Hill Park which are actually a kilometre or two away on the bank of the Swan. The hill and park are named for the cape lilac trees (*Melia azedarach*) that were planted there — one or two still survive. The preferred common name for cape lilac is now white cedar, though it is not a cedar. It is native to the Kimberley region of north-west Australia, or it was introduced there a very long time ago, and it is found in locations across Asia as far away as Iran.

Crooks (naturally bent pieces) and forks of cape lilac were favoured for making strengthening components such as knees and breasthooks in fast sailing boats raced on the Swan because the timber is light but strong.

If you are on foot, it is possible to walk from Lilac Hill Estate winery down a tree-lined track to West Swan Road without returning to Benara Road. West Swan Road is not particularly pleasant walking, but a few hundred yards along it, you can take the turn-off signposted for Mulberry Farm winery, though it's not really called that anymore. It can be called Mulberry Farm Convention Centre now but it is also Bell's Estate, although the wines that they offer there are Gloucester Ridge wines which come from Pemberton in the South-West. I liked their pinot best, as far as I can remember, but I'd stopped making notes at that stage.

From Mulberry Farm one can walk along the right bank of the Swan back towards Guildford crossing the Swan on the West Swan Road Bridge and then across the Guildford Road Bridge, to my starting point at Success Hill, thus going up the right bank and down the left bank of the lower reaches of Bennett Brook by land.

The West Swan Road Bridge is a typical jarrah log bridge. It was built in 1948, replacing a bridge built in 1900 which replaced a bridge known as Barker's Bridge built right back in 1854. Barker was a Guildford trader who left Western Australia in 1860. The timbers look to be in better condition than some of the other jarrah bridges but it is the West Swan Bridge that creaks slightly when a heavy truck goes over.

I've used the West Swan Bridge as the division between the Middle Swan and the Upper Swan but it is, of course, an artificial and arbitrary division. At Bennett Brook one is already in agricultural country because the brook marks the end of the loose sandy soils of the Bassendean dunes and the start of the clay, loam and gravel of the Swan Valley (which isn't much of a valley).

The flat and open agricultural land upstream of Bennett Brook has probably not changed much since the arrival of the colonists. On Stirling's expedition he had noted 'broad fertile flats' with park-like character. He also saw that the land around Bassendean was 'rich and romantic country' and the Swan Valley was 'undulating grassy country, thinly wooded, good loamy soil'. Fraser, the botanist who accompanied him, estimated there were ten trees per acre on average. They were looking at land that was tended and altered by Nyungar people operating a fire regime. Old photographs of the land around Bassendean and Guildford show fewer big trees than there are today and a watercolour done by Frederick Garling, the artist who accompanied Stirling, depicts the view from Bassendean, near Success Hill looking over Fish Market Reserve and shows no trees there. Today it is fairly thickly wooded.

Chapter 5

UPPER SWAN, RIGHT BANK

My survey of the right bank of the part of the river, which I regard as the Middle Swan, took two boat voyages up and downstream and a couple of visits on foot. In truth I was looking at some of the left bank too.

The week after Easter I was ready to try the Upper Swan which for me is the river above the West Swan Road bridge. But the wind blew hard from the east all week and I couldn't face the prospect of tacking all the way up Melville Water and Perth Water and rowing or tacking all the way up the Middle Swan against a stiff breeze. I'd found that the boat tacked quite well and felt safe even in strong gusty conditions if I deep reefed the sail, but beating all the way up to Maylands would have been laborious, would have taken much of a day, and I would have got thoroughly soaked by spray out on Melville Water. So I did a bit of library research and made another trip on foot instead.

To walk the river banks I could catch a train from Fremantle to a station near the Middle Swan and catch a train back from another station when I'd had enough of walking. The railway crosses the river at Fremantle and although the line links the three first settlements built on the river (Fremantle, Perth and Guildford) and runs parallel to the river, you can't actually see the river again until crossing the railway bridge between Success Hill and Guildford. Perhaps that's not quite true — you can look for the river between Mount Lawley and Maylands stations. If you stand on your seat, looking out to the right of the train heading towards Guildford, the flash of blue you see through the trees, for a split second, looking down to the end of Third Avenue might be the river.

Getting off the train at Success Hill Station, I'd walk the couple of hundred metres to the river through pleasant but dull suburban Bassendean, having travelled through similar suburbs for miles on the train.

At the Guildford Road Bridge, just down the road from the station, you can walk down a narrow path beside the bridge and suddenly you are in a completely different world. The dark untamed foliage of the melaleuca, the she-oak and marri is quite different from the polite green trees of the suburban gardens. It is impossible to reconcile the river's uncompromised idylls with the stultifying suburbs that share the same names — Maylands, Ascot, South Guildford — they don't seem like the same places at all.

The easterly winds brought beautiful clear, cloudless weather with very low humidity, but the weather had been dry all summer, and the previous winter had been unusually dry too. Perth's reservoirs were all nearly empty. Sometimes I remarked on the weather as a way of making contact with the few people I met along the river banks. 'Glorious day,' I'd say.

'Yes it is. Better if it was raining though.'

Eventually the weather forecast promised an end to the easterly weather with the prospect of a few showers and blustery southwesterly winds. *Earnest* and I could once more set off at the crack of dawn, the bright blue-check sail unfurled to a nice grey blustery morning as we went running away before the wind.

As I crossed Melville Water the sun shone through a gap in the clouds for a few minutes in a sky writhing in the change from dry summer to slightly showery autumn. It was the sort of churning sky where one moment the cloud seems to be breaking up but turn the other way and dark rain clouds filled your view. I took down the sail in a brief but chilling squall approaching Heirisson Island, and twenty minutes later, rowing past Claisebrook, I was becalmed and lathered with sweat in conditions of almost tropical humidity. I should have taken off my wet weather jacket a bit sooner.

Around the southern end of the Maylands peninsula erosion of the river banks was more evident than ever. Three small she-oaks had fallen over, three disks of roots sticking up studded with old broken bricks. The problem is inappropriately designed powerboats: big fat things that drag their big fat arses through the water and drag half the river in sharp ridges behind them. They are designed to be relatively efficient near top speed, when they almost plane on the surface of the water, but at the speeds permitted on the river they create terrible wash. There must be some way to fine or tax boats that are wrongly designed for river use. Catamarans and single-hulled vessels with elegant old-fashioned sterns are much more suitable for the river.

Commercial river cruises for tourists are provided by catamarans, all of them of near identical design with as much style as a demountable building-site office, but they don't create much wash: *River Bells, River Lady, Miss Sandalford, Lady De Vine* are all airconditioned boxes with tinted windows. Since they are not permitted to exceed eight knots anywhere, and are restricted to five knots in places, a more traditional river boat design would seem quite practical and would allow passengers to sit or stroll out on deck, shaded by awnings, and to get a bit closer to the river.

I hope that seeing a man in a real rowing boat adds a bit of interest for passengers on the cruises when I'm on the river. Rowing anything other than a racing scull, and rowing while not wearing a lycra uniform does excite some comment from men fishing from the banks. 'Looks like hard work,' is the usual comment. But it's not. Back in practice at rowing I could reply with honesty, 'It's easier than walking.' I can row gently for hours and make fifty kilometres in a day; the boat carries my tent, sleeping-bag, mat and other baggage for me. Eventually my bum gets sore from sitting on the wooden thwart and I have to go ashore for a stretch, but rowing really is very relaxing.

I was in a particularly relaxed state, rowing easily up the middle of Ascot Reach pushed by the following wind, using the oars mainly to maintain a straight course by keeping a particular tree dead astern, when I ran CRASH into a navigation beacon and scared myself witless.

Thanks to the following wind I reached the West Swan Road Bridge just after two in the afternoon. The land immediately upstream of the bridge is Lilac Hill Park and the grounds of the Guildford-Midland Cricket Club. Though it is now named a hill it used to be Preston Flats Farm and the name flats describes it much better. The cricket pitch is used at the beginning of summer for a warm-up match between visiting teams from other countries and a Chairman's Eleven of Australian cricketers, usually a mix of players who might soon be called up to join the Australian team and older players who were formerly members of the Australian team. Players of that calibre wouldn't play at Lilac Hill if it wasn't nice and flat.

I could have stopped at Mulberry Farm/Bells Estate next to Lilac Hill Park where the *River Bells* and *River Lady* cruises pull up to the jetty and the passengers go ashore for a wine-tasting, but I'd already been there when I walked around Bennett Brook. There is

Lilac Hill Cricket Ground

an important point to note about Bells Estate as a watering hole on the right bank of the river. An old shipmate and sometime drinking companion had written to me that my river project 'sounds like a good jaunt, no doubt landing places are adjacent to watering places' meaning places where you could get a proper drink. I had replied:

Alas, I shall be writing a story of a forlorn quest for the long lost riverside watering places.

Years ago I could have put into the Cape Horn Hotel (not its real name but the proprietor was a Mr Caporn) at Point Walter where the roughs who rowed the whaleboat ferries between Fremantle and Perth used to fuel up. Now there's only a modishly Mediterranean cafe/restaurant. There was the rambling old Majestic Hotel on Point Dundas now torn down and replaced by Majestic Mansions, Majestic Villas, Palazzo Majestic, Majestic Estate, Maisons Majestique, Majestic Apartments and the Majestic Mews Town Houses all crammed into a couple of acres and screaming 'look at me,' 'look at me.'

I take with me a plastic bottle full of cask red wine as a simple solace

Incredibly, following the right bank all the way from the sea, Bells Estate is the first place one reaches where one can get a drink without also having to buy a meal at a restaurant, unless you tie up among the ferries at Barrack Street Jetty. The savagely puritanical licensing laws that oppress most anglophone countries are to blame. It's no wonder that some of us are tempted to drink too much when we have the constant sensation that the authorities are trying to prevent us from ever getting a drink. And it is curious that environmentally concerned groups reliably succeed in preventing the opening of watering holes around Perth's foreshores and yet have so little success in preventing the development of far more environmentally deleterious housing estates.

A bit further upstream from Mulberry Farm the river bank is protected by ranks of signs, standing almost shoulder to shoulder, proclaiming that anyone who steps ashore on those green and bosky banks will most definitely be prosecuted on behalf of the Ministry of Justice. (That might sound like Orwellian satire, but it's true.) Above those signs, on the top of the banks, is the Riverbank Detention Centre.

Curiously, if I had gone ashore there, ignoring the prohibition, and inspected the perimeter of the Detention Centre, I'd have found that one is not prohibited from approaching its other boundaries on the road and in neighbouring vineyards. When I visited by road a couple of weeks later, an open farm gate invited me to walk down towards the river bank and view the blank grey backs of the KEEP OUT signs.

The Detention Centre seems to have been built on the site of an old homestead named Pyrton — named after the family seat of the Tanner family in Oxfordshire according to one source. But piecing together various scraps in notebooks I have constructed a much more complicated explanation of the name. Pyrton Manor was actually the name of the estate in Kent where Anne Hamersley was born and her father was rector. She married William Brockman and they migrated to Western Australia among the pioneers of 1829. I haven't found evidence that the Swan River estate named Pyrton was owned by Brockman, though he did own a number of other Swan Valley properties, most notably Herne Hill, the largest of the early estates; however Pyrton, along with neighbouring Lockeridge, was later owned by the Hamersley family. It seems that the name Pyrton was erroneously transferred to a house that had once been owned by Tanner, which he had called Lockeridge. Complicating all this, another Lockeridge, like another Pyrton, has served as a detention centre or institution for the intellectually challenged, as most of the grander colonial and federation houses have at times.

Just along the road from Riverbank Detention Centre is River bank Estate Vineyard and Winery. I asked the people there about Pyrton but they knew nothing of it, which is a little surprising because I now know that the first West Australian wine to win a medal at an international exhibition was produced right there at Hamersley's Pyrton. Riverbank Estate is a relatively small wine producer with thirty acres of vineyards but they produce a large range of grape varieties and wine styles — cabernet, shiraz, pinot noir, grenache, verdelho, semillon, chardonnay, muscat and chenin — from which they make single varietals, blends, sweet wines and a sparkling chardonnay, all quite reasonably priced and nearly all made entirely with estate grown grapes.

I'd rowed past Bells Estate and Riverbank Detention Centre intending to stop at Caversham House and stretch my legs. When I got there contractors with earthmoving machinery were excavating a car park or a space for a new building on the river bank below the house, raising clouds of dust in the process. It was an unattractive prospect and I nearly rowed straight past. But I was on a mission to investigate all historical sites so I beached *Earnest* and skirted the excavations and dust clouds to walk up to the house which sits on a small bluff over the river.

The original house is one of the oldest in the valley, however you can't see much of it from the outside because of ramshackle outhouses and more substantially designed additions, and extensions that enclose the few remains of the original structure.

The property had a number of owners during the nineteenth century, starting with Peter Cayley Shadwell who stayed only a few months in 1830. It is thought that the name Caversham Rise was probably given by Dr Richard Hinds, a naval surgeon who lived there with his family, including his interestingly named son Charles Pidley Hinds.

Caversham is the name of a village (now a suburb) near Reading in Berkshire, and Berkshire is also where the owner of Sandalford, the neighbouring property, John Septimus Roe, came from. Sandalford was the name of the home of the Montagu family, where Roe's father, the rector of Newbury, sometimes conducted services in the private chapel. Sandalford had been a priory until the Reformation.

The names Sandalford and Caversham are now linked in the name of a winery and perhaps they were linked when the names were first allocated to properties on the Swan River.

Caversham House in its current manifestation as Caversham House Function Centre is a peculiar mix of homely farmstead and glitzy function centre. There was no one there when I went ashore on a weekday afternoon, but I visited again on a Saturday a week or two later when they were busy preparing for two wedding receptions: one in the house, the other in a marquee in the garden. The place settings were very elegant, each with several cut-glass wine glasses for the different wines that would be served, and there must have been considerably more than a hundred settings crammed into the marquee and the house. There was also a rather ordinary middle-of-the-road rock band testing their PA system in the marquee. I hoped they weren't going to play 'Tie a Yellow Ribbon' and other favorites during the lavish meal but suspected it was all going to be a touch vulgar.

Sandalford Caversham, upstream from Caversham House, is a

winery of considerable historical distinction. Houghtons and Olive Farm can claim to have started commercial production earlier, but Sandalford was owned by John Septimus Roe, a man who vies with Governor Stirling as the most historically significant of all the first white settlers of Western Australia, and Roe first planted vines within a year or two of the founding of the Swan River Colony.

The Roe family did not undertake commercial wine production at Sandalford until the First World War but they maintained control of the winery from then until the 1980s. Wine production at Sandalford goes back to the 1860s when Swan Valley viticulture was just taking off and Houghtons was still very small scale. Sandalford had fallen into disuse, like several other properties, when Malachi Meagher, a ticket-of-leave convict, leased it from Roe in 1862. Employing probationer convicts he engaged in several types of agriculture, stock dealing and winemaking. By 1865 Sandalford produced 2,160 gallons (about 10,000 litres) which was fortified with seventy gallons (318.5 litres) of spirit.

Miall Meagher, who anglicised (or hebrewised) his Gaelic name to Malachi when granted his ticket-of-leave in 1860, had been a civil engineer in Limerick, Ireland. He was convicted of forgery and transported, arriving in Fremantle in 1859. His first year was spent in the Freshwater Bay work party making the Perth–Fremantle road. Once he had gained his ticket-of-leave, it is thought he went to do clerical work for John Stubberfield, licensee of a Guildford inn, and certainly he married Stubberfield's daughter Caroline in 1862. Probably his father-in-law helped him set up as an agriculturalist at Sandalford.

At the end of 1869 he gave up agriculture and bought the Guildford Hotel. During the 1870s he was a prominent member of Guildford society, serving at times on the Swan District Road Board as honorary secretary and on the Guildford Municipal Council as chairman. In 1878 he moved to Fremantle and took over the Crown and Thistle Hotel in 1880. The hotel, on the site of the later Cleopatra Hotel in High Street, became unofficially known as Meagher's Hotel. It very nearly bankrupted him within a year. In 1882 he returned to agriculture, leasing the Bassendean homestead and estate, and also returned to civic life. He retired to Perth in the 1890s and died at the farm of one of his sons near Bridgetown in 1907.

When you step ashore at Sandalford, to your right the simple farm building with wide verandahs is the original Sandalford homestead. It remains a private house and is not open to the public. The oak tree growing beside it on the track up to the winery must have been planted in the nineteenth century, perhaps when the house was first built.

Sandalford Caversham is a smart, modern winery. The majority of the wines they produce, in fact all of their premium range, are made from grapes grown in the Mount Barker and Margaret River regions where cooler conditions give a longer ripening season and better distinctive characteristics to the grapes. When I started a wine-tasting, by choosing to sample the premium range, I didn't know that I was electing to try all non-Swan Valley wines. The Classic Dry White had a lovely nose predominated by sauvignon blanc, although the label says semillon is the major component and grassy semillon is an important part of the flavour.

The verdelho was obviously picked only just ripe with very high fruit-acid content and to compensate a little sugar remains unfermented, much like a Portuguese vinho verde.

I went on to try all of the premium range except the chardonnay while chatting with an engaging young woman who was serving me. I thought the shiraz the best but the 1998 cabernet sauvignon was also very good. Having learned that I had sampled nothing produced from Swan River grapes I tried the Elements Range shiraz-cabernet blend which was pleasant enough.

Sandalford Caversham have twenty-three hectares of vineyards in the Swan Valley and buy in grapes from other vineyards.

Even on a Monday afternoon, the wine-tasting and sales were busy. A coach load of people had arrived just after I did. It became obvious that not everyone on the vineyards tour had my long familiarity with wine swilling. A lady next to me started with the delightful Classic Dry White. She took a little sip and poured the rest of the small sample into a spittoon. The woman serving us returned from finding a brochure for me. 'How did you like that?' she asked the lady.

'Well, I didn't like it really,' was her apologetic answer.

'Oh. What was it you didn't like?'

No answer.

'Was it the nose … or the acid,' she hinted, 'or the flavour?'

'It was probably the flavour.'

The flavours of other wines weren't to her liking either.

One doesn't drink enough at a tasting to get piddly, but just after leaving Sandalford I repeated my not-looking-where-I'm-going trick by ploughing into the branches of a dead tree fallen into the river.

Confusingly, the Upper Swan is crossed by the Middle Swan Road. Middle Swan in this case means the middle of the Swan Valley which starts above Guildford. The bridge is another timber bridge; it retains the original rough-hewn structure with none of the steel additions and reinforcements that most of the other bridges have accrued over the years. A sign on the Middle Swan Road Bridge warns that navigation above that point is hazardous. The river above the bridge is not dredged and not cleared of obstacles, which are mostly fallen trees. And it is very much a forgotten and ignored river — there are no jetties or landings once you have gone more than a kilometre or two above the Middle Swan Bridge.

Both banks are high in many places and where the banks are lower, they are thick with dark melaleuca and big eucalypts so one

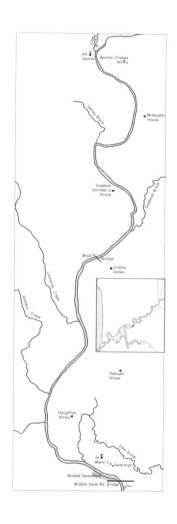

Upper Swan: Middle Swan Road Bridge to Ellen Brook

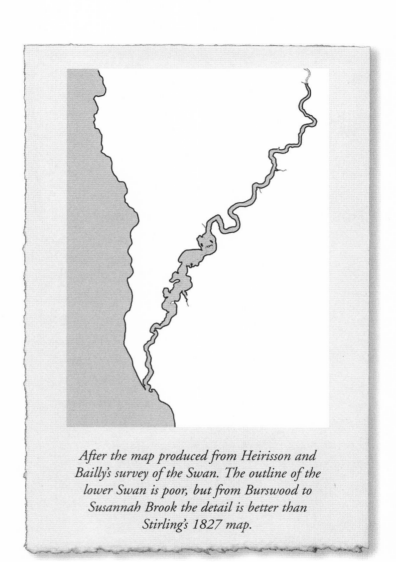

After the map produced from Heirisson and Bailly's survey of the Swan. The outline of the lower Swan is poor, but from Burswood to Susannah Brook the detail is better than Stirling's 1827 map.

can see very little of the surrounding country. I went ashore and climbed the banks to look around where I could, but the further upstream you go the more difficult that becomes because the banks are muddy and steep.

The French expedition led by Heirisson and Bailly in 1801 from the ship *Naturaliste*, Captain Hamelin, is generally believed to have explored little further than Vlamingh had in 1697. However, the chart of the Swan River produced by Heirisson and Freycinet shows that they reached some way above the Middle Swan Road Bridge, to a little above Susannah Brook in Herne Hill. Although the Lower Swan is not accurately delineated in their chart, the detail of the river from Burswood upstream is easily identified in a comparison with a modern map. The river is noticeably more accurately charted than it is in Stirling's 1827 map. Unfortunately Heirisson and Bailly made no drawings of what they saw and their written record is fairly scant, so we know little of their impressions and experiences.

A number of creeks and brooks are tributary to the Upper Swan but in autumn most of them are dry. St Leonard's Creek was just dribbling as I rowed past. I didn't go ashore near the creek but later visited the area by following George Street which is a pleasant back road running between the main road and the river.

An old farmstead, not too tarted up, which adds to its charm, near where the road crosses the creek, I took to be the St Leonard's that was originally owned by Edmund Barrett-Lennard, one of the pioneer settlers, but subsequent research seems to show that it is another homestead called Springvale. When Captain Fremantle made a short return visit to the colony in 1832 he thought Barrett-Lennard the man who had done most to get agriculture going on his selection.

Unusually, the name St Leonard was not taken from Lennard's family home in the United Kingdom (nor is it a misspelling of their name) but was the name of the barque the Barrett-Lennards had sailed out on. She was the third merchant ship to reach the Swan River, arriving after *Parmelia* and *Calista*.

Not far from St Leonard's Creek is Ambrook Wines which seems to be a small and unpretentious winery. I can't say much about their wines because, although the winery was open when I visited, there was no one other than a friendly German shepherd dog to greet me and she didn't have a corkscrew handy.

Rowing up the river as the afternoon grew late I was looking for a place to go ashore and pitch my little tent. There was no shortage of flat grassy ground, though the best sites mostly had a house fairly close by. A little before six the sky was looking very dark away to the south-west and another shower was threatening so I decided to get ashore and pitch the tent as soon as possible.

The immediate problem was a landing place. I found a spot where I could scramble up the bank and made a quick reconnaissance — there was a fine patch of thick, flattened, dried grass that looked as if it would be a very comfortable mattress, but there were three farmhouses in sight about a kilometre away. However, it was definitely going to rain, so back on the boat I hurriedly threw all the kit I needed up onto the bank, almost capsizing the boat while catching my knapsack as it tried to roll back into the river. Up on the bank I got the tent pegged out, ready to go and waited a few minutes until I judged it dark enough before erecting it. It was raining by the time the tent was up and I had the pegs for the guys pushed into the baked hard rocky soil, but it wasn't as heavy a shower as I had feared.

The hay mattress was a great disappointment — lumpy and hard — but I slept reasonably well and enjoyed the feeling of dryness and warmth while short sharp showers of rain rattled on the tent a few times during the night.

But I was uneasy about camping there without permission and it was probably that unease that caused a weirdly vivid dream. I dreamt that two men who I knew came and woke me. I got out of the tent and found that it was in a completely different spot from where I'd pitched it and gone to sleep. Instead of the bank of the river it seemed to be in a suburban backyard. I explained the oddity of the situation to my friends and one of them suggested that I might be dreaming. We investigated that possibility but it clearly wasn't true. There was too much precise and convincing detail, there was palpable texture in the setting, and there was too much time — dreams are all crammed into a few seconds of REM sleep so events and details have to be elided and concertina-ed together. We were able to inspect things in a leisurely way and were speaking in full grammatical sentences rather than the telepathy-telegraphese of dreams. We all agreed it was very much too real to be a dream. I don't remember how that hyper-real dream ended, I think it merged into a more dream-like dream.

I was up at first light and had the tent down again well before sunrise, then I sat in the square patch of dry grass where the tent had been, ate a light breakfast and watched the dawn. It was very lovely sitting there amid the vineyards beside the river on a perfect autumn morning, not a breath of wind, the air cool and almost misty. There was some cloud and some clear sky, the clouds not moving fast, and it looked to be the start of a fine day as the sun came up from behind the Darling Ranges. Autumn is a time that evokes thoughts of travel, and dreams of leaving, and wishes and longings — if the river stretched for a thousand miles …

At 7.15 I was back at the oars to find out how far the river really did stretch. A kilometre or two upstream I came to a bridge where no bridge should have been according to my new map. The steel-beam cantilever structure called Maali Bridge was newer than my new map. It is a pedestrian and cyclist bridge — 'No horses, no trail bikes allowed', a sign said, and it is too narrow for most cars. Hats off to the City of Swan for providing the footbridge. I went ashore to try it out, crossing back and forth a couple of times and admiring the view of the river it affords — in both directions.

Upstream from the bridge that joins Douglas Road and Barrett Street, the character of the river changes again. It is only ankle deep in places and many fallen trees half block the river. I tasted it to see if I had escaped the salt water. There was a hint of salt and a strangely sweet flavour like sweet corn. I wouldn't advise drinking it. Greg Stokes further upstream suggested that the flavour came from the large number of unsold watermelons dumped in the river in that season of mists and mellow fruitfulness.

Though the water is fresh, darters and cormorants, usually regarded as marine birds, live and fish right to the top of the Swan, in fact darters and also ducks are everywhere on those upper reaches. There were also pink and grey galahs and twenty-eights (brightly coloured parrots) mucking about in the same trees, a very pretty sight indeed.

Fresh water has a curious effect on a pedant's rowing, for it ceases to be rowing. Although I had been rowing on salt water, by nautical convention, the same activity is called 'sculling' on fresh water, though it seems a rather poncey name for the thing I do with *Earnest*'s chunky handmade oars. I should really have a pair of light, carefully crafted 'sculls' with thin, curved blades. Rowing is something you can't do on your own on fresh water. If one is rowing on fresh water you are operating one oar with both hands and if you do that on your own you go round in very tight circles. Operating one oar with both hands is known as 'pulling' (an oar) on salt water. 'Sculling' on salt water is an altogether different way of propelling a boat — a single oar projected aft over the stern is waggled back and forth in a figure of eight motion with the blade never leaving the water, usually while standing up. It is not often attempted without wellington boots, a beard, a pipe clamped between the teeth, a cloth cap, and a profound disdain for all things new-fangled and yachtie.

In the land to the west of the river where I sculled there were several historic homesteads, some of which still stand: Goodwood, Albion Town, Haddrill's Spring Park Farm and Richard Edward's House but I didn't see anything of them.

Above Susannah Brook there are two tight bends with short sand spits in them, a pleasant and convenient change from the muddy banks if you want to go ashore. And the river was more and more obstructed by shallows and dead trees: 'very much canoe country' I wrote in my notebook. I began to wonder how Stirling had got two large ship's boats so far up the river. I had to paddle Indian canoe fashion or row Mediterranean fashion facing forward to navigate around the dead trees, and sometimes I had to drag my boat over shallows though it only draws about three fingers of water.

The river is alternately sandy shallows and deep pools; both shallows and pools are full of little fish, and the water is clear. Every reach has a different character: some are enclosed by dark trees, some are open to the sky in a cleft between high wooded slopes, then around the next bend you row into a pastoral reach with low grassy banks and vineyards or paddocks beyond. There is a very sharp bend in the river where it is joined by Henley Brook and in the area of that confluence there is a spring line where water seeps out along the steep right bank, so the vegetation remains lush and almost tropical right through the dry summer.

There were pink dragonflies and ochre dragonflies, then I saw bright red ones, then electric blue and I stopped noting the different colours. There were large and brightly coloured dragonflies in the illustrations of the Time-Life book of dinosaurs that I had when I was a boy, and perhaps it was that association of the dragonflies that made so many of the dead branches and stumps look like ichthyosaurs rearing from the dark water.

A couple of times I had to lift the boat over fallen trees that completely blocked the whole stream. Stirling would have had his men wielding axes. The fallen trees certainly impede navigation but they are not entirely a bad thing because they protect the banks from erosion, mostly by keeping motorboats away but also by restricting most of the current's flow to the middle of the channel. They also create a habitat for the sort of creatures that live under fallen logs and branches on a river bank.

Just after the second lift over a log I reached Ellen Brook. The mouth of the brook is blocked by fallen brickwork of a weir or dam but the brook rises very steeply and would never be navigable by boat.

I decided on my second voyage to the Upper Swan that the

reach between Henley Brook and Ellen Brook is the most beautiful stretch on the whole river.

High on the banks above the confluence of Ellen Brook is All Saints, the oldest church in Western Australia and one of the smallest. It was built marking the highest point that Stirling's boats reached in 1827, and where Stirling led prayers of thanks. Construction of the church was started in 1839 on a grant of land from the selection of Captain Irwin and Judge Mackie. Richard Edwards, who managed Irwin and Mackie's farm very successfully, was also a master brickmaker and builder. He made bricks from the local clay, but to get lime for making mortar he went to Melville Water to find oyster shell and constructed a lime-burning kiln. It was Edwards who constructed the church with the help of many volunteers. It is a simple brick structure with a porch but no transept, and a little bell cote for a single bell surmounting the gable. It was significantly restored in the 1960s and a section of the original roof carpentry that has been preserved in the nearby cloisters is worth investigating for its use of ingenious locking joints and dowels rather than nails or bolts.

Names on headstones in the small graveyard include Richard Edwards and Hanna Hadrill, who was the first person christened in the church. There is a terrific view over the river from behind the church. Inside a commemorative marble plaque on the wall reads:

All Saints Church at Ellen Brook

In Memory of a Pioneer
GEORGE FLETCHER MOORE
Advocate General, Judge and Colonial Secretary
He first held divine service on this site
1831 and in winter had to swim the river
to carry out this duty.
Erected by Nephews and Nieces.

G F Moore lived just across the river so we will call on him on the way back down the left bank in the next chapter.

In the porch of All Saints there is a cash box which can easily be mistaken for an ordinary donations box. I think the old lady who dropped a coin into it was even more surprised than I was when her donation immediately started an unseen machine playing a recording of powerful organ music out of all proportion to the tiny church. There are also recorded voices to be heard in the lych gate that will tell you the history of the church.

Beside the visitors book was another book in which one could write requests for prayer. I had recently received an email containing some of the more amusing messages in the condolences book for the death of the Queen Mother. My favorite read 'I thought she would live forever, she has let us all down very badly.' There were no funnies quite that finely crafted in the prayers request book at All Saints, but I enjoyed the request from a lady that we pray for her brother's conversion, and wondered about the propriety of the request that we 'pray for our beloved cat Missy who died by a car'. I suspect that such a request could have led to charges of heresy and a remedial conflagration in times past.

Not far from All Saints, following Ellen Brook, one comes to the remains of William Connor Cruse's mill, one of the few flour mills in the early colony. Cruse arrived in 1830 as a carpenter indentured to Lt. Henry Bull; after leaving Bull's employ he went on to build his mill and run Ellen Brook farm for George Leake.

At Ellen Brook, following the Swan River upstream towards its source, one turns east to head up through the escarpment to where the river becomes the Avon River. Ellen Brook runs from many kilometres to the north and in a sense that is the original course of the Swan River. A tributary that ran in a minor fault line down from the scarp to the original river cut back further and further into the escarpment until eventually it captured or 'pirated' the Avon River, which until then had been a parallel stream draining south to north on the other side of the escarpment.

Turning eastwards towards the scarp, just upstream of the brook, I was thwarted. Not only was the river narrow and blocked by fallen trees, it was clogged with rotting weed which was not at all inviting for wading in. This was obviously where Stirling's expedition turned around and it was where I turned around too. If I had been given strong evidence that the lost city of Eldorado was just around the next bend I might have pushed on a little further. Instead I stopped and climbed up the steep bank where I found that the land was cut up by flood gullies running parallel to the main stream. The river there is a torrent in the rainy season, braided into several channels.

At about eleven o'clock I started back downstream. The return was easier because even up at Ellen Brook there is some tidal effect — the water was a few inches deeper than it had been a couple of hours earlier and those few inches made a huge difference. Sand banks that I had walked on I could now row over. Also my progress was faster because I'd become quite nonchalant about running into and sliding past the dead trees. With the tide high it was easier to understand how Stirling had got so far up the river.

A month later I made another voyage and went up on a particularly high tide. Instead of dragging the boat over fallen trees, I had trouble getting underneath some overhanging dead branches. There seems to be no way of predicting the small tides of the Upper Swan. The tidal range down at the sea is only about half a metre and the bulges of high water travel slowly upstream while other bulges are trying to flow back to the sea so that even on the Middle Swan the relationship between high tide at Fremantle and high tide at Maylands is scrambled and unpredictable. The diurnal land and sea breezes push water in and out of the river and also the water, like the mercury in a barometer, rises and falls with changes in barometric pressure.

Chapter 6

FROM THE TOP, THE LEFT BANK

Having reached the head of the Swan as a navigable river I found myself in a pensive mood with no particular feeling of triumph. What did it mean? What should I feel about it? The actuality of being in a place is seldom as perfect or clear an experience as the anticipated or recollected event. And even in the most self-congratulatory recollection, rowing to the head of the Swan is hardly a monumental achievement. Not quite in the same league as finding the source of the Nile. There was no one with whom I could share the experience either.

Rowing back downstream from the headwaters at Ellen Brook I heard a tractor up in the fields above me on the high left bank and I realised that I hadn't seen a single human being since the previous afternoon.

A little further along there stood a small, poor-looking farmhouse high over the river. I couldn't tell whether it was still inhabited though it has one of the most spectacular views of the Upper Swan.

I was unsure about whether I wanted to meet the people who lived and farmed up there. Thinking about that I realised that I felt rather as I have when I've occasionally walked into mountainous areas of terrible alienating poverty, in places such as northern Portugal where the poverty makes people seem shameful and isolated. It was the isolation and the way that the river has been left behind by history that made me feel that way, though it was quite unjustified by the reality of the Swan Valley. Up above me was rich farming land, not far from a hectic main road, but the sluggish river, cut deep into the rising land, is another place, left behind in another time.

Contributing to the feeling of grim abjection, some farm refuse still ends up in the river. One is back in an environmentally unenlightened past. Apart from rusted farm equipment and old oil drums I saw quite a lot of unwanted watermelons floating like mines and a few discarded bunches of grapes (which sink). And trees along the banks are festooned with ribbons of black plastic that have been left there by winter floods, making the trees look like the fake melaleuca with black netting foliage that attentive readers will remember Fremantle Council have threatened tree vandalisers with.

I'd read some of the history of the Upper Swan Valley before

The railway bridge crossing the Upper Swan
at Pullman Park where the river is
just a series of pools in summer

setting out and was looking for any vestiges of the pioneer homesteads that had been set up there almost before Perth and Fremantle were more than a collection of tents.

At the point where the irresolute Stirling and I had both felt obliged to halt and start a retreat, the land on the left bank is just inside the locality known as Belvoir, named after the farm of William Shaw acquired from Robert Lyon in 1830 or 1831. Downstream is Baskerville, named by William Tanner and originally assigned to Captain Fremantle who never settled in the Swan River Colony. And the next one down is George Fletcher Moore's Millendon. Originally assigned to W Lamb, it was also the approximate location of Wurerup, an important encampment for the Beelo people.

Clearly the Aborigines were the true owners of the land, as Governor King had written to his successor Governor Bligh in New South Wales, but land allocation and titles in the early days of the Swan River Colony were a mess and it is sometimes difficult to be sure who had legal rights to what land.

Before discussing the historic Upper Swan properties of the left bank I would like to share the understanding of the early cadastral law that I have grasped in trying to follow the histories of those properties.

The basis of land allocation was set out in two Colonial Office circulars published before Stirling sailed in 1829. The intention was that settlers who invested in the colony would be allocated land and later granted title to that land if they continued their investment and made use of the land.

There were six steps to gaining freehold title: assessment, selection, assignment, grant in occupation, location duties, and finally, application for 'title in fee simple'. First, an entitlement to land was determined at the rate of one acre of land for every one shilling and sixpence invested. The investment could include the value of farming equipment and stock brought to the colony and also the cost of bringing servants and indentured labourers. Documented applications were assessed by a board comprising the governor, his cousin William Stirling and Captain Currie the first harbourmaster. That board reported to the governor and if he accepted the report (of which he was an author) he wrote notifying the applicant and giving them permission to select land through the good offices of the surveyor general. If the selected land was available it would be 'assigned' to the applicant who then had twelve months to fill in a form (Land Form No. 1) describing the boundaries and supplying information such as the assignee's name. When the surveyor general accepted the completed form the land became a 'grant in occupation'. This was a title or license to occupy the land, but not ownership. The assignee had to perform 'Location Duties' which meant a further investment of one shilling and sixpence per acre. The construction of a residence was often part of that investment; purchase of stock, fencing and clearing were other possibilities. Once the location duties were fulfilled, the assignee could apply for freehold 'in fee simple', and if that application was accepted, a grant title would be issued and a location number ascribed. Ten years after assignment, any portion of the land that was not used would revert to the Crown or rent would be charged.

The system became complicated, primarily because there was much less fertile land than Stirling had hoped, and all the useful land was soon assigned, some of it to naval officers who were not likely to occupy or use it. In principle, no land could be transferred, subdivided or otherwise traded until it was owned in fee simple, but it was those assignees who had least ability to perform location duties and obtain title who had most reason to transfer their titles and who were the only potential source of land for better financed settlers who arrived after crown land allocations had run out. Governor Stirling allowed that land could be transferred once a 'Certificate of Cultivation' was issued, but since the conditions for the issue of that certificate were more or less the same as location duties that concession was no help at all.

In reality the niceties of the law were ignored and everyone was running around blithely transferring properties and mortgaging assets that they didn't own like a bunch of shonky superannuation fund managers.

Because so much land was farmed and improved by people who did not technically hold titles (including G F Moore, Commissioner of the Civil Court and Solicitor General) it was necessary for the legal system to accept the de facto property dealings.

Keeping track of who held those de facto assignments must have been impossible for the Surveyor General's Office — an office which was actually a tent. They had assigned numbers and letters to identify the land allocations that had been roughly surveyed in 1829. Because many de facto transfers, subdivisions, and some amalgamations of land assignments occurred and shifted boundaries before the assignments were converted to freehold titles, the original identification numbers could not always be used when location numbers were ascribed to the freehold titles. Roe chose to adapt the original allocation identification code rather than devise a distinctly different code so old allotment numbers and new location numbers matched in some cases and in other cases were different, and who knew which was what?

Another aspect of the problem was Stirling and Roe's contrivance for coping with the shortage of land available for allocation. All assignments were to have river frontage and Roe apportioned river frontage in very approximate proportion to the number of acres allotted, but never much more than about half a mile of river frontage to any one assignment. It appears that he sometimes measured the river frontage following the curves of the river, sometimes as a straight line between upstream and downstream boundaries, and sometimes as the shortest distance between the parallel upstream and downstream boundaries; but in any event he was well aware that he was carving up land that he had not had time to survey properly.

At best the river frontage was very short relative to the area of the large assignments. For example, R H Bland's assignment of eight thousand acres (3,240 ha) which became the Houghton property was $53^1/_3$ chains (1.07 km) wide with about 75 chains (1.50 km) of river frontage measured around the curves of the river, but it was necessarily some fifteen hundred chains long (over 30 km), stretching away over the Darling Ranges beyond Chittering — in effect beyond the edge of the known world when it was assigned. Much of it was useless to the type of agriculture practised in the 1830s and after ten years all but 572 acres (231.6 ha) of alluvial land close to the river was unused and therefore reverted to the crown. Roe was not sure that some of the land grants on the right bank of the Upper Swan did not extend out to sea. The Barrett-Lennard's grant G1 probably finished just short of the beach to the south of where Hillarys Boat Harbour has been built.

George Fletcher Moore's Millendon was another land assignment that originally stretched for miles over the Darling Ranges, and it was the Locality of Millendon that I had reached rowing downstream from Ellen Brook before I got on to the subject of land allocations.

In the first straight sunny reach where the river is not overhung by high banks and crowded trees, in a place where the slope of the left bank is gentle, a large old brick farmhouse is visible from the river. I had been looking for Millendon. If this was the Millendon homestead, built in 1831, it must be the oldest private house in Western Australia. Millendon was prominent among those pioneering farmsteads that established agriculture in the Swan Valley … or so I thought when I beached *Earnest* and climbed up the grassy bank to have a closer look.

The house has real character; the brickwork is solid and honest, perhaps the work of the same craftsmen as All Saints Church. But the house is now derelict, the roof half gone and the blind windows stripped of glass, though some window frames and sashes remain. Perhaps one of the window frames was the one scarred when a Nyungar warrior, probably Yagan, tried to spear Millendon's owner George Fletcher Moore as he stood by the newly fitted window.

The remaining window frames are certainly old and are held together entirely by dowels. Most of the brickwork appears to be sound: the walls are two bricks thick, laid in what we bricklayers call English bond (although it is probably a Dutch invention).

In the bricklaying business, bricks laid in the normal side-on way are called 'stretchers' and bricks laid with ends towards the inner and outer faces of the wall are called 'headers'. There are also 'soldiers', 'sailors', 'bull-headers' and 'bull-stretchers', but apart from the few soldiers in the segmented arches over windows, they don't appear at Millendon. There are also half-width bricks called 'closers', necessary for creating the corners in both English bond

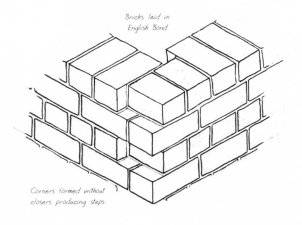

Bricks laid in
English Bond

Corners formed without
closers producing steps

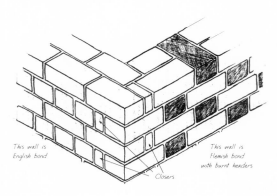

This wall is
English bond

This wall is
Flemish bond
with burnt headers

Closers

English and Flemish bond brickwork

and Flemish bond brickwork. An interesting feature of Millendon is the way that the corners of the house have been made without sufficient quantity of closers, creating indented steps in the brickwork of two corners. On three of the exterior walls of Millendon, courses of stretchers alternate with courses of headers (English bond), while in the wall away from the river, which must have been regarded as the front, there is a decorative pattern with stretchers and dark-coloured 'burnt headers' alternated in each course — a decorative form of Flemish bond.

Though most of the brickwork remains solid, in a few places the mortar has crumbled and loose bricks have been removed leaving parts of the wall unsupported. Uninhabited and partly ruined, Millendon stands as an evocative monument, but the likelihood that it would fairly soon be no more than a pile of bricks struck me as tragic.

George Fletcher Moore, whose humorous and vivacious letters written as diaries provide much the fullest picture of the pioneer's life during the first decade of the Swan River Colony was, among his many accomplishments, one of the first to grow useful quantities of wheat, and probably the first to sell locally grown wheat to the Perth market.

You can see that there were once terraced gardens stepping down from the house at Millendon towards the river. Moore's description is easily recognisable:

I have built my house upon a rising ground which first slopes rapidly, then gently down towards the river which here is about thirty yards wide, smooth, clear, and without any perceptible current ... The ground is very picturesque; on both sides it is broken at intervals into small wooded eminences ...

Moore planted lucerne in the hope of creating a green lawn, year round, from the house to the river, and he was careful to retain the native trees that shaded the house and garden for their picturesque effect.

The location of Millendon is clearly identifiable, and I was excited at having found it, but when I got back to Fremantle I began to wonder whether the house I had seen was really the original one built by Moore. It seemed too big and too well constructed to be the place that had been built, partly by Moore with his own hands, in the very first pioneering days of the colony when bare survival was the overriding concern and even public buildings such as the law court where Moore presided were mere thatched huts.

In Moore's published diaries I found a few details of the house that might allow positive identification. His intention that his house would be brick is clearly stated and later he wrote that he had added verandahs all around the house and that on those verandahs he could take a walk of 164 feet (50 m). He also recorded that his room was fifteen feet by eighteen (4.57 x 5.58 m). I calculated that if the house was fifteen feet wide and forty-nine feet (15 m) long, and the verandahs were four-and-a-half feet (1.37 m) wide, the perimeter of the verandahs would add up to exactly 164 feet.

When I returned to Millendon on a second voyage up the river I found that the house was bigger than that, but the explanation seemed to be that Moore had been (typically) modest when he claimed 164 feet of verandahs. I paced out the walls and decided the house itself was about twenty by sixty-two feet (6.1 x 18.9 m), adding up to 164 feet circumference without the verandahs, so a walk round the perimeter of the verandahs, which were actually six feet (1.83 m) wide, could have been over two hundred feet (61 m).

The house is on private land and it appeared as if the owner was either waiting for it to fall down or actively encouraging that process. No plaque or sign advertises this important piece of heritage, but above the fireplace that Moore happily described as having recesses on either side, 'for bookshelves, sideboards or what you please', a later occupant has blazoned with black spray paint 'SIMO WOZ ERE 86'.

It must have been an enchanting home and with a lot of love and attention it could be again, not to mention a winery of considerable historic distinction. Moore originally called it Hermitage, which adds possibilities for confusing naming of wines such as Hermitage Chardonnay or even Hermitage Hermitage.

Back in Fremantle I contacted the National Trust and the Heritage Council to express my concern that Millendon was falling down and ask what information they had about it. I learned that the house had been considered for Heritage Listing in 1992 but had been rejected as 'falling below heritage threshold'. The basis of the decision was that it was not the original house built by Moore but one built in the 1870s.

That didn't seem right to me. I emailed the Heritage Council.

Dear Ms Schulz,

I spoke to you on the phone this morning concerning Millendon homestead, my concern at its condition and a belief that it may be George Fletcher Moore's original 1831 homestead rather than an 1870s building.

The building is a four room house with two chimneys, brick built, English bond walls but with decorative Flemish bond using dark headers on the front wall. A number of the oldest buildings in Guildford and the Swan Valley, including the Courthouse, have the same brickwork.

The dimensions are approximately 6m by 19m (20ft x 62ft).

It has been said that G F Moore originally built a wattle and daub house: the main reason for that is his determination 'a mud edifice for me' recorded in his diary in Nov 1830. But the full context suggests that 'mud edifice' is a typically Moore example of humour and modesty recording his intention to build in brick.

'Brick and pottery clay is abundant, and they are making bricks in many places, which will soon supersede wood as a material for building. I saw a wooden house burned down some nights ago, and have therefore a dread of one — a mud edifice for me.'

If I am right in believing that Moore had a brick house built in 1831, it is unlikely that it was demolished and replaced with another brick house of very similar dimensions in the 1870s. The existing house is a simple rectangular design, the verandah roofs were separate, not extensions of the main roof, the window apertures are fairly small but tall. I might be exceeding my area of expertise but I suggest a house built in the 1870s would probably have the verandah roofing integrated with the main roof and might have wider windows.

I was exceeding my area of expertise on the subject of verandah roofs and I've edited that email to remove some information already given above, and some that turned out to be wrong, as well as a generous selection of typos.

Clare Schulz replied:

Nick

Thank you for this comprehensive information. The matter will be discussed at our next scheduled meeting of the

Register Committee on 31 May 2002, and we will advise you of the outcome in due course.

Clare Schulz
Heritage Officer (Assessment)

I also sent a copy to Philippa Rogers at the National Trust. In her reply she said, 'Of interest is a note which indicates that the Battye Library have a sketch of the house made in 1841. This may well assist in the identification.' I assumed that the sketch was by Moore himself.

At the Battye Library many of George Moore's letters to his family, written in the form of journals, are on microfilm (and extremely difficult to read). The letters are the basis of his *Diary of Ten Years of an Early Settler in Western Australia*, serialised in the *West Australian* newspaper and published in London in the 1880s, but looking at the microfilm it was soon apparent that they had been edited for publication, in part to simplify the narrative and to provide an exemplary story of industry and reward.

The original letters are peppered with tiny sketches, some of them quite charming, but Moore wasn't showing off his drawing skills because he was by no means a skilled artist. Probably his best drawing is his third attempt at Yagan's severed head, beside which is his explanation: 'couldn't get Yagan's head out of my head until I got it down on paper.'

The first drawing of his house showed a building that was quite different from the current Millendon. He drew a house with two wings connected by a lower central hall with a porch in front (like Blenheim Palace in basic shape but comprising only three rooms) and commented, 'I have partly built a brick house this is to be the shape when finished.'

A year later he wrote, 'Oh the house is advancing slowly — this is it now' and a dark splotch of ink creates a silhouette of a simple shed. Another sketch of the partially built house and a comment below it indicate that he was building using timber frame and brick noggin construction. It turned out that the timber frame was not square and doors could not be hung. I suspect that he started from scratch again in late 1832 because a sketch from January 1833 labeled, 'My intended house now' and 'Front that is to be' show something much more like the house now standing at Millendon though the chimneys are in the wrong places. A sketch from May 1833 shows one of two chimneys in the right place and an 1844 sketch shows both chimneys conforming with the current arrangement. There was no sketch by Moore after 1841.

I wrote again to Philippa Rogers and Clare Schulz:

Dear Clare,

Further to my email of 6 May about Millendon homestead. I have looked at the microfilm copies of George Fletcher Moore's letters at the Battye Library (Cat No. 263a).

There are a number of tiny sketches in his letters

showing how he originally intended his house to look and how it actually looked. The house as built is certainly similar to the one that stands beside the river in Millendon, but Moore's drawings are not good enough for positive identification.

In National Trust's file 'is a note which indicates that the Battye Library have a sketch of the house made in 1841'. I found sketches of the intended house from 1831, and sketches of the house from other dates, but none from 1841.

His original letters are significantly different from the published versions. For example, the published paragraph that starts 'I have built my house …' reads 'I will build my house …' in the original. Far from building his house before March 1831 as his published letters suggest, the house was still far from finished two years after that date.

His intention was a house with two wings connected by a lower central hall. Looking at the drawings of that intended house might have caused someone looking at his letters to conclude that the house at Millendon cannot be the one Moore built.

The house, as built, was simpler in design. The position and number of doors and windows drawn by Moore match the current building. The house now lacks the verandahs but timber attached to the exterior walls probably supported the verandah roofs. The position of that timber had led me to conclude that the verandah roofs were slightly below the level of the eaves of the main roof. That is not the case with the house that Moore drew. [Again, I was exceeding my area of expertise — if the thick thatched roof of the verandah fitted under the eaves of the main thatch it would appear that the verandah and main roofs were integrated.]

The roof line as drawn is perhaps different from the current situation — it is not really clear. The current building has a simple gabled roof whereas Moore seems to have drawn a hipped roof. His drawing of January 1833, when the house was still under construction, shows the intention that the chimneys would be in the end walls, either protruding through the hips of the roof or at the ends of the roof ridge (in which case there were no hips). The drawing of May 1833, when the house was substantially complete, shows one chimney on an interior wall protruding through the ridge of the roof. A drawing from 1844 shows two chimneys, symmetrically positioned, protruding through the roof ridge towards either end of the house. That arrangement conforms with the current house.

It is possible that Moore actually changed the chimney arrangement during construction. On the same page as his May 24, 1833 drawing he wrote: 'Today I got my old chimney snugged up for the winter.' In the crude drawing it looks rather as if he had got the State Emergency Service to throw a tarpaulin over the aperture of the original chimney on the end wall!

In summary, the house now at Millendon is the same size as the one Moore built, it has the same arrangement of apertures for doors and windows and the same placement of chimneys. It is constructed of the same material — I found a clear statement that he was building with brick. The roof line might be different, but that is not certain. Unless there is clear evidence that Moore's house (not one of his several out houses) was demolished, it would be imprudent to assume that the current Millendon house is not the one originally built by Moore.

Talking to Matt Trinca at the Western Australian Museum, who had done research on Moore and his house, I learned that the 1841 drawing in the Battye Library is by Elizabeth Irwin, not by Moore. It showed a house radically different to the one that Moore had drawn twice in 1833 and once in 1844, so the next question was how certain was it that Irwin's drawing really showed Millendon?

Julie Martin at the Battye Library checked the drawing for me and found that there was no caption and no indication of why the title 'Millendon' had been ascribed. Later, looking at the full set of Irwin's drawings we found that one of them has been identified both as Oakover and also as St Leonards, which can't be right.

I wrote a letter with illustrations summing up the information I had gathered. Clare Schulz again thanked me and reiterated the promise that the Heritage Commission would let me know the result of consideration by the Register Committee, so it would be amusing if I could now write 'and that was the last I ever heard about it'. But in the middle of June I did receive a courteous letter from Stephen Carrick, Manager of Conservation and Assessment, in which he wrote: 'It was determined that the place is likely to have cultural heritage significance at the State level and as such, has been added to our current assessment program.'

George Fletcher Moore, 1798–1886

Born County Tyrone, Ireland. Studied Law at Trinity College, Dublin and was admitted to the Irish Bar. He came to the Swan River Colony on his own initiative on the ship *Cleopatra* bringing farming equipment, capital and four servants. He had a letter of recommendation but no official appointment. He had hoped to be appointed advocate-general but another Irish lawyer, W H Mackie, beat him to the colony and to the position. Moore was appointed Commissioner of Civil Courts in 1832 making him the colony's first judge. His court sat for four days each week. Moore usually walked from his property in the Upper Swan Valley to Perth for the sittings. In 1834, following instructions from the Colonial Office in London, he and Mackie exchanged roles so he became the advocate-general (perhaps because he was a barrister while Mackie was not). As advocate-general, he was one of the four members of the Executive and Legal Councils (Parliament) and although he was a member by virtue of his official position he saw himself as representing settlers and farmers in whose interest he sometimes opposed the executive's intentions. He was not impressed by Stirling's financial management (or his honesty) and led opposition to all of Stirling's budgets which resulted in rejection of those budgets.

When Moore arrived at the Swan River Colony in 1830, almost all available land with river access had already been granted. He looked at some land on the Canning but, like almost everyone else, considered it unsuitable for agriculture, so he arranged to take half the land granted to William Lamb in the Upper Swan Valley. The arrangement was that Moore would effect improvements to the land of sufficient value that the entire grant would be granted in 'fee simple' (freehold). The land assignment of 8,119 acres (3.28 ha) must have extended inland almost as far as Northam but only a small part adjacent to the river was actually used.

At first Moore called his Swan Valley homestead Hermitage but life there was nothing like as hermetic as he had expected (during the first six months he lived there, the number of settlers living in the Swan Valley increased from ten to ninety-seven) and from late 1833 his letters refer to the large brick homestead as Millendon (sometimes Millenden) which was the Nyungar name of the place. Moore devoted considerable interest and effort to agriculture and the improvement of the property which he obviously loved. He took satisfaction in growing his own vegetables, raising stock and the sweet taste of bread made from home-grown and freshly milled wheat: 'There is no mystery in baking where fraudulent adulterations are not particularly desired.'

Moore sold the first locally produced wheat in Perth in 1832 for £1 per bushel which was about double the going rate in better supplied places, but he calculated it cost him about ten shillings- a bushel to produce.

In addition to Millendon, Moore took up land near Beverley, then exchanged it for land near York and also took up a large pastoral tract on Ellen Brook.

During the early years of the colony, when things seemed to be going badly and prospects seemed poor to almost everyone, Moore never surrendered to pessimism though he confessed to being homesick at times. He was a prolific diarist and correspondent. His published letters to his family written in the form of diaries reveal humour, humanity and lively interest about almost everything. The pity is that the published diaries were heavily edited so as to give the impression he was disinclined to record gossip, scandal and unfavourable opinions of fellow settlers.

Moore recorded Nyungar culture and vocabulary. His view of Nyungar people was not the typical establishment view: 'they are active, bold, shrewd … they are quick of apprehension, and capable of reflecting on the difference between our manners and their own, in a degree you would scarcely expect.'

He even seems to have had an inkling of something like the songlines that gave Nyungar knowledge of the extent of the Australian continent and indirect communication with the shores of the Arafura Sea. However, he was not completely above the prejudice of his time, using phrases such as 'rude savages', and in struggling to create a self-sufficient livelihood he was not above being exasperated by the Nyungars' fondness for taking his pigs. He wrote of feeling murderous on that score, 'but after all perhaps these uninformed creatures think that they have as good a right to our swine as we have to their kangaroos, and the reasoning if such there be, may be plausible enough.' There is often a Swiftian irony to his writing and his claim to murderous intentions is completely belied by his actions. He was determined 'to lay a foundation for some measure of conciliation' and in an article in the *Perth Gazette* (20 July 1833) he advocated generous compensation for loss of land and livelihood, and also a formal treaty.

He certainly witnessed barbarity toward the Nyungars. When he arrived in the colony, Colonial Secretary Peter Brown took him along on the first armed expedition to chase natives who had been stealing stock. They intercepted the Nyungars in the act of robbing a homestead — one was killed, three were injured and seven taken prisoner and brought to Perth. Yet Moore himself was obviously not perceived as inimical by the Nyungars.

In 1833 Yagan visited Moore while a fugitive with a price on his head. The following account is from Moore's *Diary of Ten Years of an Early Settler in Western Australia*, pp. 190–1.

27th [May].—On seeing several natives approach the house, I went towards them as usual, thinking they were my old friends. To my surprise, the first I met was Migo, whom I had known well at Perth, as the servant of Captain Ellis, and the friend of the chieftain Munday. On looking round I then saw Munday himself (who is proclaimed, with a price on his head): this made me look still closer, and at last I saw Ya-gan standing a little aloof, scrutinising my countenance narrowly, and my manner of receiving them. I had been taxing Migo with having been present at the murder, which he energetically denied. When my eyes first fell upon Ya-gan, I said immediately 'What name?' They all answered 'Boolgat.' I said 'No; Ya-gan.' At first he was inclined to persist in the assumed character; but seeing that I knew him perfectly, he came forward, avowed himself, and entered into a long argument and defence of his conduct, in a way that I can hardly make intelligible to you; and I confess he had almost as much of the argument as I had. Both parties seemed to consider us as respectively arguing the question. Ya-gan listened with respectful anxiety, and used bold emphatic language and graceful gesture, with abundant action he delivered himself boldly. I did not understand him but replied, 'If white man queeple (steal), white man shoot white man; if black man queeple, white man shoot black man; if black man no gydyell (kill) cow, no gydyell sheep, no gydyell pig, white man all same as brother to black man, shake hands plenty, corroboree, plenty.' Here I advanced with open hands to them, which they all ran eagerly to grasp, save the moody chief himself. They had all grouped around, evidently attending to these arguments on both sides with great interest and glad of anything like a friendly termination. Ya-gan again stepped forward, and leaning familiarly with his left hand on my shoulder, while he gesticulated with his right, delivered a sort of recitative, looking earnestly at my face. I regret that I could not understand him, but I conjectured from the tone and the manner, that the purport was this:— 'You came to our country; you have driven us from our haunts, and disturbed us in our occupations: as we walk in our own country, we are fired upon by the white men; why should the white men treat us so?'

Yagan then asked about Midgegooroo, Yagan's father who had been executed by firing squad in Perth.

I felt that the question was full of personal hazard to me, and gave no reply. Even Weeip came and anxiously asked me the same question, putting his finger to my ear, to know if I heard or understood him. I answered slowly, 'White man angry, — Governor angry.' However my men assured them that both Midgegooroo and his son [one of Midgegooroo's sons had been shot precipitating the cycle of retaliation that made Yagan and Midgegooroo fugitives; a brother, not a son, of Midgegooroo had been executed more recently] *were gone on board a ship. Ya-gan still continued to read my countenance, and when he could obtain no answer from me, he said with extraordinary vehemence of manner, distinct of utterance, and emphasis of tone, 'White man shoot Midgegooroo, Ya-gan kill three' (holding up three fingers). 'Ya-gan kill all white man, soldier man and every man kill Ya-gan.'*

A couple of years later Weeip, another noted Nyungar warrior and leader who had been with Yagan at the meeting in May 1833, was declared wanted dead or alive for the retributive murder of a soldier, and Weeip's son was imprisoned. Moore was clearly anxious that the warrant on Weeip be rescinded. He searched for Weeip and arranged that he would undertake the mission of carrying a message to Shark Bay where some whites were believed to be shipwrecked and to bring back a message if he found shipwreck survivors. Moore and Weeip discussed the seventeen hundred kilometre round trip in detail: Weeip estimated that he and his companions could do it in fifteen days though it turned out that

Weeip's intention was only to travel far enough north to make contact with Aboriginal people who could say with certainty whether there was a shipwreck and survivors. Weeip carried out the mission and learned that there was no shipwreck. Thanks to Moore's intercession, he was pardoned and his son released.

Moore became a proficient speaker of Nyungar. He was sometimes sent inland by the government as a negotiator and when there was trouble between settlers and Nyungars in the Upper Swan area he was usually asked to remain there rather than pursue his official duties in Perth.

Moore was an explorer of some note. He was probably the first white man to follow the Swan up to where it becomes the Avon (wherever one decides that is). He accompanied Dale on the 1831 expedition into the country around York. Later he discovered the river now named after him, and surveyed the land to the north of Northam. With J S Roe he waded around in the mud of the Swan River Flats, probing with sticks to determine the best position for the Causeway.

He was a noted member of the Temperance Society, but those were days when Temperance was a more temperate notion. Moore spoke at public meetings and defended the principle of temperance which for him meant nearly complete abstinence from drinking spirits, but not from drinking beer and wine. In fact he brewed beer and made wine at times.

Farming interests gradually displaced government business but he remained a respected official for more than twenty years. In 1848 he married Fanny May Jackson, the step daughter of Governor Clarke. Two years later, when both the governor and the colonial secretary fell fatally ill, he was obliged to take up the role of colonial secretary and de facto governorship.

In 1852 he applied for leave to visit his ailing father in Ireland and when he went to the Colonial Office in London to apply for an extension of leave he felt he was treated unfairly and discourteously. He resigned and never returned to Australia, partly because of his wife's protracted illness which led to her death in 1863, though he still owned twenty-four thousand acres (9,720 ha) of land in Western Australia at the end of his long life.

The Millendon property was passed to his nephew W D Moore, then to A W Moore, who sold it to another noted merchant, William Padbury. It was then subdivided. The boundaries of the suburb or locality called Millendon are the boundaries of the original grant after Moore had let the large unused portion revert to the crown in exchange for better land on Ellen Brook.

Having become very interested in G F Moore's old homestead, I returned by road and found that the Millendon homestead is only a couple of hundred metres from Olive Road. What you see from the road, but don't see from the river, is a largish modern house on the rise above the old house, almost obscuring it from the road. I looked around for someone to ask about the old house but there was no one home.

Not far away at Baxter-Stokes Winery I met Greg Stokes, who about ten years ago had tried to buy the old homestead with the intention of restoring it and still watches its slow deterioration.

Baxter-Stokes' vineyards are on the left bank directly opposite

All Saints Church where Stirling and I turned round. Greg and his wife Lucy run an inviting example of a small-scale Swan Valley winery, crushing twelve to sixteen tonnes of fruit per year (0.001 percent of the total Australian crush) and selling all the production through cellar door sales on weekends.

I mentioned that Greg's basket press doesn't look much bigger than the one my dad uses for making wine at home. He explained that Lucy, the accountant, has calculated that he can crush four tonnes in a morning and only uses the press four mornings a year, so it is an appropriate level of technology and capitalisation.

The small winery owners in the Upper Swan cooperate and help each other in ways reminiscent of small farming communities in older wine-producing areas of southern Europe.

'One year I had a cold and had no sense of smell so Dorham Mann came over to check things for me — sniffed it and said, "Yep, that's all right". We lend each other equipment and you can turn to the expert older winemakers like Dorham for advice.'

The small-scale grower-producers are also relatively protected from the adverse effects of glut and over-production which occur cyclically, whereas larger-scale, uncontracted growers who rely on selling to winemakers were in serious trouble in 2002.

I spent rather longer than I'd intended leaning on a barrel out the front of Greg's winery one sunny Saturday in autumn talking about the Swan and Millendon, about winemaking and local characters. Greg talks about his wines in a relaxed and straightforward way, but his enthusiasm and the satisfaction he obviously derives from winemaking shine through.

Eventually I allowed myself to be persuaded by Greg's hospitable invitations to try a couple of his wines. I was a little reluctant because I was cycling and couldn't purchase any wines since I couldn't carry them.

Greg's vines have all been planted in the last decade so they are developing rapidly, and he pointed out the changing character from one vintage to the next and explained some of his experiments with different techniques. I was interested to learn that powdered milk is sometimes used as finings to pull out the flocculent stuff in suspension when the wine has been fermented on the skins. His unusual blend of shiraz and pinot noir can be sampled both unwooded and wooded with American oak. I thought it worked, even unwooded where the farmyardy flavours of the pinot stand very well in place of the woody elements.

Nearly all the vineyards in the Swan Valley are irrigated these days. Greg did tell me of an Italian gentleman who grows superb grenache unirrigated on the gravel-land below the escarpment. 'The vines look dead by this time of the year but there's a lot of competition for his grapes.' A bore for irrigation has to go down at least one hundred metres these days; above that the water is too saline.

When George Fletcher Moore first sank a well in 1831 he found good sweet water at sixteen feet (4.8m), only a few years later he had to go to twice that depth. On the other hand, in Moore's time, the river was brackish all the way to Ellen Brook before the winter rains, whereas nowadays the slight run-off from the irrigation displaces the salt water.

Something that impresses and gladdens me visiting the wineries these days is how genial and hospitable Australians in places like the Swan Valley have become toward visitors and tourists. When I first visited the Swan Valley a decade or two back, people in small wineries could be quite surly. Resenting or ridiculing tourists was thought to be clever and amusing in much of Australia (not least in Darwin where I lived at the time). Of course some tourists can be annoying, demanding and plain stupid but there's no honour or virtue in being rude to them. A gracious and hospitable people are infinitely more deserving of honour and respect. I would suggest that the world is a better place thanks to the example offered by the profoundly cultured and exalted Balinese.

To return to the story of my downriver voyage: I tied up to a dead tree, scrambled up the bank — nearly falling back into the river when a rotten tree stump gave way and enraged a vicious stinging ant that bit me on the waist — to look for the grave of Susannah Smithers.

Mrs Smithers died suddenly in April 1839 and our friend George Fletcher Moore was asked to read the burial service. He wrote: 'They have chosen a picturesque place, not far from the house, for her burial.' I was looking for the grave and if I was in the right place, there was now nothing to mark it unless three olive trees among the eucalypts serve that office.

Curiously, the place where the grave was reported to be was on the opposite bank to the Smithers' property. I thought perhaps there was a custom of burial on neighbouring property. When William Keates or Keating from Henry Bull's Ellen Brook property was buried, it was on the opposite side of the river in the Shaw's land. But the truth is that I had been misdirected and the stone marking Susannah Smithers' grave still lies in a paddock on the right bank where W H Smithers took a small property after being caught up in the disastrous failure of Peel's attempt to settle at Woodman's Point and further south.

Continuing downstream, back at Maali Bridge I went ashore again and walked to Sittella Winery, set in perfect rolling Swan Valley vineyard country, but on that weekday afternoon the winery was closed and there was no one there. I'd seen several horses during the morning but still hadn't seen a single person. I supposed that in the season after the frantic activity of the vintage, the farmers were probably taking well-earned rest.

Sittella Winery is named after the little off-white-breasted birds, small flocks of which flit and chatter incessantly in the melaleuca scrub, and which viticulturists constantly persecute with shotguns to keep the little buggers from ruining the grapes. The last part of that description probably isn't true — I made it up and I don't know what sittellas eat.

Sittella Winery struck me as well worth a return visit. It has an elegant but unpretentious restaurant with views panning round from the Darling scarp to the river. Anyone canoeing or boating on the Upper Swan on a weekend would be foolish not to put ashore there for lunch. Though the first vintage was as recent as 1998, their wines are impressive, they all have a well-developed fruity nose. I especially liked the fragrant verdelho, which is not a big wine but is everything that verdelho should be, and I liked the sparkling chenin — warm yeasty flavours and a crisp dry finish. Both excellent lunch wines. You, dear reader, must take me there for lunch one day; and, dear vigneron, I will happily accept a case or two in thanks for these comments.

The next winery I thought to visit was at Oakover. Oakover Winery and Cafe is not far from the river but if you were trying to get to it from the river you'd have to use a Global Positioning System to work out where to go ashore and you'd then have to march across farmland. You can't see any sign of it from the river. I did make a visit to Oakover by land one weekend during April which is the 'Taste of the Swan' festival month.

That particularly Saturday the fourth annual Swan Valley Olympics were held — a series of slightly sporting events conducted between wine-tastings, wine slurpings and beer guzzlings, by a bus load of very good humoured yahoos.

It was getting towards midafternoon when I encountered them at Oakover during the finals of the splash around in the ornamental pond event. The bus driver explained that there were four teams competing: Irish, Brazilian, Swedish and Russian. A contingent of the Swedish team were chanting

> *Russians take it up the arse*
> *Doo dah, doo dah*
> *Russians take it up the arse*
> *Doo dah, doo dah, day.*

Which very nearly led to an impromptu throw-each-other-in-the-pond event but some clearly set-out rules of decorum were invoked and the ruckus was stopped with a firm word or two from a big bloke. The whole thing was an impressive combination of contained rowdiness and genial good fun.

Once the Olympic athletes had been herded back into the bus and things had quietened down, I tried the '99 verdelho which is bigger than the Sittella verdelho but less interesting to my taste; and I tried the 2000 shiraz which the tasting notes recommended cellaring for eight to twelve years. It was not a bad wine by any means but seemed to be a good example of the contemporary fruity, drink-now style, so I couldn't see why it needed that much cellaring.

Oakover is yet another of the pioneer farming properties started in the 1830s. According to the winery's brochure the land 'was extensively cleared and farmed by convict labour in the 1840s' which was very pioneering indeed since the convicts didn't arrive until the 1850s. The land (Swan Selection 10) was originally assigned or at least offered to D H MacLeod and then to Ensign Dale of the 63rd Regiment detachment. Neither of those men made improvements to the property and it was sold to Samuel Moore (brother of George Fletcher Moore) in 1834.

Moore bought properties on both sides of the Swan, which he called East Oakover and West Oakover, and he had a bridge, wide enough for a cart, built over the river connecting the properties. The date that it was built seems not to be known with certainty: it might have been the first bridge built over the Swan, if it was built before the Causeway Bridge (1841–42), but it was damaged in the floods of 1847 and never repaired.

The original Oakover homestead was a simple, single-storey, eight-room house with a wide verandah and a separate kitchen. It was built of earth rammed between wooden shuttering.

Samuel Moore suffered coronary problems in 1848 and correctly fearing his impending demise he wrote a detailed calendar of plantings, harvesting, manuring and fertilising for his family to follow when he was gone. It lists a very wide range of crops including several stock-feed crops such as mangel-wurzel and cow cabbage (kale).

By the early 1850s, after Samuel Moore's death, grapes from the vineyards at Oakover were used to produce wines in commercial quantities. The only serious competition at the time was from E P Barrett-Lennard's St Leonard's across the river to the north of West Oakover.

I had thought I'd go ashore at Houghton's Winery. It is the largest of the Swan River wineries, has a long history (by Western Australian standards) and produces some estimable wines. But there is no landing at Houghton's and no connection between the winery and the river, although the winery is close to the river and is very popular for picnics. When I first visited Houghton's in the late 1980s you could walk down to the river. Now the way is barred by a number of fences and a 'Private Keep Out' sign.

With navigation above Middle Swan Bridge hazardous, it would be irresponsible for Houghton's to encourage people to approach their property by boat, but it wasn't always that way. There used to be a jetty. On the river bank adjacent to Houghton's you can see the remains of a largish wooden boat which was noted and photographed in a survey of Swan River wrecks in 1980. It has deteriorated little since then — probably built of Western Australian jarrah.

Houghton's Winery has beautiful gardens, the 1863 homestead

is restored and maintained with a shingle roof, there is a museum of old winemaking equipment; the approach road runs through lovely country which is a mix of vineyards and woodland such as Wild Flower Ridge where Houghton's are revegetating and creating a conservation area for native species. They are taking great care of the land and heritage, yet they seem to have sold off, or leased, all the land between the winery and the river, entirely turning their back on that aspect of their history. Of course the river doesn't mind.

Since I make a habit of finding out how places got their names I had better tell you that Colonel Houghton, who bought the property in consortium with two other army officers, never got closer to Western Australia than service in India.

The land was originally selected by Revett Henry Bland. He entered an arrangement with another noted pioneer, Thomas Newte Yule, an ex-army officer, who was in the consortium with Houghton, whereby Yule would take half Bland's assignment of eight thousand acres (3,240 ha) in return for performing the location duties for the whole property (those duties for eight thousand acres of land would require £600 worth of improvements). At the same time or earlier — and this was before the land was granted freehold — Bland, who lived and farmed up at York, had sold the other (southern) half of the land to a Dr Joseph Harris (or Strelley-Harris), apparently without any proper documentation of the sale. Two months after the freehold title was granted to Bland, Harris obtained a private mortgage on the property from William Tanner, but it was not until three years later that the transfer from Bland to Harris was legally registered.

Both Harris and Yule undertook the expense of location duties on their four thousand acres (1,620 ha) only to have more than ninety percent of the acreage revert to the crown, unused, within a year or two of obtaining the freehold titles. They would have received remission certificates to the value of one shilling and sixpence per acre resumed by the crown that could be used as credit in purchasing other land beyond the Darling escarpment.

Yule took up the management of the Houghton property in 1836 and remained there for twenty-three years, according to the official Houghton's Winery history, although in fact he spent some of those years living at Toodyay. He started working for the government as Swan District Resident (Magistrate) in 1838 and became Acting Colonial Secretary in 1849. He married Lucy, the daughter of Dr Harris next door, and moved in with the Harrises. Sadly Lucy died some months after giving birth to a son, but Yule continued to live at Strelley for some time and it was there that his son was brought up by a grandmother and aunts.

During the 1840s the 322 acres (130.4 ha) of Houghton that had not been resumed were short-term leased to a number of men but increasingly fell into disuse, as did much of the land in the Swan Valley during an economic depression. The consortium that Yule represented was assigned tracts of land far larger than the Houghton property up in the Avon valley.

It is not known whether Charles Pidley Hinds who lived on the opposite side of the river was often piddley, but Thomas Newte Yule was celebratedly pissed as a newt or mightily hungover with some regularity. He served as a magistrate and a sweet story tells of the time that he was trying a well-known drunk, 'Tom the Rat'. Tom spoke in his own defence saying in his Irish brogue, 'Well, Your Worship, it's all very well for the Police to say I was drunk, but I can assure Your Worship that, this time, I was no more drunk than Your Worship is at the present time, now that is a fact Your Worship.' Thanks to that ambiguous mitigation he got off with a caution.

Yule returned to England in poor health in 1862 and the land-owning partnership was wound up.

Yule's southern neighbour, Dr Harris, appointed to the official position of Colonial Surgeon, clearly drank more than was good for him since he died with delirium tremens.

The next owner of Houghton, Dr John Ferguson, appointed Colonial Surgeon after the death of Dr Harris, bought the property for £350 in 1859, and it is said that he sold the first commercial wine production in that year. Since only twenty-five gallons (113.75 L) was produced, an amount that most men could knock over in six months, we can assume that the doctor was not a big drinker.

In 1863 he bought Harris' property, Strelley, and his sixteen-year-old son Charles took up management of the combined properties. Charles built up the wine production and reputation during the next fifty years, working with George Mann, a wine and brandy maker from South Australia.

From 1930 until 1971, his son, Jack Mann, was the head winemaker; his best-known creation is Houghton's White Burgundy, a blend of chardonnay and semillon with something else added; it used to be tokay but I believe it is chenin these days.

The year 1859 was particularly notable for Swan River wines. In the year that Dr Ferguson bought Houghton, William Harris, son of Dr Joseph Harris from Strelley, leased Rainsworth on the other side of the river and started planting vines. He later bought the property and developed it as a major winery. Also, in that very same year, 1859, Dr Alfred Waylen, son of pioneer Alfred Waylen, started a vineyard and winery at Garden Hill, and the following year, a wine was made at Edward Hamersley's Pyrton that won a medal at the 1862 Great Exhibition in London.

Following the river downstream from Houghton one turns eastwards, inland, back towards the Darling Ranges for a kilometre or more. Towards the downstream end of that reach one can see a church and some old buildings less than two hundred metres from the river. The modern rectory sits between St Mary's Church and the river and it certainly doesn't enhance the view, but the rectory is a low building and not too obtrusive.

Immediately downstream of the church is the complex of Swanleigh Residential College which has two impressive buildings adjacent to the church but is a bit of a sprawl. I suppose that 'Residential College' means boarding school.

The church was built in 1869 on the site of an 1839 church. It is a fairly simple building with no tower or spire, but it does have transepts that were added early in the twentieth century. It is honestly built with decorative brickwork that is wearing well (unlike some of the later brickwork at adjacent Swanleigh) and there are several fine stained-glass windows. The triptych window 'Suffer little children' is from 1869 while the others were installed nearly a century later. Like All Saints at the top of the valley, St Mary's has a lych gate.

Once the rector's dog has got used to you and stops barking through the fence, St Mary's well-tended graveyard is a restful and shaded spot to contemplate the times when the Swan Valley's first church was built. The graveyard contains headstones which bear the names of several of the pioneers of Swan Valley agriculture. The oldest grave, that of Lucy Yule, predates the first church. Samuel Viveash and his family, several of the Blands, Lefroys, Barrett-Lennards, J G Meares and William Locke Brockman are all there, along with Reverend William Michell, said to be the first clergyman of Swan Parish though it could be argued that Louis Giustiniani had that honour during his brief tenure.

The Reverend Doctor Louis Giustiniani

Captain Irwin, on a visit home in the mid-1830s, urged the Missionary Society in Dublin to provide a missionary for the conversion of the Swan River Aborigines. In England a society was formed with the purpose of sending a mission to Western Australia. The Reverend Dr Louis Giustiniani arrived in July 1836 with his wife, a catechist named Fredrick Waldek and Waldek's fiancée.

Some sources state that he was Roman Catholic, but he was certainly operating as an Anglican at that stage of his life. He had been brought up a Catholic, of aristocratic Venetian descent, qualified as a physician in Rome, trained as a Jesuit, married a German and had become a Lutheran, then a Methodist, but he reached Western Australia as an Anglican missionary, burning to bring the Lord's blessings to the Aborigines.

Giustiniani, like Robert Lyons before him, objected vehemently in the press to the treatment of the Aborigines by the colonial authorities. He wrote frequently to Lord Glenelg, the British Colonial Secretary, detailing atrocities against the Aborigines and he was never deflected by diplomatic niceties from expressing his views in the strongest terms.

He wrote an essay intended for publication in the local press about the establishment of the mission to Western Australia, showing that it had been achieved largely through his exertions and apparently denigrating Captain Irwin's role. Possibly he made other more invidious comments or accusations about Irwin. Irwin was still in Britain at the time, but his friend and relative William Mackie got to see the essay and became very angry and hostile towards Giustiniani. G F Moore, a friend to fellow Irish Protestants Irwin and Mackie, also tried to warn off Giustiniani.

It was while those ructions were developing that Giustiniani attempted to defend in court three Aboriginal men accused of theft. But it was in the court of Justice Mackie that Giustiniani argued that, for the same reasons that the law dealt differently with minors, it was wrong to try the men who had not been instructed in the culture that decreed their actions to be wrong. Mackie interrupted and contradicted him during his presentation of the defence and then sentenced the men to appallingly harsh sentences — seven years transportation for stealing a lump of dough in one case. (Sentences of transportation were regularly given in the Swan River Colony in the decades before convicts were transported into Western Australia. Convicts were sent to New South Wales.)

Giustiniani left the colony in February 1838.

Fredrick Waldek remained; he was a tailor and later a merchant, and was the progenitor of a noted Fremantle family.

The oldest building at Swanleigh is Brown House, named after the Reverend Canon James Brown, MA, 'Rector of the Swan' — probably it was his rectory. Built in 1874 (or 1876) it is now rather spoiled by having its upstairs balconies shabbily enclosed with fibreboard and large windows. The main building, adjacent to Brown House, has fared better, though there seems to be a touch of rot in the original timber balconies; in places the mortar is falling out of the brickwork and some of the bricks are decrepitating in an alarming way. The foundations of this building were laid in 1904. The attractive neo-Georgian front has vines climbing up it.

A little beyond Swanleigh the inland flowing reach ends and the river turns south and passes under the Middle Swan Bridge, also called Whiteman Bridge. Having passed back under the bridge, back into the officially navigable Swan, one encounters on the left bank the Middle Swan Industrial Estate.

There have been brickworks in the area since the nineteenth century and some of the broken wastepipes that run down the river banks look as if they have been there since then. Because of the moderately high wooded banks the industry doesn't impinge greatly on the look of the river, but there was a strong burnt sugar smell like a sugar mill as I rowed past, though there is no sugar mill there. Are bricks glazed with treacle?

After the industrial estate one passes the Reg Bond Reserve, farmland, then Ray Marshall Park.

Reg Bond Reserve is in the small suburb of Viveash named after Dr Samuel Waterman Viveash, the owner of the land in this area in the 1840s. Viveash arrived in the Swan River Colony with his family in December 1838 and took up land in the Avon district. William Tanner, one of the more successful gentleman farmer pioneers in the Swan River Colony, was married to one of the Viveash family and he bequeathed his Swan River properties, including Wexcombe where the industrial estate now is, to Oriel Viveash.

There is a creek, actually an artificial cut or drain, that runs a kilometre or so east on the upstream side of Ray Marshall Park. I didn't follow it all the way to where it drains Blackadder Creek because the mosquitoes were overly attentive in the late afternoon, but it is deep and straight, and probably navigable right to the end for a small boat. It would certainly be a better location than the Helena River if one were making a documentary film about exploring the Helena River by boat. The stratigraphy of old bricks and beer bottles in the banks suggests that the area was once a rubbish dump. The land designated as Ray Marshall Park is believed to have once been a corroboree site. It now encompasses a football field and it is popular and noisy at times.

Downstream of Ray M's Park there is a ghetto of schools: the Governor Stirling Senior High, Guildford Grammar Preparatory School and Guildford Grammar, which I understood to be a boys' school but there must be a girls' school too because I saw two schoolgirls sitting almost completely hidden in some low bushes on the river bank like a pair of nesting waders. Though they weren't smoking they were clearly embarrassed to be seen and I affected to ignore them.

The most striking building on that part of the Swan is Woodbridge, a really large nineteenth-century house overlooking the river. Woodbridge was the name of Governor Stirling's in-laws' mansion near Guildford in Surrey, England. In the 1830s Stirling

Woodbridge House
Courtesy Ross Shardlow

built a country home on the large property he called Woodbridge centred around the settlement of Guildford, but he never attempted farming, even through the agency of a farm manager, preferring to let Woodbridge to others.

The current Woodbridge House isn't the place where Stirling built his country cottage. Charles Harper, a successful agriculturalist, parliamentarian, and pioneer of the pearling industry in north-western Australia, first leased, then bought, the Lower Woodbridge Farm in the early 1880s. In 1883 he started the construction of the house, about which, the following year, *The Inquirer* declared, 'the handsomest private residence that has as yet been erected in the Colony and the design reflects the greatest credit upon the architects' (*The Inquirer* was particularly well placed to access full details of the building since Harper had a financial interest in the newspaper).

It is a grand house. The design illustrates the end of a conservatism in Western Australian colonial architecture. Woodbridge exemplifies a shift from relatively simple shape and restrained ornamentation which can be seen as reflecting Georgian aesthetics, to the late-Victorian taste for revivalisms and extravagant ornamentation that one sees in the Western Australian gold rush architecture of the 1890s.

The house is owned by the National Trust and open to the public most afternoons, as are the appended 'Coach House Tea Rooms'. The rooms are splendidly furnished in fussy but elegant late Victorian-style. Some of the furniture and trimmings are original and overall the internal decoration feels cohesive and appropriate; there are good examples of the late-Victorian taste for oriental, including Japanese, design.

In 1896 Charles Harper opened a school for his own children and those of neighbours and friends in the billiard room, so that room quite correctly lacks a billiard table and has a large number of child-sized wicker chairs arranged round the edge. The class in the billiard room led to a larger school in an outbuilding and eventually to the establishment of Guildford Grammar School. In 1921 the house was leased and became the Preparatory School of Guildford Grammar. You can see some graffiti from that era: for example, scratched into the Brick:

M H JR.

1920–1924

It's a quality of graffito, or *sgraffito* since it is scratched, that you don't get in these days of the aerosol can; the letters are carefully formed with exaggerated serifs and quite probably young M H junior was caned with exaggerated precision for his pains.

In 1942 Woodbridge became a home for aged women. In 1964 it reverted to school use, providing overflow classrooms for local high schools and demolition was apparently imminent, but in 1968 the National Trust applied to the government to be granted the house, the government complied, and it has been open to the public since the 1970s.

Downstream of the schools the left bank is agricultural again, low flat land as you approach Guildford, and looking back across the swampy meadows one can contemplate a very English scene with the western facade and spires of the chapel of St Mary and St George, the chapel of Guildford Grammar, rising above the trees. It is regarded as a fine piece of English Gothic Revival, built using stone brought from Donnybrook, or so I read.

Being a pedant I'm inclined to quibble and say that even if Gothic is a nearly meaningless term, Gothic doesn't include Romanesque and the two turrets flanking the gable at the west end are Norman Romanesque in inspiration. It seems to be a building that was designed to be seen rising above the trees over the meadows because, seen from the road, it appears disproportionately tall and the walls of the lower half of the building are extremely plain. It actually looks as if the original intention was to build a wider church with aisles on either side of the nave but for reasons of economy it ended up with a simple rectangular floor plan and no ornamentation designed for the nave walls.

Closer to the river, just upstream of Barkers Bridge, is the St Charles Seminary, which was built as Garden Hill House in 1895.

Garden Hill was one of the properties of Alfred Waylen, a very notable pioneer settler. The house was built for his son Dr Alfred

Waylen who had a successful vineyard there, and in 1918 it was bought by another notable family, the Padburys. The house with its gardens running down to the river must have seen some spectacular balls and garden parties in the first half of the twentieth century but it is a very staid seminary now.

Chapter 7

THE MIDDLE SWAN, LEFT BANK

Guildford Town Wharf was once a very busy wharf where pioneering traders supervised loading and unloading, always keeping an eye to the opportunity for arranging the sinking and capsizing of each other's over-laden barges while the skippers swaggered at the bar of the Rose and Crown. The river trade was the crux of Guildford's existence, prosperity or penury.

The wharf is also known as Moulton's Landing for a Mr Moulton, a river trader who had a store right beside the river. In the depression of the 1840s he diversified into the newly developed sandalwood trade. In 1846 he chartered the ship *Paul Jones* to take himself and a large shipment of sandalwood to Hong Kong. The Malay crew mutinied and Moulton was murdered with a harpoon driven through him.

The historic wharf is restored and maintained but largely forgotten and isolated. You can't actually see the town from the river and, by an unhappy coincidence, you can't see the river from the town either, so they have become historically disassociated from each other. This is not unusual. J K Jerome was describing Walton-on-Thames when he wrote 'As with all riverside places, only the tiniest corner of it comes down to the water, so that from the boat you might fancy it was a village of some half dozen houses, all told.' But it could easily be Guildford Jerome was describing, and his sentence discussing the town of Reading is just as apposite if altered to read, 'Even the industrial side of Midland, though it does its best to spoil and sully and make hideous as much of the Swan River as it can reach, is good-natured enough to keep its ugly face a good deal out of sight.'

Guildford never really achieved the importance that was envisaged when the town was proclaimed and mapped out. Fremantle in 1832 wrote of the 'Town of Guildford (or rather where Guildford is to be)' and that unprosperous start is only part of the reason for its scattered appearance. First the railway, and more recently the Great Eastern Highway have cut through the middle of Guildford so it no longer knows where its centre is.

In one of fractured Guildford's centres you can still go to the Rose and Crown, Western Australia's oldest pub, which opened in 1841, the year that service was first held at All Saints Church. But you won't find any ruffians from the river barges there these days. The Rose and Crown operates more as a restaurant and function centre, so the ruffians are there for weddings, showing off hired tuxedos and their best behaviour, and in truth it's not the same building that opened for business in 1841.

Guildford was named by Governor James Stirling after the town in Surrey, England, where his father-in-law presided as Sheriff of the County. Probably Stirling would have called the Swan the Wey River if it had not already gained an established name, because, to quote J K Jerome again, 'the Wey [is] a pretty little stream, navigable for small boats up to Guildford ...'

Guildford is like the goldrush towns and agricultural centres further inland in that its boom days are long past and the large and magnificently decorated pubs or hotels on each corner dwarf the bric-a-brac and antiques shops huddled between them. Fremantle at the mouth of the river is another boomtown of the same era but it is thriving again and the exuberant architecture is part of the zest rather than a faded glory.

There are plenty of historic buildings and sites in Guildford, and it has a museum, open on Sundays, housed in the old Court House. Much of the museum's collection is rather tatty and inconsequential compared to the stuff at Woodbridge: there is a display of 1960s fashions, but not fab Carnaby Street gear, just the everyday clothes worn by ladies going to the shops in the suburbs. There are interesting tools and household utensils displayed out the back in the old gaol and in the corner of the backyard there is Taylor's Cottage — a tiny two-room shack from the early twentieth century built of cleft and rough sawn timber with hessian walls and mostly homemade furniture — a sad reminder of the shanty-town poverty that decent but hard-up families in Australia lived in less than one hundred years ago, and to which they will return if the harder-nosed capitalists and the economic rationalists get their way.

I started my survey of the left bank from Guildford downstream fairly early in the morning, taking things at a resolutely leisurely pace. Resolute leisure was absolutely essential because even my unsophisticated little boat, rowed limply, had turned out to be too efficient a means of travel. I enjoyed the rowing and once I got going found it difficult to stop and explore the shore, but on that day I was determined to do things properly, so I stopped after a couple of hundred yards at Fish Market Reserve.

The area was surveyed by Sutherland (Roe's assistant surveyor) when Guildford was first laid out, with the intention that it would be a general market for produce, including cattle. He mapped out a fish market right on the point, and separate markets for meat, pigs, poultry, corn, fruit and vegetables spread around the reserve. It was anticipated that the produce would be brought in from the agricultural area and also brought upstream from Fremantle and Perth, but the area was only used for selling fish.

The river was certainly full of fish in the early days. George Moore recorded catching about ten thousand fish with a single haul of a seine net in Melville Water. But I wonder how many

Fishmarket Reserve from Success Hill

fish were available for marketing so far upriver?

There appears to be a law of supply and propinquity that says the further you get from the source of a product the better value it will be. The law works most perfectly with wine which is always cheaper at a suburban supermarket than it is at the cellar door, and in the case of Australian wines, cheapest at supermarkets in London. Similarly, it is cheaper to buy your fruit and vegetables down in the fishing port of Fremantle than it is at the Fruit and Veggies Growers Market in Midland, and if the seafood in Fremantle seems too expensive, head away from the coast to look for the little van selling cooked prawns for $6.80 per kilogram beside the railway line in Guildford (nowhere near the Fishmarket Reserve).

The reserve is a pleasant wooded park with particularly good white sand beaches. Most of it was sold to Messrs Whitfield and Tanner in 1833, but it has been returned to public ownership.

I walked around the park and looked at the neighbouring houses on Swan Street, particularly looking for the ancient olive trees in the garden of Bebo Moro. The trees are said to have been planted by Spanish Benedictine monks billeted there in the early 1850s. They had been evicted at gunpoint from their mission at New Norcia and had walked the seventy miles to Guildford with little more than the habits they stood up in because of a power struggle within the Catholic Church that should not have involved them at all.

I rowed the kilometre downstream from Fish Market to Kings Meadow Oval. The name Kings Meadow sounds historic, and in a way it is, though there's nothing there to enhance any sense of history.

There is a belief that it was named for a local bootmaker and merchant, George Ogilsby (or Oglesby) King, rather than Captain Phillip Parker King, King George IV, Elvis Presley or William IV. In fact, when Sutherland mapped Guildford in 1829 he marked four areas of public open space and labelled each of them King's Meadow, meaning crown land. (Kings Park, adjacent to Perth, probably got its name in the same way. The area was set aside as public land in the early days of the colony and was often known as Perth Park. It was first gazetted as public open space in 1871 and opened as 'Perth Park' by Sir John Forrest in 1895. By the early twentieth century it was Kings Park, perhaps to celebrate the accession to the throne of Edward VII.)

Kings Meadow Oval is surrounded by an unsealed track which is popular with young men who like to fill their cars with their spotty mates and then practise handbrake turns and other methods of raising the dust.

When the hoons aren't there practising their bad-driving skills, the most notable thing is the disreputable bird life. For someone born outside of Australia and living in an urban environment where there's no contact with wombats, numbats or thylacaleo, the bird life is the most obviously exotic element of the Australian environment. It's almost shocking to see parrots, even budgies that ought to be in cages in old people's homes, flitting from tree to tree as if it were the most natural thing to do.

There are big mobs of parrots, specifically corellas which are cockatoos, hanging around Kings Meadow Oval and Point Reserve across the river. When a really big mob of corellas, all screeching like maniacs, come swooping fast on their stiff mechanical wings up the middle of the river, straight at you, it's like a scene from Hitchcock's *The Birds*.

Early in the morning the cockatoos start calling to each other — they don't seem to have anything else to do and I wonder when they feed. Early in the day they really seem to be calling to each other to say 'we're here' and they do it in a relatively collected way. It actually sounds a bit as if they're going, ''ere, 'ere, we're 'ere, 'ere, we're 'ere ...' They call and call and attract more and more corellas to come and perch in the branches of the same tree until the tree is full of screeching white rags, then one of them flies off screeching to another tree and the process starts all over again. By midmorning they're all just screeching their heads off and taking no notice of each other, or so it seems. If you get close to a tree full of shrieking corellas it turns out that many of them are demure couples sitting quietly taking no part in the rabble. The ones that screech make a fantastic noise: anyone who tried to imitate a corella at full volume for a couple of minutes would lose their voice for a week.

There are also mobs of magpies at Kings Meadow. They are vicious birds with big sharp beaks. They are dangerous in the nesting season when they will mob humans, especially children, and occasionally blind someone by spearing the eye with their beak. They also drive away seagulls, which speaks volumes about what thugs they are since the seagulls that hang around picnic spots are hard nuts themselves, not easily driven off by humans or dogs.

The Kings Meadow magpies all wear metal bracelets or bangles that add to their piratical look. Many have two metal rings on each leg and some even have three on one leg. If it weren't for their covering of feathers they'd probably get tattooed too. With their multiple rings they jangle around like dancers wearing ankle rattles.

A gaggle of geese from a house just downstream from Point Reserve sometimes visit Kings Meadow.

The mouth of the Helena River is beside Kings Meadow. Apart from the Canning, the Helena is the largest tributary of the Swan. Though it's called a river you can't go very far up the Helena by boat unless it's in flood. If you do go up the Helena you will find an island in the middle of the stream a short way up. It is possible to go either side of the island but you will find a clearer passage if you follow the left bank. The Helena is only ankle deep in places and, like Bennett Brook, obstructed by fallen melaleucas.

I turned round just a little upstream of the Great Eastern

Highway/Johnson Road bridge. The bridge is yet another jarrah log bridge. There are no weight restrictions on its use, but having paddled under it and seen the rotting timbers I would advise anyone driving a heavy truck to think about emulating the three wise men and go home by another route.

It seems to me that the waterfowl — the ducks and drakes and moorhens — are less wary of humans in the narrow tributaries such as Bennett Brook and the Helena. Out on the Swan if you approach them, no matter how slowly and quietly, they will fly away making you feel guilty for disturbing them. On the Helena you can drift along with a group of ducks swimming just ahead like tugs.

Olive Farm Winery. Is there a nicer riverside spot for lunch anywhere on the river? Unfortunately I was there too early for lunch despite loitering in Kings Meadow and Fish Market Reserve thinking up ways to slander the birds. The lawn sweeps down to the river from the limestone terrace where the dining tables are shaded by awnings. Across the river no suburban sprawl spoils the view because one looks across to Pickering Park.

Vines were first planted at Olive Farm in 1829 or 1830, in the first days of the colony, by Thomas Waters. Viticulture hasn't been continuous there since Waters' time, but the Yurisich family who bought the property and planted vines in 1933 are still running the winemaking. Until a few years ago they grew some unusual varietals, notably Muscat of Alexandria which made a somewhat riesling-like wine. They also made a white port when white ports were not fashionable.

On my recent visit I tried their Classic White which is verdelho based and very good. I'm not sure whether I preferred it to the sauvignon blanc/semillon blend which has a particularly delicious nose. After a quick wine-tasting I bought a glass of the cabernet sauvignon/shiraz merlot which is a good rich wine with plenty of oak, enough tannin, and a hint of portiness. It seems to me that Olive Farm wines are warmly flavoured because they are unashamedly hot-climate wines — and there is nothing wrong with that.

The light-lunch menu offers some very reasonable plates based on a range of freshly baked breads. I wish I lived next door. Olive Farm makes a very nice farewell to the Swan River wine-producing area if you are travelling by boat. On the road it is too close to an ugly light industrial area to feel like part of the vineyard country.

At the downstream end of the Olive Farm Reach, where the river turns sharply to the west, it runs very close to Redcliffe Industrial Area and a very large and obtrusive shed. The name Redcliffe comes from a farmstead built there long ago on land originally selected by Captain Currie, who was briefly Fremantle's first harbour master and then Commissioner of Counsel and Audit. Despite the name there are only the smallest cliffs, red or any colour, close to Garvey Park, while there are several places on other parts of the river that could have appropriately been called Redcliffe. Indeed there was another Redcliffe on the Canning.

Fauntleroy Avenue, that leads from the river to the domestic terminal at the airport, is named after Robert Fauntleroy who bought Redcliffe in 1852.

Having hung around Olive Farm and taken my rather early glass of wine I rowed even more slowly and reached Garvey Park about lunchtime. I took lunch on board *Earnest*, tied up to the bank in the shade under a she-oak tree.

Lunch was bread and cheese, a lemon from the old garden near Sandy Beach Reserve, and a mug of wine from a flagon of Olive Farm's quaffing red that I had acquired as a souvenir. Drinking more wine was probably not a brilliant idea out in the sun in the middle of a particularly hot day.

The ducks were all hiding from the midday sun in the shaded patches of water under the she-oak trees across on the Ron Courtney Island shore, the parrots had given up squawking, but the shags still stood out in the sun on dead branches, piles, rocks, and anywhere they could watch the river while sunning their never-dry wings.

After lunch I probably should have had a snooze under a tree but I rowed on languidly downstream passing the Ascot Inn, where I didn't fancy stopping for a drink.

There is foot access to most of the river bank from Fish Market Reserve downstream, but the path is cut by the Helena River and some creeks. The cyclepath follows the Great Eastern Highway until Garvey Park. From there you can cycle or walk close to the river until the Burswood peninsula where extensive wetlands end the riverside paths. However, you can cross the peninsula and from there follow the left bank of the river with almost no interruption all the way to Fremantle Harbour.

Two notable breaks in the riverside path go around the Ascot Inn and the Sandringham Hotel. These are the only two licensed premises with river frontage, and they each have their own jetty. I suppose we cyclists should blame ourselves for the publicans' antipathy to cyclepaths. We either go to the pub too infrequently or just don't take our bikes with us when we go to the pub.

On the officially navigable reaches of the Swan there are navigation beacons marking the deepwater channel wherever they are needed and there are signs warning of hazards to navigation.

The most unusual sign warns navigators to keep clear of a horse swimming area downstream of the Tonkin Highway Bridge and you really do see people taking their horses for a swim in that horsey area close to Ascot Racecourse. The horses seem to enjoy a swim — what the owners and trainers don't tell them is that sharks like swimming in that part of the river and a racehorse has been bitten by a shark in the horse swimming area.

The first record of horseracing in the Ascot area is from 1848. In 1852 the Western Australian Turf Club was formed and its headquarters have always been at Ascot, though it was not always called Ascot. The racetrack is beside the river, but the only racetrack building that can be seen over the fence from close to water level is styled like a Madurese mosque with a three-tiered pyramidal-pagoda roof. I don't know if that was the architect's intention but the Madurese are famously fond of racing. They hold races for pigeons and for buffaloes dragging wheel-less chariots, and they seem to gamble although they are devout Moslems whose religion prohibits gambling.

Downstream of Ascot Racecourse and the Garratt Road Bridge a new island has been created by cutting a canal through the wetlands on the left bank and round the back of a low hill that used to be Ascot rubbish tip. The rubbish tip has been rehabilitated and the island will remain as a nature reserve, while on the eastern side of the canal there was (yet another) new housing estate under construction.

Currently the housing estate, Ascot Waters, is too much architecture and too few trees but it will probably look better in a year or three. There's rather too much public relations blather too. One of the larger houses under construction was billed as 'a masterpiece of modern contemporary living' and another billboard explains that Ascot Waters is a community based on

Ronsea Island where, Crusoe-like, I stayed in solitude
for several hours

'New Urbanism (or Traditional Neighbourhood Design) principles' which makes it clear that new urbanism isn't new and probably isn't a properly articulated concept either.

I think one is supposed to imagine that these new housing estates will develop all the best aspects of Coronation Street thanks to some new design concept, but you'll be wasting your time if you try to find a corner store, friendly or otherwise, in Ascot Waters or any of the other 'self-contained urban villages'.

The new island doesn't seem to have been given a name. Nick Burningham Island is a bit of a mouthful, too many syllables. Short names are better and long ones generally get abbreviated. I've already contracted Ron Courtney Island to Ron C Island and now write it Ronsey or Ronsea Island in my notebook.

Subsidiary channels run off from the canal into the wetlands on the northern side of the island and can be explored by small boat. There is a low headroom footbridge over the canal — I had to duck slightly when rowing under it — and a road bridge with a little more headroom towards the southern end of the canal. A sealed road runs on to the island but doesn't go very far and motor vehicles are banned.

On the edge of the housing estate is a pond with some wetland vegetation, separated from the canal by a rubble stone wall. Pelicans obviously like the pond; there were four of them standing contentedly on piles, preening and escaping the heat of the afternoon with their head and long beak tucked under a wing.

Mind you, pelicans aren't terribly fastidious: you can see plenty of them around the ponds of waste water at Cockburn rubbish tip, which is still in use as a rubbish dump.

I was told at Maylands that a pair of black swans bred last year in the wetlands on the western side of the island. It is said to be several decades since black swans last bred on the river that was named after them. In places one can see flocks of twenty or more black swans, although usually one sees only one or two at a time, but back in the floods of 1830 Ann Whatley described how, 'The black swans now sail up and down the river most majestically in parties of fifty or more …' and there must have been many swans when Willem de Vlamingh's men caught them.

The Ascot area was originally farmed as Grove Farm by John Wall Hardey, the older brother of Joseph Hardey who lived across the river at Tranby House. Swan Location 33 was originally allocated to James Henty, then to Phillip Haymen Dod who swapped it for the original Tranby House in Fremantle. In 1854 J W Hardey added neighbouring Belmont Farm (Swan Location 34) to his property. His son Robert Davy Hardey later bought Swan Locations 30, 31 and 32 and built Belmont House on the high bank of the river downstream of the Sandringham Hotel. At that time the Hardeys had all the left bank from Burswood to where the Tonkin Highway now crosses the river.

The Left Bank Hardey

John Wall Hardey owned two selections on the Maylands peninsula where his brother Joseph built Tranby House, but he lived and farmed on the opposite side of the river. With Joseph he also owned large tracts of land on the Avon near York. John Wall accompanied Ensign Dale on the first expedition over the Darling Ranges in 1830 and identified land with good agricultural potential. Late in 1830 he was a member of a larger party including James Stirling who surveyed the land for allocation to settlers.

Living on the southern side of the river, J W Hardey had particular interest in seeing a causeway and bridge built over the Swan at Heirisson's Islands and as chairman of the Roads Trust he was well placed to see it happen. Curiously, he and his friend and fellow Methodist Mr Clarkson were the only persons to attend the official opening of the Causeway Perth Bridge in 1843.

In 1855 Hardey was appointed as an 'unofficial' or 'non-official' member of the Legislative Council. Originally the Legislative Council, and the Executive Council, had comprised only the governor, the colonial secretary, the surveyor general and the advocate general — all government officials and thus 'official members'. During Governor Hutt's term, as a token response to public pressure for an elected assembly, four unofficial members were added to the Legislative Council, appointed by the governor.

It was Governor Hampton who appointed J W Hardey. They got on together well and J W was adept at making speeches flattering the governor and praising his legislative initiatives. Hardey was a great help to the governor in maintaining his resistance to pressure for government by elected representatives and in 1867 Hardy resigned in protest when Hampton acceded to informal election of six members who he would then formally appoint.

To that end six electoral districts were designated. Hardey stood for the Swan District but got only a handful of votes. The Champion Bay District (now Geraldton) refused to accept a 'Claytons' democracy and boycotted the ballot. Hampton decided to appoint a representative. His choice of loudly undemocratic John Wall Hardey inflamed the protests and Hampton resigned. His successor Governor Weld did not immediately replace the Champion Bay representative but he did reform the Council with two-thirds elected members, a reform that Hardey voted against.

Elisabeth, John Wall's wife, was ten years his junior but predeceased him at the age of sixty-one in 1873. During the following twelve years leading to his death he seems to have been more or less completely estranged from his three daughters and son. Increasingly paralysed, he lived with old friends, Mr and Mrs George Lazenby.

The left bank running from the Sandringham Hotel to the Burswood peninsula is high and steep and there is a very pleasant walk or cyclepath running along much of it. There are several tiny beaches where people sit and fish in the shade under tall trees, and where the path ascends to the top of the bank (and peters out) there are fine views of the river and across the Maylands peninsula.

Cracknell Park is a small terraced park running up the steep bank. From the river, the park appears to be the grounds of the adjacent large white house with a belvedere; probably the park once was the house's grounds. The house, called St Columban's, looks very elegant from the river. Close up it's marred by fibreboard additions.

Because (at the time of writing) the path just petered out into a dusty vacant lot that might be called Hardey Park towards the eastern end of the reach, you can only find the riverside path by approaching from the western end — by going through the water-ski boat launch ramp area downstream of Cracknell Park which is thoroughly sordid. It's another example of what happens if a road and parking are provided right beside the river with easy access from a major road. KFC wrappers and plastic bags that once contained ice are strewn everywhere.

Since there is also a water ski area on the downstream side of Burswood peninsula it seems unnecessary to allow water skiing on this relatively narrow and fragile part of the river where the banks are not protected (and not spoiled) by concrete embankments.

River bank erosion on the Maylands side of the river is worse than anywhere else; every time I pass there are more she-oaks fallen. It's not just the ski boats that cause the problem: most powerboats are of designs that cause excessive wash, and many boats exceed the speed limits on the river, but it is the waterskiers that just go round and round in circles on the same patch of river, hour after hour, causing cumulative damage.

She-oaks and melaleuca do fall into the river through a natural process on other parts of the river: the layer of topsoil gradually slides like a glacier into the river taking shallow-rooted trees with it. However the fallen trees around Maylands have fallen away from the river, not into it.

Burrswood (with two Rs) was the property of Henry Camfield, and was named, in the usual way, after his family home in the old country. There were extensive shallows and swamps upstream of Heirisson's Islands and the swampy Burswood peninsula was only connected to dry land by a narrow isthmus.

A canal was cut through the isthmus in the first decade of the Swan River Colony creating Burrswood or Camfield Island. The Burswood Park Golf Course is partly on reclaimed land and partly on the land that was formerly the Burswood sewage filter beds: the golf course's ponds or water traps represent the remains of the arm of the river that cut into the peninsula and created the narrow isthmus. Most of the land where the casino and associated temples now stand is reclaimed.

The northern end of the Burswood peninsula is the site of Belmont Park Racecourse and, as with many attractive river bank sites, it used to be a rubbish dump. In the days when the rubbish dump and sewage beds operated, an earlier racecourse called Goodwood was positioned in the middle of the peninsula. Belmont Park Racecourse, like Ascot Racecourse, is a horseracing course and just across the river there is another one at Gloucester

Park. Why do they need three horseracing courses within three kilometres of each other? Every year or two one hears on the radio or TV a spokesman for 'the horseracing industry' whining that they need more government support for 'this important industry that earns so much for the state'. Probably Ascot is for horses that run clockwise and Belmont for horses that run the other way, or vice versa.

Belmont Racecourse is surrounded by fairly extensive wetlands which provide habitat for a range of birds including spoonbills. It's a wonderful thing to see such rare and curious-looking birds feeding and breeding in undisturbed tranquillity little more than a kilometre from the city centre.

The very northern tip of the peninsula is Garling Point, named for the young artist, Frederick Garling, who accompanied Stirling on his first Swan River expedition. Several of Garling's watercolours from that expedition are now in the collection of the Art Gallery of Western Australia. One shows a clearly recognisable Mount Eliza, others are less securely identifiable and there are contending opinions as to which parts of the river they show.

Garling was a good watercolourist and provides a reliable record. It is often said that the artists who came to Australia in the early days of colonisation could not paint Australian trees, that their Australian landscapes look more like English parks. Garling, however, seems to have had no trouble painting convincing eucalypts.

Following the left bank around the western side of the peninsula, after the golf course there is a park called Kagoshima Park, not Ron Kagoshima Park, just Kagoshima Park, so it is probably not named after a local councillor who had a fondness for football. In the park is a bronze statue of a large-framed but gaunt gentleman in seventeenth-century costume dancing a quadrille with a swan.

I was there when the statue was unveiled by Crown Prince Willem-Alexander of the Netherlands in January 1997 to celebrate the three-hundredth anniversary of the first historically recorded visit to the Swan River by Willem de Vlamingh and his crew.

Willem de Vlamingh's visit to Western Australia in 1797

The first historically recorded visit to the Swan River was made by men from the three ships commanded by Willem de Vlamingh of the Dutch East India Company (Veerinigde Oost-Indische Compagnie or VOC) in March 1797. Vlamingh's ships were named *Geelvinck* (Goldfinch), *Nijptang* (Pliers or Pincers) and *Weseltje* (Little Weasel). His voyage was purportedly organised to look for survivors of *Ridderschap van Hollandt*, a ship that had gone missing after leaving Cape Town two years earlier; it was also to be a voyage of exploration and scientific survey.

The voyage was promoted by Nicholaes Witsen, Mayor of Amsterdam and a scientist, in the days when very few scientists were specialists and most felt at liberty to speculate in mathematics, medicine, engineering, optics and anything else that took their fancy.

It has been suggested that the funding of Vlamingh's expedition was really motivated by a perceived need to consolidate Dutch claims of discovery in Australia and the southern seas. The English buccaneer William Dampier had visited a part of New Holland (Australia) and was preparing another expedition with the Royal Navy. Vlamingh's mission was to nail up plaques and signs proclaiming Dutch discoveries in places such as Tristan da Cunha in the South Atlantic and St Paul and Amsterdam islands in the Southern Ocean.

He landed at Dirk Hartog Island on Australia's west coast and seemingly found an inscribed pewter plate left there by Hartog, whose landing in 1616 is the first recorded landing in Western Australia. Vlamingh took Hartog's plate back to the Netherlands. Curiously, it had its inscription all bunched in the upper half of the plate leaving the lower part blank. Vlamingh replaced it with a strikingly similar plate which copied Hartog's inscription squeezed into the upper part and gave more detail of Vlamingh's visit in the lower half. It looks suspiciously as though the Hartog plate was actually Vlamingh's first attempt at a plate on which they were trying to engrave too much information.

Whatever the truth of the plates, both Hartog and Vlamingh landed at Dirk Hartog Island and there is no doubt that Vlamingh's men walked over the hills from Cottesloe to the Swan River and later took a boat up the river where they saw the black swans. They named the river *Zwaaneriviere* (Swan River) and captured some black swans to take away with them.

From Kagoshima a series of adjoining parks carry broad green lawns right around the South Perth foreshore. Almost all the parkland and the casino grounds are reclaimed from the river. The parks around the Burswood Casino — Kagoshima and Charles Patterson — are very popular for picnics and family outings; the trees are full of tangled kites, and cones of traditional frozen whipped petroleum by-product are sold as ice-cream from antique pink vans.

Downstream of the Causeway, McCallum and Sir James Mitchell parks continue the lawns. There are patches of melaleuca and she-oak, ponds, and a small circumscribed swamp as landscape features. It might not be a completely natural environment but the huge flocks of waterbirds obviously love it.

The flood-prone alluvial flats behind the parks were used for market gardening and dairy farming before the parklands were reclaimed and the old foreshore became suburban housing estates. Sir James Mitchell Park could have been named Douglas Park with some justification. The Douglases were the third family to settle in what is now South Perth. Thomas and Phoebe Douglas migrated from Cambridgeshire to Western Australia with their two sons, William and Frederick, in 1852. A third son, Alfred, was born that year.

Thomas took up much of the floodplain land along the South Perth shore where he planted orchards and gardens. Probably he had worked in similar alluvial plain horticulture in the flat fen lands of Cambridgeshire and perhaps he had taken produce to market rowing his boat down the fen canals and ditches in the same way that he rowed the produce to market over Perth Water. Later he set up a shop on the site where Perth Town Hall now stands.

The Douglases were a boatie family: young William used to row across the river every morning to attend Bishop Hale's Perth Boys School. At the age of twenty he married Emma Matilda Barratt, daughter of the head government gardener. Thomas worked as a driver on the Perth–Albany mail coach and he moved to Albany with his wife. Soon he left the mail coach and went to sea. By 1873 he was owner of the cutter *Victory*. Later he bought the steam launch *Perseverance* and in 1896 he bought the tug *Dunskey* from Sydney.

With *Dunskey* he rescued and salvaged the freighter *Gertie* in 1898 and in 1899, working from Fremantle, Douglas, with a crew including his son Clem, performed a very heroic rescue of the crew of the sailing ship *City of York* that had run aground on the northern side of Rottnest Island in heavy winter weather. Early in the twentieth century he bought the Fremantle-built barquentine *Iris* from J and W Bateman.

Fred Douglas moved to Albany about the same time as his older brother and worked on some of his brother's vessels. In 1881 he bought a forty-three ton fore and aft schooner *Agnes* which he operated successfully in the coastal trade. He had the contract to carry the mail to Esperance.

In 1892 *Agnes* was wrecked in heavy weather at Bremer Bay when parted from her three anchor cables, the windlass pulled right out of the foredeck. Fred then bought a larger schooner, *Grace Darling*. She was a very fine-looking ship with a deep square topsail and topgallant on the foremast. Douglas sailed her hard and took her in and out of tiny coves and bays to supply settlers along the southern coast. In 1894 Captain Douglas rescued the crew and 196 passengers from the steamer *Rodondo* that had sunk after striking Pollock Reef.

The Narrows, separating Perth Water from Melville Water, is created by Point Lewis over on the Perth shore and the point of land that stretches towards it on the South Perth side. That point was called Belches Point for Peter Belches, 3rd lieutenant on HMS *Success* in 1827; it was also called Point of Perth on some maps, but it has long been popularly known as Mill Point because there has been a mill there since 1833.

It is now accepted that Mill Point is the western side of the Point of Perth and Point Belches is on the eastern side, while the point itself, hidden under the Narrows Bridge, now lacks a name, but really they are all the same point.

The mill was built to the design of William Kernot Shenton and a second, larger mill was built on the same site for him in 1835. That second mill has been restored by the National Trust and it still stands there on Mill Point. Even ten years ago you could see it quite clearly but now the trees and buildings have grown up around it so densely that it has virtually disappeared.

I had come to the conclusion the mill had probably become a feature in the lobby of a hotel built over the top of it. But the windmill is still there: you can still find it and it is supposed to be open to the public most days of the week, but on the two Saturdays that I have been there it has been closed.

W K Shenton who owned the mill, and his brother George, came to the Swan River Colony in 1829. William, an engineer, brought a disassembled sawmill. He took up land on the Helena River and he started the newspaper that became known as the *Perth Gazette*. In 1831 he built a horse-powered flour mill at Fremantle, probably using parts from the sawmill mechanism. Horses for driving the mill were not readily available so operation of the mill was expensive. It was converted to wind power within a year.

The first mill built at Point Belches was a timber structure. George Shenton was there on his own when it was successfully raided by a large mob of Nyungars from the Mandurah or Murray River region in April 1834. The door of the current mill is said to show scars from the 1834 raid.

So many conflicting versions of what occurred have been published that it is worth reading George Shenton's own account.

George Shenton, of Point Belches, near Perth, in the said

Colony, gentleman, being sworn, saith on Thursday last, the twenty-fourth instant, about nine o'clock in the forenoon, a party of natives at least thirty in number came up to the Mill, at Point Belches in which I reside. I was then entirely by myself, no other person being on the same side of the river within some miles, to my knowledge. I was in the Mill when I saw them coming, and as I recognised them to be Murray River natives (they themselves having told me so a day or two before) I shut the door of the Mill. They came up and wanted me to go and call Captain Ellis, for the purpose of taking them across the river in his boat, but as I suspected they merely wanted to get me out of the Mill and then to rob it, I did not move. By promising two of them some flour if the others went away, I persuaded them all to leave the door except two, but I found shortly after that they did not go away further than one hundred yards from the Mill, when they concealed themselves behind the bushes. I gave the two who remained some flour, one of them went away to get some water. I then went out of the Mill and shook hands with the one who remained. He wanted me very much to sit down with him, this I declined, and had just turned round to get into the Mill again when I saw several other natives with their heads just above the grass, as if in ambush. I immediately jumped into the Mill, the man with whom I had shaken hands tried to catch hold of me, and jumped up to the Mill door after me; but I jambed his fingers between the door and door frame, and he let go. The two, to whom I had given flour, sat down at a fire close to the Mill, making dampers, and continued, for the space of half an hour, trying to persuade me to leave the Mill, and go and sit down with them. At length the others, who had been concealed, to the number of about thirty, came up to the door, and began to be very riotous, making attempts to get in at various parts of the Mill, and in one place pulled off part of the weather boarding. I kept them at bay by closing the door, for full half an hour, and then promised them, if they went away I would give them all some. I began to give each of them a small portion through a narrow framed window, but while my attention was engaged at the window, they forcibly broke open the door, by breaking the hasp, and a strong piece of cord by which the door had been secured. Several entered the Mill together, and immediately one of them seized the only gun in the Mill (which was unloaded, there being no ammunition in the Mill) and handed it one to the other; while the rest of those who had entered surrounded me, and pushed me out among the main body outside. Some of them cried out 'gidgul' (meaning to spear me) and others said 'No, no,' but laid hold of me and made me lie down on the ground where they kept me until they had carried away every article of flour and pollard, and were beginning to take the wheat when I cried out that the white men were coming (but there was not in reality any boat or assistance in sight) to frighten them, and they then desisted. They carried away eight bags, two baskets, several pots and pans, and in short, every vessel about the Mill which could hold flour. The whole quantity of flour carried by them amounts to nine hundred and eighty pounds weight. Every one of them carried off as much flour as he appeared able to carry. I am quite confident that I could recognise without the least hesitation, several of those most active in the robbery; in particular the two who so long tried to persuade me to leave the Mill, and also the individual who first entered the Mill by force and seized the gun, and also, I believe, was the person who called out to spear me.

Immediately that the natives let go of me, and were making off into the bush, I ran down to the water's edge, and called across to Captain Ellis who very soon came over, and shortly after him, the Reverend Mr. Wittenoom and Mr. Armstrong, who at my request went back to the Perth side, and brought back two of the Swan River natives, who examined the footsteps in the Mill among the flour spilled on the floor, and they immediately gave the names of several of the Murray River men, whose footsteps they pointed out. Mr. Wittenoom, who was then present, took down the names so given. A party of military under Captain Beete of the 21st soon arrived and accompanied by Captain Ellis pursued the track of the Murray River men for some hours, without coming up with them.

(Sgd.) GEORGE SHENTON.

Sworn before me at Perth aforesaid, the first day of May, 1834. W. H. Mackie.

The Murray River Nyungars were regarded by the settlers as aggressive and well organised. The warrior identified as their leader by the colonial authorities was Calyute (Kalyoot, etc.). After the attack on the mill and the initial unsuccessful attempt to intercept the Nyungars, a contingent of the mounted police were dispatched by Lt. Governor Captain Daniell. (Stirling, who was away in Albany, had instituted this troop which included Aboriginal trackers to protect settlers.) They captured Calyute and others whose part in the mill raid were confirmed by George Shenton back in Perth. Calyute was whipped and imprisoned for a month, whipped again and then released.

In July 1834 Calyute and his mob lured two young settlers called Nesbitt and Barron into the bush and speared them. Nesbitt was murdered but Barron escaped and survived. Captain Daniell did not retaliate but waited for Stirling's return. Stirling and others were cautious about confronting Calyute and the Murray River

Nyungars. Before doing so, Stirling negotiated a treaty with Weeip of the Swan River Nyungars so that Weeip and Calyute would not ally to form an axis of evil against the settlers. It is unlikely that either Weeip or Calyute could have led such an alliance but Stirling was acting according to European ideas of diplomacy and strategy.

On 28 October 1834, Stirling, Captain Ellis (superintendent of the mounted police) with soldiers and armed civilians making a party of twenty-four attacked and trapped in crossfire a group of about eighty Murray Nyungar men, women and children at Pinjarra. According to the official account fifteen Nyungars were killed and Captain Ellis also died a week later as a result of being speared in the head. Calyute escaped the massacre but his youngest wife and a child were killed. Another account estimates that about thirty Aborigines were known to have been killed and others, dead or dying, were probably washed away in the river. A third account says ten men, three women and one child were killed.

With most of the Murray men killed or fugitive, the police corps is said to have protected the surviving women and children from neighbouring Nyungar groups who would otherwise have forcibly subsumed those survivors into their groups.

The mill at Mill Point fell into disuse later in the nineteenth century and was restored as Alta Tower in the late 1870s. It was given a 'grand balcony two yards wide' outside the first-floor dining and reading room and a gallery on top adjoining the 'smoking room and snuggery ... from which a view of unsurpassed beauty [was] obtained' according to an advertisement for the Alta Gardens pleasure resort.

There was also a spacious hall for dances, music, weddings and other parties, and a hotel with commodious rooms, winter quarters for invalids, boating facilities, and nearly two acres of gardens with swings, merry-go-rounds, croquet, archery and cricket.

The resort was developed by an expiree (former convict) Thomas Henry Johnson Browne who had been slowly accumulating capital through hard work as a land agent, despite some obstruction from government officials. He was also an architect and civil engineer and developed a scheme for the building of a sheltered harbour in the mouth of the Swan River, but antipathy from the director of Public Works (also surveyor general) Malcolm Fraser, who had alternative plans for a harbour, meant that he had no chance of being involved in any public projects. Browne leased the Mill Point land from the Hamersley Estate.

Alta Gardens 'became the most fashionable social centre for the elite' but it didn't do well financially. In 1882 Browne was sued by a creditor and the case was transferred from the Civil Court to the Criminal Court, though no reason for that transfer was offered. During the case fraud was alleged though no evidence was produced and the defence witnesses were apparently dissuaded from giving evidence. Browne was found guilty in what looked very much like a judicial conspiracy against him and committed suicide by taking strychnine. The pleasure resort became a poultry farm.

Browne was not the only well-educated convict with a respectable background. Like most convicts of that description he had been convicted of forgery. Browne claimed that he had sacrificed himself to protect his wife. All the educated and successful expirees seem to have suffered some degree of obstruction or bullying from government officials; Browne seems to have been less able to tolerate and overcome that obstruction than others.

The shore that runs approximately straight from Mill Point south to the Canning River mouth is thoroughly blighted by the Kwinana Freeway that runs parallel to it only a few metres inland from the beach. Currently there are claims that the freeway will be made uglier by the addition of a mooted railway line running up the middle of it, but I can hardly imagine that the freeway with railway will be a significantly worse aesthetic and physical disruption of the South Perth and Como shores.

The freeway is not an entirely bad thing for the river shore environment; it creates a very strong physical and psychological barrier between the suburban hinterland and the beach, keeping people away. The beach and foreshore form Milyu Nature Reserve, and the adjacent waters which are shallow and unnavigable 'foul ground' are Milyu Marine Reserve. The reserves are particularly important to migratory waders, including plovers, curlews, shanks and stints, but in late autumn when I sailed past, the stints and all their mates were away for the northern summer on the tundra shores of Siberia and Alaska.

It is said that the remains of an Aboriginal stone weir fish trap on the Como shore used to be visible on a low tide.

To the south of Milyu there are three large pedestrian bridges over the freeway, all within a few hundred metres of each other. Their construction has been criticised as unnecessary or profligate but they create an interesting visual effect and to some extent re-connect Como with the river after years of having been severed by the horrible freeway.

The flashiest and most architectonic of the three bridges restores the connection between Preston Street and the Como jetty, the longest jetty on the Swan. There is a shaded viewing platform with smart stainless steel benches overlooking the river. Brass lettering set into the polished paving like giant cloisonné work, both on the platform and on the bridge itself, provide contextual information. Reading that information is meant to be a structured experience, and if you start on the river side, as I did, you are starting at the wrong end and what you read doesn't make much sense. First I read the names of several headlands and landmarks that I could see, the lettering pointing in about the direction of each location, but there was also the name of a headland that can't be seen from the bridge. Next I read an etched stainless steel plaque bearing an image of tangled rope and these words in single inverted commas: 'THE TRAM PUTS VISITORS DOWN NEAR THE SPLENDID PROMENADE JETTY … THE LONGEST ON THE SWAN RIVER.'

Starting from the landward end, as one is expected to do, the first thing one reads is SWAN RIVER FERRIES and then set into the paving the names of many of the famous ferries of times past. Across the bridge one reads JETTIES AND LANDINGS, and then the names of many of the jetties and landings where the ferries used to embark and disembark passengers, including the selection of headlands and landmarks that I had first read. Anyway, it's a very nice bridge even if it did have me perplexed for a while.

Not far south of Como jetty is the mouth of the Canning: another river, another voyage and another chapter for me.

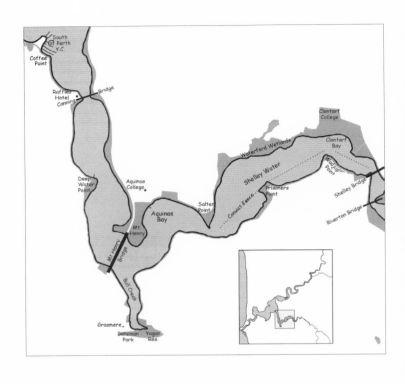

*The Lower Canning: South of Perth Yacht Club
to Riverton Bridge*

Chapter 8

THE CANNING RIVER

In late May I set out for the Canning. There had been some significant rain by then. The land was washed clean, most trees were noticeably greener than they had been at the beginning of the month and everywhere the grass was almost fluorescent with new shoots. I set out on a day when some showers were forecast for the afternoon, hoping to use the westerly winds before the passage of a cold front to go upstream and to return on the south-easterlies after the front had passed on the following day.

In Perth the problem with outings during the weeks leading up to the winter solstice is not the occasional showers nor the cold — the maximum temperatures were still over 20°C most days — but the days are short; there are less than twelve hours of daylight.

Alarm clock set for six, I got up and packed while it was still dark. As I walked down to the river the eastern horizon was glaring pink-red as it should on a day with showers forecast and a cold front impending ('red sky in the morning: sailor's warning') and I was out on the river just before the sun was up.

The weather forecast had promised moderate to fresh northwesterlies backing south-west, which would have been very helpful. Unfortunately, there was a light easterly: a headwind that I rowed against under an almost cloudless sky all the way to Point Heathcote, taking two hours with the help of a flood tide. It was warm with the sun on my back, though my feet down in the damp bilge were cold until I replaced the shoes and socks I'd taken off to launch the boat.

Off Point Heathcote I stopped rowing to jot a few notes, to eat a sandwich that I'd intended to keep until at least eleven o'clock, and ponder the question, where does the Canning begin or end? A generous allowance would divide the Canning from the Swan with a line from Point Heathcote to Como jetty. The official boundary might have been a line drawn eastwards from Coffee Point to the opposite bank, but Coffee Point has ceased to be a point because South of Perth Yacht Club jetties, land reclamation and lawns projecting further into the river than the point. The yacht club's race starting line probably marks the current boundary between Swan and Canning.

The first European expedition to take note of the Canning, the French expedition from the ship *Naturaliste* commanded by Hamelin, decided that the Canning River led to the sea, that it was another outlet of the Swan. They named it Entrée Moreau. Some locals now believe that 'Moreau' is archaic French for 'sea water', another theory is that a midshipman called Moreau was on the French expedition that investigated the Swan, but the correct story is probably that the Entrée was named for Napoleon's General Moreau of Hohenlinden, killed at the Battle of Dresden.

The Canning River was named for Thomas Canning, formerly treasurer of the admiralty, and/or his brother George Canning, member of parliament, foreign secretary, and briefly, in the months before his death in 1827, prime minister. As foreign secretary during the first part of the Napoleonic Wars he had employed the Royal Navy as a decisive implement of foreign policy, most noticeably in the first and second bombardments of the neutral Danish capital, Copenhagen. His political career was interrupted in 1809 when he quarrelled with the secretary of war, Viscount Castlereagh, to the extent of fighting a duel.

The Canning Stock Route in north-western Australia was not named for either of the bellicose Canning brothers but for the explorer Albert Canning.

It is much less widely known that the Canning Highway, which crosses the Canning River near its mouth and follows the old southern route from Fremantle to Perth on the south side of the Lower Swan, has a Nyungar name. Canning or Kanning means 'south' in Nyungar. That origin of the name is not well known because, while the etymology is based in fact and recorded in

G F Moore's *Descriptive Dictionary of the Language of the Aborigines*, it's my own invention.

The Canning Bridge that carries the Canning Highway over the Lower Canning River is a notable example of the timber bridges built from logs, because unlike most of the others, it still has a humpbacked carriageway. Like Fremantle Traffic Bridge, it has a catwalk out to the central piers for access by anglers. The Canning Bridge's catwalk extends from the eastern bank.

During the Great Depression, there was a camp of shanties and tents to the south of the bridge on that eastern shore, created by homeless and dispossessed families who scraped a living partly by netting fish.

The men who built the first Canning Bridge included convicts who lived in a small encampment beside the bridge on the other bank and spent many years doing almost nothing to improve the Fremantle Road, according to contemporary complaints.

On the windless morning that I set out to investigate the Canning I rested on the oars and let the tide carry me silently under the bridge, surprising a couple of restful anglers. The light easterly had fallen to a flat calm and it was nearly hot as I rowed towards Mount Henry.

Unless you like the noise of heavy traffic, this beautiful reach of the river is slightly blighted by the traffic on the Kwinana Freeway, especially if you are following the right bank. There's traffic racing up and down the freeway, traffic pouring across the

Canning Bridge and traffic charging across the Mount Henry Bridge at the other end of the reach.

The right bank has a very pleasant foreshore, if you ignore the stream of the traffic just beyond it. White sandy beaches are backed by luxuriant melaleuca and she-oak: a combination that is rare on the Swan where melaleuca fringes are usually combined with sticky black mud. A former Aquinas College student tells me that the pleasant banks of the Canning downstream of the college were known as 'The Shells' and that they were famous for an activity known as nooky.

I have asserted that most river bank scenes are best appreciated from close under the shore, but the large old brick building with tower and turrets (a part of the extensive campus of Aquinas College) standing on the wooded hill above the freeway is so imposing and attractively set among the trees that it is best seen across the full width of the river from the opposite shore.

Directly underneath the Mount Henry Bridge you are almost completely shielded from the traffic noise by the thousands of tons of concrete hanging over your head, and there are lovely views back up the Mount Pleasant reach and across to Mount Henry. It is a much longer bridge than any of the three big concrete bridges over the Swan and there are wonderful views from the cycle tracks slung on either side below the main carriageway — the problem is deciding which side to cycle since you must choose either the upstream or downstream view.

The Shells, a secluded spot with erotic associations
for several generations of schoolboys

Mount Henry is not a naval admonishment invoked by Captain Stirling as some of my gay friends claim to believe. Second Lt. James Henry from HMS *Challenger* led an expedition up the Canning in June 1829, subsequent to Captain M J Currie's excursion that had been curtailed on its first day when one of his party shot him in the head. It was Lt. Henry's expedition that traced the Canning to its source in the Darling Range.

Mount Henry is little more than a hillock by most standards, but it has a nicely rounded shape and a covering of dark native vegetation, totally unsullied by car parks, public lavatories and other buildings. Hidden by the trees there is a cross-country running track that has been used to torture generations of schoolboys.

The hill has long been owned by the Christian Brothers, part of the grounds of Aquinas College and, as such, it is private property. However, I did see a couple of anglers who'd found their way in as I rowed around the southern shore and opened the view of Aquinas Bay on its eastern side — a delightful tranquil bay.

On a weekday in winter when there is no river traffic, this broad part of the Canning offers an undisturbed peace that is rare on the Lower and Middle Swan. It was wonderfully peaceful on that late autumn morning until a waterskier and ski-boat turned up.

Having previously offered one or two negative comments about waterski boats I should make it clear that I am not against waterskiers. Waterskiing is the most marvellously uncomplicated and uncompromised way of showing off and it provides a fine sport for those who are compelled to demand attention. But there is a proper place for waterskiing and that place is the tailings dam of a uranium mine, not the Canning River.

At the eastern end of the Mount Henry Nature Reserve, where the Aquinas College campus comes down to the water's edge and their rowing club is located, there stand the remains of a ruined timber jetty. The Canning is full of historic timber remains, many of them embellished by grave pelicans keeping watch over the river. There were five dignified pelicans on the piles of the jetty, each keeping a jaundiced eye on the ski-boat as I drifted past.

The other side of Aquinas Bay is Salter Point where there used to be a large jetty for loading firewood into barges. Mr Salter was a contractor involved in the shipment of firewood from there and timber from Mason's Mill further upstream early in the development of that trade.

A convict camp, picturesquely called Fig Trees, was established on the Canning opposite Salter Point in 1865. Most of the convicts were employed in aspects of timber getting, processing, and transport to Perth and Fremantle.

The 'convict fence', a long line of timber stumps sticking up out of the water from Salter Point all the way around past Prisoners Point and Wadjup Point to another jetty near the current Shelley Bridge, can still be seen in the Canning. The timber stakes originally retained a mud embankment on the edge of a deepwater channel dredged by the dredger *Black Swan* in the 1870s. Convicts propelled the timber laden barges by poling them along the fence or by towing them from the embankment.

If the embankment has not been maintained or repaired since the nineteenth century, the stakes, which are said to be jarrah, must be over one hundred years old; and since the visible parts of the stakes are at that most injurious level for timber — between wind and water — they must be made from a wonderfully durable timber. Perhaps the embankment was maintained more recently, though I can find no direct evidence of that.

Thanks to the Great Depression, the use of manpower to tow and pole laden barges lasted well into the twentieth century in some parts of England. It was my privilege to meet and talk with Harold Gibson who remembers those days and is now living in Western Australia.

Harold was brought up in the city of Hull in the East Riding of Yorkshire, and left school at fourteen, not long before the outbreak of the Second World War. He took an apprenticeship as a fitter with a company called Barracloughs, whose fleet of small cargo vessels included a number of sailing barges, known (and rigged) as sloops, working on the Humber estuary and the rivers and canals feeding the River Humber.

At Barracloughs it was felt that some experience on the unmechanised barges was a useful part of a fitter's apprenticeship.

Harold was assigned to the steel-hulled sloop *Rhoda B*, and probably because of the labour shortage created by the war, he stayed with her until 1942 when he misrepresented his age and was taken into the Royal Navy to train as a landing-barge coxswain.

Rhoda B could load about 110 tons of cargo with her side decks awash, yet she was handled by a crew of just two: young Harold and the skipper, who rejoiced in the superb name of Nabs Horsefall, and was a Lincolnshire man as many of the bargees were. The skipper and his mate were not paid wages but received a third of any profit from each voyage, so they were anxious to make at least one paying voyage per week and also to keep costs as low as possible.

Manoeuvring in docks and canal locks was done mainly with two long ashwood poles. The longer pole, called the 'stoure', with a hook at one end and a wooden pad called a 'shoulder button' at the other, was used mainly for pushing, while the shorter boathook pole was used to catch on to any convenient line, chain or piling to pull the sloop along.

Like all the Humber sloops, *Rhoda B* set a large gaff mainsail and a single foresail from a mast that was stepped in a tabernacle (called a 'lutchet' by the Humber bargees) so that it could be lowered for passing under bridges. Sail was used mainly on the broad Humber estuary. On smaller rivers and on canals, once the mast was lowered to pass under a bridge it was unlikely to be raised again unless a good fair breeze and a long run to the next bridge were promised.

A typical trip would see the *Rhoda B* sail up the Humber estuary from the seaport city of Hull to the inland port of Goole on one flood tide, even if they had to tack against a headwind, raising and lowering the heavy leeboards on every change of tack. The Humber estuary has powerful, swirling tides. They could spend the night at Goole, and if they were bound up the Aire and Calder Canal to the flour mill or the coal pit at Knottingley, they would have to set out very early the next morning with the mast lowered.

The canal had a towpath intended for horses to tow canal barges, but in the 1930s sloops like *Rhoda B* working on slender margins of profit hired no tow horse. 'Beau', as Nabs Horsefall called his young mate, was set in a hessian halter at the end of the half-inch diameter plaited cotton line made fast to the winch, and it was his job to tow the sloop the ten miles up the canal to Knottingley. This process was known as 'bow yanking'. The skipper helped get the vessel under way by poling with the stoure, although old Nabs Horsefall, who had a hernia that, in Harold's words, 'hung out like a half-inflated football bladder,' couldn't have offered very much help. Once under way, it was possible to keep the sloop moving at a slow trudge. Any following wind was a help and sometimes the large plank called the lutchet board, which sealed the hatch aft of the tabernacle when the mast was stepped, was stood on end in the lutchet to serve as a small sail.

The only respite came at the 'lock pits' where Harold had to help the lock keeper operate the sluice gates for 'penning up' or 'penning down'; and where the towpath was interrupted by road or rail bridges the tow line could be cast off for a minute while the skipper poled the sloop under the bridge.

There were no other stops until Knottingley was reached at the end of a very long day because anywhere they put a line ashore they had to pay. Fortunately for Harold, the canal was shallow so *Rhoda B* could load little more than eighty tons when bound to or from Knottingley.

The convict fence on the Canning runs absolutely straight from point to point, out in the middle of the river, except at Prisoners Point where it is lost under reclaim. I followed a less direct course, around the northern shore past the undramatically suburban suburb of Waterford, and then past the thick old-growth melaleuca stands of Waterford's extensive foreshore and wetlands conservation area.

There were pelicans, black swans and musk ducks all fishing together. The musk ducks, which are good divers, seem to swim around the pelicans' long beaks as they sift in the sediment searching for whatever they eat. I was able to watch the birds while sitting back and quietly progressing under sail for about twenty minutes, thanks to a moderate south-westerly breeze that had come up.

Under Wadjup Point I was becalmed again and needed to unstep the mast to get under a water main that bridges the river just downstream of Shelley Bridge. Had I not set the sail at all, I would have rowed into Clontarf Bay as I had intended to do before the excitement of sailing took hold.

I had seen some attractive buildings through the trees of what I took to be Centenary Park. What I was looking at was actually Clontarf Aboriginal College which includes a large Italianate church with a tall square campanile. It is another Christian Brothers edifice. Clontarf was set up as an 'orphanage' for Aboriginal children in the days when Aboriginal parents didn't need to be anything like dead for their offspring to be taken away as orphans.

Some non-Aboriginal boys were also sent to Clontarf for a bit of remedial Christian Brothers discipline. It is said to have a dark history for which the Christian Brothers are now striving to make amends in the running of the current college.

I don't know whether one can see the tower of Aquinas from the tower of Clontarf but it looked to me as if the brothers had been building a string of fortifiable towers in line of sight from each other (Heathcote — Aquinas — Clontarf) like a feudal mediaeval pope securing the lands surrounding Rome or Avignon. Unfortunately for that poetic hypothesis, it turns out that the tower at Point Heathcote was built after the government had bought the land from the Christian Brothers.

Centenary Park, to the south of Clontarf, is a grassed-over landfill rubbish dump and not particularly pretty or inviting. Shelley Bridge is a very ordinary concrete bridge that carries the Leach Highway; although I've been under it a number of times I can't actually recall what it looks like. Upstream from it is Riverton Bridge, another one of the old timber bridges with the same basic structure as all the others, but much lower. With only five feet of headroom it provides an opportunity to inspect closely the detail of the carpentry or even to head butt it from a boat.

Just above Shelley Bridge the Lower Canning River ends in much the way that the Lower Swan once ended at 'the flats' and Heirisson's Islands, with the river divided or braided into several channels that snake though swampy wetlands.

According to my maps there were three channels, but down at water level it looked like rather more than that. Following my 'right bank up, left bank down rule' I took the northernmost channel. Almost immediately I was lost in an Everglade-like maze, fighting past fallen trees thick with hairy lichen and swatting mosquitoes the size and colour of little pied cormorants. Stirling had noted a similar experience when forcing a passage through the flats of the Swan: 'Of all the places I have visited I think this place contains the greatest number of mosquitoes.'

When I came to a ruined footbridge, its narrow steel-mesh carriageway leaning over at forty-five-degrees and with only two

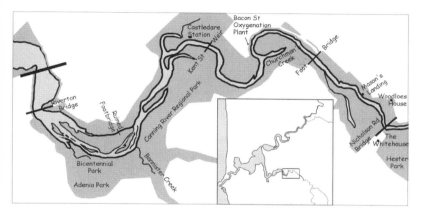

The Middle Canning: Riverton Bridge
to Nicholson Road Bridge

inches (50.8 mm) of headroom under it, I should have turned back. Instead I decided to drag poor *Earnest* over the bridge, doing horrible violence to what remained of the scratched paint on his/her bottom and straining myself too.

Having eventually got over the bridge I noticed that the channel was completely blocked just ahead by a large fallen tree. I would either have to turn back and heave heavy *Earnie* back over the bridge or find a way through. The trees on the banks, grown rank and leaning at all angles, were much too close together for portage to be possible.

Despairing, I rowed the few strokes to the fallen tree. Between a projecting branch and an upwards bend in the prostrated trunk there was a slit of unobstructed water a couple of feet wide, but *Earnest* is rather more than twice that width. I climbed out and onto the tree trunk and hauled *Earnie* into the gap, turning her on his side as I did so.

Balancing on the log, lifting and dragging at an awkward angle, I could move the boat a few inches at a time, stopping between lifts to whimper and curse with vexation, or to apologise to *Earnest* while getting my breath back. The further I dragged my poor boat through, the more she jammed in the cleft, but eventually I got her to the other side and swung myself down onto a thwart.

I was relieved to find the straining and distortion had not started any new leaks even if it had pulled a muscle in my side. The slow leak from the centreboard case didn't seem any worse than usual.

A minute or two of rowing and poling brought *Earnest* and me out of the northern channel at the point where the three channels recombine in a broad pool.

I do not recommend the northern channel.

Just ahead the river divided again. I thought I remembered from the map that I should take the southern channel this time. In fact the map shows that you can take either channel, but in truth that southern channel is now a dead end. You can see through the trees to where it used to rejoin the main stream, as I discovered before I exercised the discretion born of recent experience and turned round.

Despite the obstructions and diversions, it was still only one o'clock when I rowed out of the tangled, primeval forest to find myself, like Gulliver waking in Lilliput, beside a little jetty and a miniature railway station called Castledare Station.

This was a surprise worth investigating: I tied up and put ashore for lunch and a snoop around. The railway station has a proper signal box with levers to operate the old-fashioned semaphore signals and to switch points. The railway line appeared to be about 200mm gauge (it is actually $7^1/_4$ inch gauge — 184.15mm) which looked much too small to haul carriages that children could sit in, but since the line wanders for five kilometres through otherwise inaccessible wetland and riverside scrub I supposed it had to be enjoyed by passengers.

There are a number of bridges, including a model Bailey

Bridge that also looked too small for passengers. Nevertheless, Castledare Miniature Railway does carry passengers on the first Sunday in each month. Those passengers are both children and the adults who must accompany the children. They are not permitted to lean out of the carriages but I would think there would be more problem of parents bulging out of the carriages. Some parents are certainly too wide hipped to get into the carriages in the first place.

Castledare is named for the large house there, originally an 'orphanage' run by … 'not the Spanish Inquisition' … the Christian Brothers. It does not have a tall tower that could communicate with Clontarf and, as far as I can discover, it never did.

A short row from Castledare Station, just past Wilson Station at the southern end of the miniature railway line, one comes to Kent Street Weir Park, a place where one might expect to find Kent Street Weir. I had been expecting that I would have to drag *Earnest* up the bank, over the cycle track abutment of a bridge and back to the water on the upstream side to get around the weir, so I was confused to find no weir, only a footbridge. The weir had been opened. Perhaps they do that every year at the start of winter?

The Canning River has been the subject of serious experimentation to reduce the problems of toxic algal blooms and anaerobic water. These problems have something to do with phosphate fertilisers washing into the river, very low oxygen levels in the stagnant river water when flow stops during summer, and a wedge of dense salt water lying under the fresh or less brackish surface water. No doubt the operation of Kent Street Weir is connected with the experiments to remedy the problems.

As I rowed past the weir, biology students from Curtin University were preparing to launch aluminium dinghies from which they were going to sample riverbed water for plankton and oxygen content, salinity and temperature, the boys driving the outboard motors and the girls doing the sampling.

Not far upstream of Kent Street one starts to encounter a very long black water serpent whose arching plastic back undulates in and out of the water in regular curves like some representations of the Loch Ness monster. This Canning monster is rather longer than the Loch Ness version and in places there are two black serpents intertwined.

Around the next meander, still keeping an eye on the endless black serpent, I consulted the map to decide which channel to follow at another branching of the river. I took the northern branch which looks like a backwater. The southern branch, called Churchman's Creek, is wider and runs relatively straight but, as the map shows, it is a dead end. Rather than dig out the map I could have just followed the serpent's undulations.

Just past that branching of the river the serpents go ashore to the Bacon Street Oxygenation Plant. The big black plastic pipes run upstream and downstream about a kilometre in each direction from the Oxygenation Plant. One pipe draws in the stagnant

Mason's Landing is now a very
pleasant riverside park

water from the riverbed, the other pipe returns the water refreshed with pure oxygen.

A little further upstream one passes the end of Mason Street leading down towards the river. Benjamin Mason, apart from being a bridge builder, was the owner of a sawmill which processed timber, mainly jarrah, brought down from the Darling Ranges.

In 1870 Ben Mason supplied sixteen thousand jarrah sleepers for the Indian railway system. The sleepers, about fifteen hundred tonnes in total, were loaded into barges at Mason's Landing and lightered out to the iron-hulled clipper *Dharwar* lying in Gage Roads; the whole lading taking fifty days.

Dharwar also loaded fifty-nine horses for the Indian Army but all but two of them were injured and had to be put down after the ship was caught by a tropical cyclone in the Indian Ocean.

Benjamin Mason was the contractor who undertook the construction of the first road bridges at Fremantle and Guildford and he was also registered as the builder of a ketch, seventy-seven feet three inches long by nineteen feet beam (24.25 x 5.79 m), probably a large sailing barge, launched at Riverton in 1885.

The street adjacent to Mason Street was Wharf Street until very recently, presumably commemorating a timber loading wharf that used to be there, but in the last year or two it has become Civic Street commemorating the civic power to change the name of the street.

Mason's Landing where Mason and Bird Timber Company had their main timber mill is somewhat further upstream. There, Pioneer Park is a shady park on the sloping bank with wood-burning barbecues, toilets, a play area, and a memorial obelisk dedicated to Mason and the other pioneers of the Canning who, it says, 'will never be forgotten' (until someone changes the name of the park).

Mason's Landing was located at the upstream limit of navigation in summer for the laden barges because there were shallows and slight rapids just beyond it. The river has been cleared and dredged since then.

Though it was only two o'clock in the afternoon as I left Mason's Landing and approached the Nicholson Road Bridge I was beginning to think about possible places to pitch a tent for the night. I knew that just after Mason's Landing and before I reached the Nicholson Road Bridge there would be on the right bank a large old house, no longer privately owned, with grounds stretching down to the river. Since no one lives there now, it might provide a pleasant spot to return to at dusk if nowhere further upstream looked suitable.

Woodloes House Museum (open to the public on Sunday afternoons) is, according to a sign outside, the first architect-designed house to have been built south of the river. Presumably that means south of the Swan River since Woodloes is on the north

Woodloes House

bank of the Canning River. It was built in 1874 for Francis Bird, Mason's partner in the timber business.

Seen from the road, it is an attractive, shingle-roofed house with wide verandahs and carefully tended gardens. I imagined the lawns, smooth and green as a billiard table, and very much softer, sweeping down to the river bank, and surely a fine lawn once did that, but Woodloes is another place that now hides itself from the writhing black river serpents. Far from an inviting lawn open to visitors from the river, at the bottom of Woodloes' garden there is the thickest darkest jungle thicket anywhere on the Swan or Canning. You couldn't see a tiger burning brightly through it, let alone a lawn.

Nicholson Bridge is another of the Swan and Canning bridges that turns out to be two bridges — one concrete bridge and one lower timber bridge — when one rows under it. That there were two bridges was something I had never noticed from the road. Later I asked a friend who drives taxis about Nicholson Bridge: he was quite adamant that there was only one bridge. Yet, when you row underneath there are clearly two.

I had no idea what to expect upstream of Nicholson Bridge. Some people had told me that you can't even get that far by boat. I'd never been to whatever suburbs or shires were there, as far as I could remember, and if I had been there, I hadn't been aware that a river was there. And even if I had been, you can very rarely see a suburb from the river or vice versa.

My first impression of that unknown stretch of the Canning was that houses came down closer to the river than elsewhere, but there were not many houses.

I also noticed a few exotic plant species including a weeping willow. Almost everywhere else the sclerophyllically correct *Melaleuca sp.* and *Casuarina sp.* have been replanted while politically incorrect trees of European origin such as willows have been expunged, but up in the forgotten headwaters of the Canning, more nineteenth-century sensibilities still pertain: or so my inconsequential musings went.

In places the river was partially blocked by fallen trees but nowhere was it impassable and it was evident that someone with a saw had been pruning the fallen trees to keep the river open.

What surprised me, as I rowed pleasantly on into the dappled sunlight of a mild sunny afternoon that was showing no sign of the forecast showers … what surprised me was that I seemed to be travelling into the countryside no less than one is in the Upper Swan Valley. I had thought myself to be rowing into deepest suburbia, yet beyond the fringe of river-bank trees on the right bank there were bright green paddocks of fresh winter grass rolling gently between spinneys of tall trees; and the blue-grey hills of the Darling escarpment were not far away on the port bow.

The left bank was too high for me to see what lay beyond the wooded rise carpeted with newly sprouted wild irises. I was composing a pastoral idyll along those lines when, glancing over my port shoulder to avoid entanglement with fallen trees, I caught sight of a bright new sign:

TEMPORARY RIVER CROSSING
150m AHEAD
NO THROUGH ACCESS UNTIL
DECEMBER 2002

'Ophar King Sheet,' I exclaimed to myself, for strange and unwarranted words come to me unbidden in moments of angst. And just round the next bend, blocking the river's tenebrous tunnel of trees, there was a bigger surprise than a miniature railway station — there was a huge, bright yellow, surrealistic wall of sand and limestone rubble right across the river, stretching away in either direction to infinity.

I don't know whether people other than characters in Enid Blyton's children's stories really do rub their eyes with disbelief but I came very close to it before rowing up to the barrier. It was definitely solid and real, and beyond it, on the left bank (if a river continued on the other side of the barrier) towered a colossal pile-driving pylon. I got out the map again.

There, where I calculated *Earnest* and I had reached, was a pair of dotted lines marked 'Proposed Roe Hwy Extension'. So there it was, site of another massive concrete bridge that would link eastern suburbs with a new Fremantle bypass, except that the

Fremantle bypass (that would have bypassed Fremantle by going through Fremantle) had been cancelled.

There were three pipes of about four-foot (1.22 m) diameter through the rubble bund. I tried to back *Earnest* into the one closest to current river level but *Earnest* had a little too much beam to fit through the pipe. I considered that I might just get through by half sinking *Earnest* to bring the widest point of the beam down to exactly the widest point of the pipe but I wasn't quite that eager to get through and find myself under the pile driver. If I did get through and the river level rose during the night I'd never be able to get back again.

Glumly reflecting that I was victim of the unhealthy western obsession with the motor car, once again I turned around and headed slowly back downstream, despondent and directionless. I had hoped to be able to go at least another four or five kilometres upstream to the point where the Canning and Southern rivers divide, and at that point to be really quite close to the hills. Like Captain Currie, who I had thought ridiculous, I was forced to turn back on the first day of my Canning expedition.

On the first part of my gloomy retreat I looked carefully for the confluence of Yule Creek, named after our old friend Thomas Newte Yule, but in that season nothing recognisable as a creek flowed into the Canning. It was still only 2.30 in the afternoon. I'd already decided that if I was going to camp out it would either be well upstream of the wetlands or well downstream of them. I didn't fancy pitching or striking a tent in the twilight with the attention of those wetlands mosquitoes. They had been quite fierce enough even in the middle of a sunny day and could probably tear holes in a tent.

The flood tide that had been helping me upstream all morning had now turned and was pulling me back towards the wetlands which I reached before four o'clock, so I kept going, following an athletic canoeist through the wide southern passage. I started to row faster in the hope of getting to Bull Creek, where I wanted to spend some time investigating, before dark.

The trees in that broad spread of wetlands where the Canning braids into several channels provide roosts to hundreds of sacred ibis (*Threskiornis aethiopica*). With their long stilt legs they don't look like tree-roosting birds but there they were — big flocks suddenly descending on favoured riverside trees all around me in the late afternoon.

I kept rowing doggedly. Back on the broad water, clear of the wetlands, downstream of Shelley Bridge, I didn't know it at the time but I was rowing through the Shelley Gap, an anomalous stretch of water, rather like the Timor Gap. It is a riverine equivalent of no-man's-land where riverbed boundaries are seemingly unresolved. Upstream of the gap, the border between the suburbs of Riverton and Wilson runs on the southern bank of the river so that the river itself is in Wilson. Downstream the border between Shelley and Waterford runs down the middle of Shelley Water, but between Shelley and Wilson?

It was at about five, with the sun very low in the sky, that I got back to Wadjup Point and met the south-westerly funnelling fairly freshly up Shelley Water. I stepped the mast and set sail to make a board, as we nautical types like to say.

Making a board is sailing on one tack, then changing tack and sailing back a similar distance on the other tack — making one zig and one zag in the series of zigzags by which a sailing vessel makes progress against the wind. I sailed across to the Waterford shore on port tack — the wind coming over the port bow where I would have boarded (hauled taut) the rope called the port tack if my small boat were square rigged — passing a team of schoolgirls in a coxed four and their coach who was talking to them rather than bellowing at them. About a mile away downstream I could hear a male coach with a loudhailer employing the more normal technique.

By the time I put about on to starboard tack the sun was kissing the trees on the ridge running up to Mount Henry and the breeze was fading. I sailed back past the rowers again (they had covered some distance in the intervening minutes) going slower and slower.

Back on the Shelley shore, having made less than a kilometre, I dropped the sail once more and started rowing a little wearily against the fading breeze following the convict fence to make the shortest course. It was almost dark and flat calm when I got to Bull Creek.

Sitting out in the middle of the stream, I broke out my plastic bottle of cheap red wine and opened a Tupperware container of rice and lentils cooked with garlic sausage and tomato. While I slumped in the bottom of the boat and ate a comforting meal a light breeze returned. After dinner and a couple of large mugs of wine I set the sail and sailed very slowly downwind past Deepwater Point. I was lying in the bottom of the boat, almost dozing, and steering by back bearing rather than looking ahead, and so it was that I repeated my trick of sailing straight into a navigation beacon.

I sailed on, looking ahead towards the bright lights of the Raffles Hotel at Applecross. Singapore famously has its Raffles Hotel. The left bank of the Canning River at Applecross has its Raffles Hotel too, and not only that, it also has a Raffles Motel round the back of the hotel. The Raffles Hotel replaced a fine, old, sprawling, colonial hotel called the Canning Bridge Hotel. The Raffles is Art Deco, and like nearly all Art Deco looks a bit tatty unless the render has been freshly patched and painted — the large illuminated signs advertising Swan beer erected on the roof don't lend it much class neiver.

I have considered forming a Society for the Eradication of Art Deco Architecture but I couldn't support the demolition of Raffles Hotel which the owners are said to desire. Though its outward form doesn't much appeal to me, internally it has a solid and venerable feel. I've had the honour of addressing a couple of Booragoon Rotary meetings there and I can report that the dinners are authentically Anglo-Australian Art Deco — smooth damp vegies with the flavour gently steamed out of them, gravy thick as wet plaster rounding the terraced slices of roast meat, limp roast potatoes with no crisp or angular edges, and very few trimmings.

Raffles Hotel has a fantastic location on the river bank and the accommodation could be upgraded to something above *Psycho* motel standards. The appearance suggests that the owners would prefer to let it run down and replace it with some glittering tower. (That perception wasn't quite right. In the following months developers made permission for the construction of a seventeen-storey hotel on the motel site a condition of preserving the hotel.)

Earnest was self-steering very nicely in the light following wind and was able to glide right through the Canning Bridge without any assistance from me, a trick that earned *Earnest* a murmur of applause from half-a-dozen Vietnamese anglers under the bridge.

Beyond the bridge I was becalmed once more so it was back to the oars. I rowed unenthusiastically past the South of Perth Yacht Club, round Point Heathcote and set course across a perfectly flat Melville Water for Point Walter. To the north a first quarter moon rode a sky clear of cloud bar a few light cirrus, and beside me its reflected twin slid across the polished black water.

But an hour later, as I slowly approached the Attadale shore, the sky was clouding up quickly with cloud flying from the south-west and a breeze started again. It looked curiously as if there was rain to windward over Fremantle, so I dug out my wet weather gear. Five minutes later I put it on, five minutes after that I was rowing briskly to windward in cold torrential rain, but after another five minutes I was able to take the jacket off.

At Point Walter sand-spit I managed to beach *Earnest*, jump ashore from the bow, haul the boat across the spit, climb back on board, and row away without getting my shoes and socks wet. Luckily the tide was still with me, indeed the ebb was pouring out and I just used the oars to keep steerage in the middle of the stream and let it suck me down to Fremantle where I beached at 2210, exactly fifteen hours after getting under way.

I had been keen to find out how far the Canning was navigable, not only for narrative purposes and personal boating purposes but also to understand how rational or misguided Governor Stirling's original plans for an Upper Canning River settlement had been. Stirling's intention was to create four settlements — Fremantle at the mouth of the Swan, Perth probably at the confluence of the Swan and Canning, Guildford somewhere on the Upper Swan, and Kelmscott on the Upper Canning.

Governor Stirling, his Surveyor General John Septimus Roe, and the Colonial Secretary Peter Broun all publicly stated that Kelmscott was named by Stirling to honour the Oxfordshire birthplace of the Reverend Thomas Hobbes Scott, former

Archdeacon of Sydney whose return to Britain via Western Australia on HMS *Success* had been protracted by an extended visit to the newly founded Swan River Colony when *Success* went aground and was badly damaged on Carnac Island at the entrance to Cockburn Sound.

However, Stirling seems to have hit on the name Kelmscott before the Rev. Hobbes Scott reached Western Australia in late November of 1829. Earlier in the month Stirling had been up the Canning and had chosen the site of the town.

There is an intriguing map in the Department of Lands' Archive of Historical Plans (No. 411). It is a copy of the promotional map used by Stirling in 1828 selling the idea of the Swan River Colony to the British government and to potential settlers. On this particular copy Thomas Peel's vast selections are carefully marked with a fine cartographer's pen. With a thicker-nibbed pen, in a more freehand style, five town sites are marked and named. These thick-nibbed annotations are believed to be in Governor Stirling's own hand.

The map shows Peel's intended Clarence town site south of Woodman's Point on the shore of Cockburn Sound; Fremantle is shown in its proper place, but Perth is on the north shore of Melville Water where Dalkeith is now situated, Guildford is on the south shore of Perth Water where Burswood Casino now stands, and Kelmscott is somewhere up a very elongated and distorted Canning River.

If Stirling marked and named the settlements, including Kelmscott, before the locations of Perth and Guildford were finally fixed in August 1829, and before the real length and direction of the Canning were known, he must have done so on the voyage out or, more likely since Fremantle is named, in the very first weeks after arrival in June 1829, perhaps while waiting on Garden Island for the winter storms to abate.

Kelmscott as a township made little progress in the early decades of the colony. It proved to be too isolated and 'difficult of access in the summer' when the river was low. But did difficult of access mean completely impossible? Or did it mean only possible for small boats? Was Stirling just slightly overoptimistic in his planning or, faced with an unbridgeable disparity between the real availability of accessible fertile land and what he had promised the settlers, was his promotion of Kelmscott and the Upper Canning a wild attempt to deny reality — the sort of thing one might expect of a beleaguered politician at a hostile press conference?

Kelmscott is certainly a long way upstream of the point where the Southern River divides from the Canning and where the river appears to diminish to a narrow stream on the map.

Stirling's original intentions, shown on the map mentioned above, that Kelmscott should be on the broadwaters of the Canning but nearly twenty miles south-south-east of Point Heathcote, were founded on a greatly exaggerated representation of the length and volume of the Canning River. As Captain Fremantle wrote after a precursory reconnoitre:

The Course of the Canning is decidedly wrongly laid down on Captain Stirling's Chart as it trends much more directly to the Mountains and then runs along the foot of them to its source.

Writing about his 1827 exploration of the Swan River, Stirling noted:

… I had discovered, from the top of a high hill that a branch of the river that the French had named 'Entrée Moreau' and called an 'arm of the sea', extended for seven or eight miles to the SSE. I determined therefore, to ascertain its nature, and I despatched Mr Belches in the gig to explore it: this he accordingly did, and on his return two days afterwards I learned that after tracing it for 20 miles, he found it to be a freshwater river, similar in every respect to the one we had just descended.

It was on 16 March 1827 that Stirling despatched Lt. Belches and the high hill from which he descried the course of the Canning is always assumed to be the hillock of Point Heathcote (which was named after a midshipman on HMS *Success*). If that assumption is correct, Stirling was obviously exaggerating what he saw from the hill at Point Heathcote. Seven or eight miles (12–13 km) to the south-southeast of Point Heathcote is the eastern side of Jandakot Airport, almost eight miles west of the true course of the river to Kelmscott. The river actually runs more like east-south-east and my suspicion was that you could not see more than a mile or two upstream from Point Heathcote.

When I climbed to the top of the hill I discovered that you can't see anything like that far — you can't see much beyond the Canning Bridge, partly because there are trees in the way. Quite probably there were fewer trees back in 1827, thanks to Nyungar land stewardship, and perhaps Stirling got a midshipman to climb one of the few trees at the top of Heathcote's hill for a clearer view.

I tried climbing a tree on the south-east side of the hill but that didn't help at all. So I asked Melville Council staff for permission to climb to the top of the clock tower on the top of the hill. From there I could see over the tops of all the trees and the views were splendid in every direction, but I still couldn't see any part of the Canning River further than one mile (1.61 km) away. Looking in the direction the river flowed I could just see the spires of the Christian Brothers' Aquinas College on top of the ridge behind Mount Henry.

Back down at ground level I talked with the gentleman who had unbolted the doors of the clock tower for me and it was he who started my speculation about the Christian Brothers building a string of fortified towers when he told me that, like the Aquinas College, the tall clock tower and associated buildings on Point Heathcote were originally owned by the Christian Brothers.

Since Stirling had not explicitly stated that he viewed the Canning from Point Heathcote hill, I returned to Mount Eliza on the right bank of the Swan which is the highest hill in the area. From Mount Eliza in Kings Park you can see a long way. You can see the smoke stacks of Kwinana nearly forty kilometres away, and there is a clear view up the Canning as far as Mount Henry and Bull Creek. But there didn't seem to be any hint of where the river went beyond there.

Perhaps there might be some way of getting a glimpse of a small patch of Shelley Water. I tried climbing a tree near the top of Mount Eliza, but I couldn't find a climbable tree with an unobstructed view.

The DNA Observation Tower with its double-helix stairway is much easier to climb but the problem was the same — the tree beside the tower has outgrown the DNA and obstructs the view to the south.

I didn't note whether it was a tuart or a marri, but in either case it shows you why climbing a tuart or marri in Kings Park is no help for surveying the rivers — you can't see out through the luxuriant foliage. And you definitely can't see seven or eight miles up the Canning from any hill: Stirling's memory was playing him false or he was making it up.

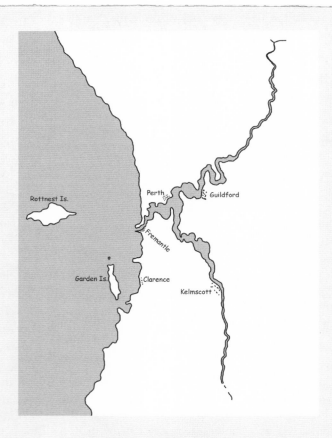

*After Stirling's hand-annotated map showing Swan and
Canning Rivers as presented to potential Swan River
Colony settlers, and showing early intentions for town
locations.*

Distances and location of Kelmscott
according to Stirling's Promotional Map of the Swan and Canning rivers based on his 1827 survey.

This analysis uses the distance from Rottnest to Garden Island as the datum for measuring other distances. That distance between the islands should have been known reasonably accurately to Stirling and his officers because they undertook a survey of Cockburn Sound, Rottnest Island, Garden Island and Carnac Island, and they should have been relatively familiar with the techniques of surveying coastal geography. The distance between Rottnest and Garden islands, measured to the nearest kilometre on a modern map is nineteen kilometres and should represent about the same distance on Stirling's map.

The settlement marked Kelmscott on Stirling's map is on the western bank of the Canning at the point where the river narrows from a flooded estuary valley to a river confined within banks. The Canning narrows in this way a little upstream of Riverton Bridge.

The actual settlement of Kelmscott was established much further upstream.

Stirling's map only slightly exaggerated the distance from the coast to Kelmscott (and the Darling Ranges) but it greatly exaggerated the distance inland of the end of the estuary broadwaters where Kelmscott was notionally situated. Similarly, the distance from Point Heathcote to Kelmscott was not too wildly exaggerated, but the distance from Point Heathcote to the end of the estuary was hugely distorted.

Tracing the stream to its source, from Point Heathcote to the point where one would start to ascend the Darling Ranges, the length of the Canning River was grossly exaggerated, far in excess of the 'twenty miles' (32 km) reportedly covered by Lt. Belches which was itself an overestimate. The length of the Swan was also grossly exaggerated, though not to the same extent as the Canning. The two rivers were made to be nearly identical in length.

The direction of the Canning River was also misrepresented. It was shown running about south-south-east whereas it runs about east-south-east for much of its navigable extent. As a result, the position of Kelmscott was shown not much further inland than its actual position but it was shown very much further south than it really is.

Distance measured from map	Actual Distance	Distance scaled from Stirling's Map	Distortion
Rottnest to Garden Island	19km	19km	0%
Coast to Kelmscott	21.5km	24km	111.6%
Point Heathcote to Kelmscott	21km	27.5km	131%
Heathcote to Ellen Brook (Swan River)	28km	60km	214%
Heathcote to Salter Point	4km	9.5km	237.5%
Heathcote to head of Canning River*	22km	61km	277%
Heathcote to head of Canning broad waters	6.5km	24.5km	375%

*   The river is drawn up to where it emerges from the Darling Ranges escarpment.

Settlers who took up land at Kelmscott must have understood that the river was nothing like as long, wide or navigable as had been represented because by the time they were able to register their selections Lt. Henry had explored the upper river on foot.

Three of those early Kelmscott settlers also took up land at Bull Creek, which they identified as a potential port for the trans shipment of cargoes from large river craft to smaller boats for use on the Canning. John Adams, Lt. Henry Bull and Thomas Middleton all selected land on the Upper Canning and at the creek that would become known as Bull's Creek.

Bull held his Bull Creek land in partnership with William Wood but it was John Adams with whom Bull worked in partnership, with the intention of developing a Canning transport business based at the Creek. Adams had 3400 hectares at Kelmscott, but abandoned it in late 1830 because of attacks by Aborigines and the firing of his barn. He left the colony in 1831.

Thomas Middleton farmed the Bull Creek property with one of his two sons while the elder son ran the Kelmscott property. They too built a house and barn at Kelmscott in 1830 but these were burned down the following year, so the Middletons also consolidated at Bull Creek. Even the Bull Creek settlement was all but forsaken within a couple of years, despite a small military contingent provided for its protection. The Middletons moved across the river to farm Mount Henry.

Kelmscott had a military detachment of seventeen men; their

barracks was the first building erected at the townsite on the eastern bank of the Canning.

The soil in the area was, and still is, relatively fertile. The settlement survived through agriculture and timber getting, and because it was on the track from Perth to Albany and other settlements in the south. When the Perth–Bunbury railway opened in 1898 the commercial centre moved from Kelmscott to Armadale, which was still known as Narrogin Inn at that time.

There were also early settlements along the river between Bull Creek and Kelmscott. In the 1830s Major William Nairn built a fine brick homestead beside the Canning at Maddington Park, more or less bankrupting himself in the process. Nairn's Maddington Park farm had been started and developed by John Randell Phillips, despite his having been seriously injured when speared in October 1831. Two of Nairn's shepherd boys were speared in 1833, apparently for refusing to give bread to a Nyungar called Buoyeen and his wife.

Thomas Newte Yule, in financial consortium with Houghton and Lewis, took up a Middle Canning Location which became known as The Rapids. It had a brook flowing through it, at least during the rainy season, which became known as Yule Brook. Just upstream of Yule Brook's confluence with the Canning there was a small stretch of rapids but the rock bar that produced them has been removed.

Because I had raced down the left bank of the Canning in failing light taking little note of the features, and since I could not take *Earnest* to the highest navigable point on the Canning, I would have to explore, like Lt. Henry, by land.

On Sundays, like all good Christian folk, I take myself out of the house to avoid the procession of mendicant callers who come soliciting funds for highly unlikely donkey sanctuaries in the Northern Territory or for the under-eights team of the local primary school to compete in the Southern Hemisphere Junior Polo Championships in Paraguay.

On Trinity Sunday, the first Sunday after my abbreviated voyage up the Canning, armed with a new Bike Map for Canning and Armadale, I set out to further explore the Canning, particularly that portion above the Roe Highway Extension Obstruction.

The whole length of the left bank of the Canning from Point Heathcote to the confluence of the Southern and Canning rivers, and the Southern River for several kilometres beyond that, can be followed on cycle and walking paths with no significant breaks. I thoroughly recommend it to anyone looking for a reason to get out of the house on a sunny winter's day.

The lower reaches of the Canning are deservedly popular. On a Sunday, particularly following the shores of the first reach from the mouth of the Canning to Bull Creek, a cyclist has to manoeuvre slowly and carefully to avoid getting entangled in dog leads or clobbered by the swinging fists of power walkers. If there are enough of you cycling and properly dressed in lycra it is probably better to wobble down the middle of the road obstructing the traffic than it is to mix with the walkers.

At Bateman Park, at the end of Bull Creek, a timber bridge through the swamp had been burned in the fierce bush fire of the previous summer and had not been replaced, so a short diversion following the Leach Highway cycle track was necessary.

The Shelley foreshore is pleasant if distinctly suburban. You could avoid it by crossing the Mount Henry Bridge and, having skirted the Aquinas College campus, enjoy the Waterford suburban foreshore and then the dense dark forest of the Waterford conservation area before following Centenary Avenue round to Shelley Bridge and regaining the left bank.

In research, before I set out on my notebook-brandishing explorations of the rivers, I had listed the names of a full one hundred parks, reserves and gardens that line the river banks. There turn out to be more park names than there are parks because on the Canning's banks upstream from Shelley and Riverton bridges there are parks that have more than one name. Canning River Regional Park seems to be the overall name for a series of conjoined parks. The first part that one walks or bikes through on the Riverton bank of the river is also called both Bicentennial Park and Adenia Park. All three names appeared on adjacent signs. I hope each naming was a funding opportunity.

All along the Riverton and Ferndale banks of the river the

Canning Regional Park preserves a wide ribbon of the native paperbark swamp environment, and in places there are high bulrushes (not native) screening the river. Even when you think you have caught a glimpse of the river through the screening vegetation you are probably looking at a cut-off meander — an oxbow lake as they are sometimes called.

One is not encouraged to explore the swamps and scrub. A sign at Bannister Creek shows a large snake and advises: 'This is my home. To keep us both safe please stay on the track.' I did stay on the track and I'd biked more than half the distance between Riverton Bridge and Nicholson Road Bridge before I got a glimpse of the Canning. Going through those left bank parks one correctly gets the impression that it is a secret and hidden river. I had gone ashore on the left-bank in a couple of places when I rowed that stretch, but the land is swampy and difficult to walk. During wet winters, large areas become broad shallow ponds, and as the waters retreat hundreds of fish are sometimes left flopping around hopelessly in the shrinking pools.

Crossing Nicholson Road and finding the continuation of the cycle track on the other side is something of a test. Cycle tracks and cycle routes are being improved but signposting remains very inconsistent and there are many dead ends that would never be tolerated by motorists.

Having got across Nicholson Road, I was surprised to find that the very large white house on the upstream side of the bridge is not just a white painted motel but a genuine colonial brick house called The White House. At least some part of the structure was originally W G Brockman's homestead called River View, built in 1889. Brockman, descended from a pioneer family, did well during the goldrush of the 1890s and was later Mayor of Perth. His River View estate was a big, well-financed, model farm.

The White House is now apparently a church though it looks like a motel. It is on the north-east corner of Hester Park which was named for the not-always-lucky Hester family, who first took up the land a little further upstream (Canning River Location 19) in 1830. Within a year of arrival, two of the Hesters' servants had died, Mrs Sophia Hester had died in childbirth and the infant died a few days later. Thomas Hester was left with five children to bring up and he was going blind from opthalmia. The charity of neighbours and also the local Nyungar people kept them from starving; they persevered and Thomas Hester regained his sight.

T N Yule in a letter in 1840 commented that 'old Hester is getting on better' and went on to say 'Miss Hester is I think although very awkward and untaught the prettiest and altogether the finest girl in the colony.' Thomas Hester was later a pioneer settler at Bridgetown.

Above Hester Park the river-fringing parks and reserves of the left bank are quite narrow in places, but I hadn't seen that from the river because of the steep banks. I had to take a diversion around the Roe Highway Impertinence and a bit further on the riverside

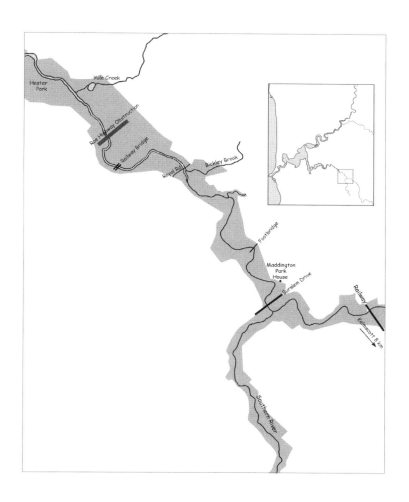

Labels on map: Hester Park, Yule Creek, Roe Highway Obstruction, Railway Bridge, Royal Rd, Bickley Brook, Footbridge, Maddington Park House, Burslem Drive, Railway, Kelmscott 8 km, Southern River

Upper Canning and part of the Southern River:
Hester Park to Gosnells

cycle track passed under a double railway bridge. From there the park or reserve is a little more extensive, full of Arcadian charm and exotic species. Native flooded gum and marri still predominate with the regular melaleuca on the edge of the river, but there are also cape lilac, jacaranda, figs and blackberry thickets. There are walking tracks through the wooded land on the banks of the river which must be particularly lovely in spring when the irises are in bloom. There are several tracks and it is always worth following any tracks closer to the river rather than the track closest to the line of bungalows, particularly above the Spring Road/Royal Street Bridge.

At Royal Street Bridge the river is quite narrow and the banks are very muddy, but it is still navigable for a small boat. A little further up are the first really shallow shallows and the stream starts to rise above sea level at a perceptible rate — it is no longer even a very small river, it is just a brook swirling and chuckling down a gentle slope, and the wooded banks are, perhaps, even more lovely.

Hidden from the river, but not far away on the right bank just before Burslem Drive Bridge is Maddington Park House. Almost certainly the oldest private house in Perth, it is the one that Major Nairn nearly bankrupted himself building in the 1830s. It is a two-storey house built of rendered limestone with brickwork around the door and window apertures. Nearly surrounded by citrus groves, the garden around the house is still attractive, if a bit overgrown.

The house is no longer inhabited and most of the windows are boarded up — and have been vandalised. It could be restored, in fact there didn't seem to be much wrong with it other than boarded-up windows. A bit damp and musty, but still sound. In the kitchen there is an old wood-burning range that looks as if it was used until a few years ago. It is only a couple of hundred metres from the windowless Maddington Metro Shopping Centre where thousands of paunchy people get their weekly exercise walking listlessly between endless rows of shelves each weekend, but this beautiful house and garden are lost in the trees, behind an orange grove, unregarded and forgotten.

How hopeless we are at looking after the little heritage we have. I recently worked in Ravenna, in north-east Italy: a small city of about 100,000 population with no great tourist industry. Ravenna has at least a dozen buildings built more than a thousand years ago in the late-Roman and early-Byzantine periods, and there are a great many more mediaeval buildings, plus renaissance, baroque, rococo, and even some fine fascist mediaeval revivalism; all well preserved, and well loved, in precincts protected from developers' depredations. It is very difficult to imagine that the civilised Italians would have it any other way, yet we barbarians …

Just above the Burslem Drive Bridge, the Southern River and the Canning River join or divide depending which way you look at it. You can walk on paths through the woodland and cross the two streams on bridges formed by fallen trees to find the confluence. In late autumn the streams were of very similar size and the Southern seemed to have a little more flow than the

Canning. Both rivers or brooks run from the south for several kilometres, parallel to the Darling Ranges and to each other a couple of kilometres apart, but it is the Southern River that the parkland reserves and cycle track follow.

I cycled on the tracks and in places on suburban streets as far as Southern River Road where, curiously, the river seemed to be wider and faster flowing than it had been at the confluence with the Canning. Presumably the waters are absorbed into the sandy soils the river flows over. There was a cormorant watching for fish in the pool under the Southern River Road bridge.

From there I cycled up the road to Gosnells to find the Canning again. The Canning, too, is distinctly broader at Gosnells than it is a few kilometres downstream. Presumably the rivers soak into the sandy soil of the plain below the Darling Ranges. However, the Canning at Gosnells is not a river navigable even for a small boat carrying a sack or two of wheat nor ever could it be. No doubt there is more water in late winter but the rate of flow would make an upstream passage extremely difficult. Kelmscott, which is a little further upstream, can never have been a useful river port settlement.

A few days after discovering the Roe Highway Extension Barrier on the Middle Canning I returned to Bull Creek, rowing all the way from Fremantle on another beautiful, clear, calm, sunny autumn day.

Once again I was struck by the way that looking back on the land from the water everything looks different. The prettiest stretches of the river are beguiling and even the tawdry bits are not too infuriating. One enjoys a pleasant detachment out on the river. Even the tragic depredations of the property developers can seem to be just comic follies when drenched with enough sunlight and framed by acres of blue blue sky and bluer blue river.

Having said that, I suppose I should admit that I don't always row along in a daze of benign contentment. Between brief moments of looking outwards and enjoying the scenery I retract inside my head, composing rancorous letters to newspaper editors, fatuous daydreams of fame and admiration or of revenge and justification until I run into a navigation beacon. On the very few trips when I've stayed away on the rivers for three and four days I've gradually settled into a more placid frame of mind, eventually able to think about even Philip Ruddock without bitter excess of spleen and bile.

The problem with exploring a local river is resisting the temptation to pop home and water the plants and check that you haven't been burgled. Holidays and travel are more complete where bookings, distance and parsimony prevent thought of premature return. Yet, a few decades ago when life and transport were slower, Perth families had the composure necessary to enjoy weeks of summer camping on the undeveloped shores of Melville Water almost in sight of their homes.

Pondering these changes in the pace of life and the scale of the

The Swan River ferry Mayflower
Courtesy Ross Shardlow

world, I was down to Bull Creek almost before I noticed I was on the river. There are a couple of wrecks lying in the shallows of Bull Creek that I hoped to look at.

The Swan River ferry *Mayflower* is said to lie somewhere on the western side of the creek but the only wreck I could find there looked too small to be the remains of *Mayflower*. The wreck, showing a timber sternpost and a couple of steel frames projecting above the water, lies at the bottom of a private garden. A much larger wreck, the remains of a flat or barge, lies at the very southern end of the creek. At low tide it is exposed. Only the flat bottom of the barge and the stubs of the futtocks — the parts of the timber frames that strengthened the sides of the hull — remain. A simple but elegant double-ended shape is evident.

Barges of over one hundred tonnes carrying capacity were built at Preston Point, Perth and even up at Guildford when the river was the main channel of bulk transport.

Beyond the end of the creek is a melaleuca swamp, partly called Bateman Park and partly Yagan Reserve, that was burned out by a fierce bushfire during the summer of 2002. The trees were all blackened and almost devoid of vegetation but some of the larger trees were starting to bud again.

The big, mature, melaleucas across the river in the Waterford conservation area show signs of having been burned in the past and have obviously recovered so, hopefully, the Bull Creek swamp will do the same.

To the south-west of the creek on rising land above the swamp stands Grasmere, one of the finest examples of nineteenth century homestead architecture. It is built on land originally selected by Thomas Middleton.

Middleton was the third pioneer settler in the Bull Creek area and at Kelmscott. When he found that John Adams, the second settler, already had the land he wanted at Bull Creek (Canning Location 27, to the south-west of the creek), he took the land adjacent to Adams' to the west, Location 28. Lt. Henry Bull, a naval officer, was the first settler.

Like his business partner, William Wood, and others, Bull used Royal Navy (or Army) half-pay pension entitlements to invest in the Swan Colony. Wood and Bull jointly acquired 17,530 acres (7,100 h) in various locations. They were allocated Canning Location 26 in April 1830, on the south-east side of the creek, three months after requesting it. Bull immediately started planting and building a house. In 1831 he built a substantial jetty at Bull Creek with the intention of developing a Canning River transport business.

Bull's Bull Creek property was the first freehold title granted in what is now Melville municipality. Title was granted in 1834, but by that time Bull had moved his home to a property on Ellen's Brook in the Upper Swan Valley.

One of Bull's men, Puckrin, was a brewer and he was brewing beer at Bull Creek in 1830, which Bull sold for three shillings a gallon. After Puckrin left Bull's service he operated cargo boats on the river.

Lt. Henry Bull

One of the most energetic and enterprising of the early settlers but he seems to have been unable to settle anywhere for more than two or three years.

Bull had a more conciliatory attitude toward Aboriginal people than many of the settlers. He was Justice of the Peace of the Upper Swan where a small contingent of soldiers was stationed to protect settlers from theft and attack by Aborigines. Bull repeatedly refused to sanction retributive expeditions by the soldiers, which brought him into conflict with some of the more bellicose neighbouring landowners. In one confrontation over his failure to appreciate the perceived need to teach the Aborigines a lesson in savagery, he would have been shot by Samuel Burges from Brook Mount if Burges' pistol had not misfired.

Bull was very popular with his employees, who he treated on equal terms. In 1836 he was offered command of HM Colonial schooner *Champion*. He gave up the command two years later, sent his wife home to England for a holiday, and started setting up a property near Bunbury. His wife returned and had a rather public affair. He packed her off to Batavia (now Jakarta) with an allowance of £50 per year, sold up much of his Western Australian property and returned to England where he died in 1848. He left the Bull Creek property to his nephew, John Islip, who bequeathed it to his only heir, Elizabeth James, who was living in England; she in turn bequeathed it to her three unmarried daughters.

The Bull Creek settlement made a promising start thanks to the energy of the pioneer settlers but the soil was poor, the settlement was small and isolated and the Nyungars were hostile to the appropriation of their land. A small military detachment was stationed at Bull Creek because of the problem of Aboriginal hostility and firing but it could not save the settlement.

The Middletons moved across the Canning to Mount Henry after their house was burned down, Bull went to Ellen Brook and John Adams left the colony. Adams' cottage at Bull Creek became the Leyson Arms Tavern. There was business for a tavern because Bull Creek was on the southern land route from Fremantle to Guildford. The Leyson Arms Tavern was burnt out in 1835.

There was a ferry across the creek to avoid a long detour south of the swamps in winter before a bridge was built over the swamp 1853. From Bull Creek the route continued east to ford the Canning at Yule's Crossing, also known as the Rapids (a bit upstream of Nicholson Road), then turned northwards. In 1836 the government gave up running an irregular ferry to Bull Creek and that was the end of the Bull Creek settlement for some years.

In 1835 Middleton mortgaged his Bull Creek land to acquire livestock. Many Melville properties ended up mortgaged to finance developments elsewhere because it was not prosperous land. Little other than temporary agistment of cattle and firewood cutting were developed in Melville until the late nineteenth century.

In 1850 Middleton sold his Bull Creek lands, which he had been unable to lease, to Alexander Francisco for £500. David Bras Francisco, Alexander's son, inherited a one-third share of the property in 1878. Although he was in financial difficulties, he borrowed money to buy out the shares of his mother, sister and a nephew. As soon as he had title he mortgaged it to John Bateman for £300 at eight percent interest. When he defaulted on payment, Bateman, the progenitor of a noted Fremantle trading dynasty, auctioned the land. It was bought by his son John Wesley Bateman.

In 1886 the Batemans built a jetty for unloading bricks and other materials, and then started construction of Grasmere. The original intention was that Grasmere would be a weekend retreat: it was built in a style that would have been seen as slightly old-fashioned and rustic in the late 1880s. With high ceilings, large rooms and surrounded by wide verandahs it was a very comfortable house and soon became the permanent home of uncle William Augustus Bateman, who had retired from commerce. Employing a number of labourers he cut firewood and farmed the land very successfully.

By 1928 the farming had declined and all but sixteen acres (6.48 h) surrounding the house were sold. More land has been sold off since then but the house was still standing with distinction in May 2002. Unfortunately, the remaining land around the house had been subdivided into twenty-four blocks each of which will soon be crammed with some gimmicky postmodern stately mansionette.

The road that leads past Grasmere, Spinaway Crescent is named after a beautiful sailing ship, built at Sunderland in 1874 for the Batemans' fleet. Bob 'Spinaway' Howson, the master shipwright who constructed *Spinaway*, has a couple of streets named after him, though neither are in the suburb of Bull Creek.

Howson sailed out to Fremantle with *Spinaway* on her maiden voyage to work for the Batemans. He built and repaired some fine ships in Fremantle. *Spinaway* was the pride of Bateman's fleet; her rival as queen of Fremantle shipping was Walter Padbury's *Charlotte Padbury*, also built in 1874.

Having poked around the niches of Bull Creek, I was able to sail back down to the mouth of the Canning past the land granted to Lionel Lukin in May 1830, including Point Heathcote and Coffee Point, the area now occupied by the South of Perth Yacht Club. Lukin also had land at North Fremantle and he put more energy into that land and developing a river transport business.

At the end of the nineteenth century there was a shipyard building river ferries, barges and luggers at Coffee Point. It was established at the bidding of Alexander Perceval Matheson who was subdividing and developing two new suburbs to be called Applecross and Attadale on the southern shore of Melville Water between the Canning and Point Walter. Matheson's projected

Melville Waters Park Estate housing developments were isolated in the scrub between Fremantle and South Perth and could only succeed as suburban developments if there was convenient transport. That was why he established a boat yard at Coffee Point to provide ferries for the Applecross Steam Ferry Service or Melville Park Steamer Co.

The first ferries were *Harley* and *Helena*, paddle-steamers built by Edwards & Co. of Millwall, London, and reassembled at Coffee Point in 1897. They were reasonably fast but narrow and unstable. They were replaced in 1906 by *Silver Star*, also built in England and reassembled at Coffee Point by A W Grey, or built from the keel up by head shipwright D Weir at Coffee Point according to another source.

Silver Star measured 30 x 5 x 1.2 metres and had a well-stocked bar. She was a good-looking ferry with an elegant elliptical counter stern (an overhanging stern aft of the sternpost) but was probably too big for river use and was sold to Albany in 1908 where she ended up in the hands of the Douglases who were descended from the pioneers of South Perth.

In 1935 Clem Douglas sold *Silver Star* to the Cossack Lighter Company with delivery to Fremantle part of the contract. He had given her an auxiliary ketch rig for fishing a year or two previously and she made excellent speed on a south-wester coming up the coast. In Fremantle Douglas worked converting the old ferry for work as a lighter.

She had been replaced on the river by the motor launch *Mayflower* which was almost certainly built by Peter Andersen and George MacCarter at Coffee Point. A year later, 1909, the Melville Park Steamer Co. went out of business.

South and Olsen took over the Applecross ferry run with *Valkerie* and *Valhalla* (first of their several 'Val' boats that carried generations of passengers on the Swan). Their operations were subsidised by Melville Roads Board (i.e. the Council).

When a bus service to Perth started in 1920, the ferry business declined.

The several jetties at the South of Perth Yacht Club, crowded with motorboats and many sailing boats too, are floodlit at night for security reasons, especially the northern jetty where the most expensive powerboats live.

The big floodlights on the tops of steel poles provide excellent platforms for pelicans to stand and watch the water below. (They also like to stand on top of the big lights over the freeway along the Como shore.) It's diverting, even fascinating, to watch the pelicans coming in to make a landing on one of the floodlights. They are very big birds (the Australian pelican is the largest of pelicans) with plenty of momentum and their webbed feet probably don't provide much grip, so they don't usually make a successful landing on the first attempt.

A wonderful bird is the pelican

His bill will hold more than his belican,

He can take in his beak

Food enough for a week,

But I'm damned if I know how the helican.

(Dixon Lanier Merritt. Famously used by John Gilroy
in a 1935 Guinness advertising poster.)

But I've never seen Australian pelicans fishing by straining distended beaks full of water.

The most remarkable thing about the Australian pelicans is the way they fly. When seen on the ground or flying close by, they do appear big bodied, but they have huge wings with much more aerofoil curve than other birds and they glide and ride thermals with incredible grace.

The very last of the Swan and Canning River commercial fishing boats can be seen moored in the shallows just upstream of the yacht club. It is a long, low, grey painted, open rowing boat with its registration number LFBP106EX94 on the bow. The hull is fibreglass but was obviously made using an old timber hull to create a mould.

I have not managed to meet up with the fishermen but the arrangement of the single thole pins (rather than rowlocks) suggest that they are of Mediterranean origin.

Fishing on Melville Water and the Lower Canning has been a commercial business since Fremantle fish merchant Robert Partridge financed a number of fishing boats in the 1830s. Salted and smoked herring were exported to India. Only the best timbers, such as oak and jarrah can be used for smoking fish. Old packing cases and particle board will give a terrible bitter taste. Somewhere in my researches I remember reading that using dried cow dung rather than sawdust gives the fish a better colour and a rich flavour.

The last commercial fishing boat working on the Canning River

Chapter 9

MELVILLE WATER AND BACK TO FREMANTLE

The final leg of my river exploration was the left bank from Heathcote Point at the mouth of the Canning around the southern shores of Melville Water, through Blackwall Reach and back to Fremantle. Melville Water is a beautiful, often sparkling, body of water. I have sailed on it frequently while yacht racing, but that is no way to look at the river and its banks.

I sometimes sail from the South of Perth Yacht Club on Saturdays between one and five o'clock in the afternoon when everyone from every yacht club takes their sailing boat out to race around the buoys and around each other. For those four hours Melville Water is thick with sailing boats thrashing to windward and careering downwind under brightly coloured spinnakers and only just under control. Collisions are not uncommon, partly because racing yachts' sails are cut so that you can't see what's ahead on the leeward side of the bow. If you are sailing on port tack you don't need to keep a look out because yachts on starboard tack have right of way and will yell 'STARBOARD' to let you know if you are on collision course.

It is well known that yacht racing involves a lot of yelling. Usually the bloke who owns the boat and steers it does most of the yelling. I crew on a 'classic' yacht (*Solquest*, a Randell Gemini built in the 1950s) where yelling is rare. We, the crew, take care to impugn the skipper, Tony's, competence, judgement, manhood, honesty and education before leaving the marina berth and then do our best to keep him on the backfoot throughout the afternoon.

When the boat has a clean bottom, and we don't make any stupid mistakes, *Solquest* is quite competitive, particularly in a stiff breeze. We usually make a stupid mistake with the course, missing one of the buoys that we are supposed to round. Angela is usually nominated as navigator and if Tony always checked with her what buoy he should head for next there would be few mistakes, but, to exasperate Tony, I have encouraged Angela to pretend she's lost and always nominate the buoy that we have just rounded as the one we should be heading for. He has coped manfully with the insults and annoyances for a couple of years but in recent months his psyche has been crumbling and he seems vengeful.

Last time we raced, I was on the foredeck after a failed spinnaker hoist, disentangling the spinnaker halliard (the line that hoists the sail) that I'd got caught up ('fouled' as we say) around the spinnaker boom topping lift (the line that holds up the boom which holds out one corner of the spinnaker). While I was doing it Tony quietly asked for the topping lift to be slacked off. The result was that in the next couple of seconds of weird slow-motion action the boom dropped, the spinnaker dropped into the water, caught a couple of tonnes of water like a parachute brake, thrust the spinnaker boom aft like a hydraulic ram and splintered it around the shrouds which somehow left me with a dislocated finger.

Len Randell, who designed the Gemini, as well as many other yachts, powerboats, various types of commercial fishing vessel, tugs, and Western Australia's Sail Training Ship *Leeuwin*, is a man whose knighthood and Order of Australia are well overdue. Some years past seventy, he is still a championship-winning glider pilot and a thoroughly delightful man to talk with.

At Len's house overlooking Blackwall Reach, with views across to Freshwater Bay and Dalkeith on one side and around to Rocky Bay on the other, I asked whether he was related to the George Randell who had owned and part-owned in various partnerships most of the early steamers on the Swan including *Les Trois Amis, Lady Stirling, Friends* and *City of Perth*.

It turned out that he is related to another pioneer of steamers, Captain Bill Randell, who owned river shipping, not on the Swan but on the Murray and Darling rivers in South Australia. The family originally came to Australia from south Devon, that most maritime of English counties. Len's more immediate ancestors in Western Australia were entirely un-nautical. He grew up in Inglewood with Maylands the nearest riverside suburb and has been fascinated by boats since he was very young, sailing tin canoes with hessian sails and any other boat he could get his hands on.

Len won a scholarship to Perth Modern School but, in the last years of the Depression, at the age of fifteen, had to leave school to work at the state government Department of Works as an apprentice mechanical electrician. During the war he tried to join the Royal Australian Navy but as a Department of Works electrician and working on the electricals of the Allied Forces units including the Catalina flying boats on the river, he was in a reserved occupation. By the time he was twenty-two he was supervisor of electrical works for three-quarters of Western Australia, but the work was not creative, not satisfying, and not boats. He returned from an arduous trip around the state to find his desk thatched over with a huge pile of files, gave a month's notice and with no savings to depend on, set up as a naval architect.

It was a time, as Len says, when almost no one in the state knew what a naval architect was. Most vessels were designed by the boatbuilders whether that meant designing on paper or sculpting the hull by eye. Len says he was lucky enough to get into designing cray boats when the crayfishing industry was taking off. Of course it wasn't just good luck. He made himself very useful, even indispensable to the industry. At that time, cray fishermen were using motorised sailing boats that chugged along making five or six knots at best. Len designed the first semi-planing plywood cray boat. It was relatively cheap and easy to build, made twice the speed of the other boats with the same engine and was a good sea boat too.

Over the years bigger and better cray boats, developed from that original design, were his bread and butter. Many of the older cray boats that Len designed are now used on the Swan and offshore for recreational fishing, and they have become vintage watercraft.

Earning formal credentials as a naval architect is far from easy and normally requires years of university study. Len blithely recalls that he had been reading books about naval architecture and the mathematics (formidably difficult for most people) were no problem to him — 'So I wrote a thesis and submitted plans to the Royal Institute of Naval Architects in London and was admitted: I was able to put the letters after my name from then on.' He showed me a certificate from the Institute acknowledging forty-five years of membership and added that he will be getting to fifty years soon.

In that long career Len has designed almost everything — fisheries patrol boats; *Hydroflite,* the first high-speed Rottnest Island ferry; successful racing yachts and government work boats. I observed to him that if one looks at any copy of *Trade-a-Boat* (the so-called Dreamers' Bible that lists thousands of boats for sale in every issue) there are probably more Randell-designed vessels listed than vessels from any other naval architect, partly because of the diversity of Len's designs, partly because of the duration of his career as a freelance naval architect, partly because of the practicality and success of his designs, and because owners are proud to list their vessels as Randell designs. He added that some of the boats listed as Randell designs are no such thing, but the owners pretend they are in the hope of increasing the value of hopeless old clunkers.

His designs are successful and, equally importantly for many boat owners, they look right; they are elegant. I wondered whether for him designing is mostly application of theory or is it more application of informed intuition.

'It's just about all intuition. Theory tells you how to analyse things but it doesn't tell you how to solve the interconnected problems that each set of design requirements presents. You do the maths, which is drudgery, afterwards, to check the design. I learned about boat design by sailing and looking at boats when I was young. You sail boats and see how they perform, look at the design and say, "Ah, that's how that works."'

Another thing I wanted to ask Len about was the design of motorboats that cause so much damage to river banks because of their wash.

'It's madness. They're overloaded with freezers and furniture and video players and microwaves and washing machines so they need bigger engines and great big fuel tanks. But it's what they [the clients] want because it's no good if their mate can get to Rottnest Island two minutes quicker. And they can afford it. I designed many of them myself.

'You could design beautiful river boats with low-speed hulls that don't create any wash, but nobody wants them. We used to anchor to go crabbing or catch fish. You can't anchor anywhere on the river now because of the wash — it's continuous.'

I encouraged Len to continue in that curmudgeonly vein but he tends to look on the bright side and observed that although crab and fish numbers seem lower than they were years ago, the river is healthier than it was.

When I sailed to Point Heathcote in *Earnest* and rowed slowly back to Fremantle following the southern shore, not only did I see things I'd never noticed before, but Melville Water seemed to become a quite differently shaped body of water. The several bays and headlands, and the limestone hills and ridges behind them, overlap and slide past each other, opening up changing views as one sails around the shores. It is very attractive but it has to be admitted that the character of the shores from Point Heathcote to Alfred Cove is largely wooded suburban.

The Point Heathcote area was seriously considered by Stirling as the site for Perth, the capital of Western Australia. He had told the Colonial Office that Perth would be situated at the confluence of the Swan and Canning rivers.

Below the hill of Point Heathcote, the wreck of a barge can be seen in the shallows on very low tides. The bay to the west of the point is known as Waylen Bay and also known as Frenchman's Bay.

Alfred Waylen acquired all the properties from Deepwater Point on the Canning to Point Heathcote and all the way round Melville Water to Point Walter (the entire southern shore of Melville Water) during the 1830s, but he wasn't much interested in farming the area. In March 1831 Waylen departed the colony for two years, leaving his servants to run his several properties and enterprises. Then in 1841 Waylen leased everything and went to England for a decade while his children were schooled.

John Wellard first leased and then in 1856 bought most of Waylen's Melville lands. He ran an abattoir and butchery business in Fremantle and used the land mostly for short-term cattle grazing. An impediment to agricultural development in the Melville area and elsewhere was Aboriginal burning in late summer which destroyed crops, orchards and even buildings, but the greatest problem was the arid sandy soil. Wellard went bankrupt in 1865. His extensive Melville land was then bought for £250 by George and Silas Pearse who also listed butchery among their several enterprises.

It was Alexander Perceval Matheson, a Scot, whose Melville

Waters Park Estate Company first developed the Applecross and Attadale areas as residential suburbs. Applecross and Attadale were names of parts of the vast family estate in the highlands of Scotland. He bought all the lands once owned by Alfred Waylen except the Point Walter estate (Swan Locations 61, 73 and 74) for £50,000. It was claimed that the value of the timber he cleared from the Attadale area covered all the costs of putting in roads and subdivision, but Matheson's plans were only partly successful. Many blocks were unsold and remained that way for half a century. Attadale and Applecross were regarded as too remote from the metropolitan centres of Perth and Fremantle. Even the offer of a free block for the construction of a hotel was not taken up.

In 1897, to lend prestige to Applecross, Matheson invited the governor, Sir Gerard Smith, to accept a large block of land with a commanding location on Point Dundas. Matheson then funded the building of a large house intended as a vice-regal summer residence on the point. Smith never took up residence; his term of office as governor would soon be brought to an end and was already clouded by accusations of inappropriate connections.

Matheson eventually sold the property to a dentist, G C D Forster, who lived there for a few years. When Grafton Forster moved out in 1904 he applied for a provisional licence for the property which became the Hotel Melville. The ferry *Decoy* made nightly runs from Perth to the Hotel Melville, and for some years it was a very fashionable watering hole. In 1925, after a refurbishment, the hotel was renamed the Majestic Hotel. Over the years it became somewhat run-down but remained a hugely popular spot, not least with river-borne visitors who beached their boats on the shore below the hotel. Popularity often invites exploitation.

A succession of proposals for redeveloping the Majestic Hotel and its grounds on Point Dundas was derailed by public protest. In 1969, a resort in the form of a phony Mediterranean seaside townscape was proposed. In 1974 a casino, hotel, marina and an exclusive yacht club were on the drawing board.

The Majestic Hotel and grounds were bought by Bond Corp. for $5 million in 1978. They proposed building just one hotel, of thirty-two storeys, on the site but even that moderate proposal was rejected. They next proposed a high-density housing development and marina which were also rejected. They put the property up for sale and seemed to have sold it to a Japanese investment company for $17 million, but the deal did not go through. They put it up for sale again in 1989.

Back in 1973 Melville Council had accepted that the 'skyline of the Point must be retained to a great extent. Thus any development would physically need to blend in to the topography of this magnificent site.' In 1978, before the Bond Corp. purchase, the council established a requirement that any residential development would see half the land surrendered to the council, presumably for public use. Yet it is now entirely covered by a chaos of pompous mansions, each of which might look all right standing in its own grounds, but they are all packed together as densely as the shambles of a mediaeval slum.

Actually, the architecture looks quite attractive and interesting seen from a couple of hundred metres off the north-eastern side of the point on a sunny morning but it strikes me as mean and contemptible that Point Dundas, a prominent headland on Melville Water, should not be public open space crowned with trees.

Sir Paul Hasluck, in his 1970 foreword to George Seddon's *Swan Landscapes,* warned 'Beauty is fragile. So many of our precious possessions have "just come to pieces in our hands".' He wrote of Canberra spending millions to beautify its lakesides and Perth spending similar sums on ruining its river banks. In some ways things have improved since then but there is no end to the building in of the river banks. There are guidelines about the kind of development that should be allowed by municipal authorities but no suggestion that there should ever be an end to building. Back in 1964, protesting the reclamation of Mounts Bay, Bessie Rischbieth said, 'This is without the consent of the electors. If we let this go by there will be no end to it.' There has been no end to it.

Municipal authorities are always faced with a dilemma — the revenue that allows them to exercise power comes from rates and there are no rates from undeveloped land. Melville Council has more river shore in their domain than any other Perth local government authority. They accede to public protestations, rejecting development proposals, agreeing that lands such as Point Dundas must be retained as public open space; then a few years later they run another proposal so the individuals and groups who spent time and energy convincing council of the value of the public open space must start their campaign all over again, and eventually battle fatigue or the trusting belief that the council could never get away with any such proposal allows an unworthy project to get past them.

Despite the commercial pressures, there are still undeveloped shores in Melville. Attadale foreshore was another Swan River rubbish dump until fairly recently. The river has often been preserved by neglect, rather than the attention of the authorities and entrepreneurs. (The same has been said of Fremantle.)

Attadale foreshore and adjacent Alfred Cove in the corner of Lucky Bay are the largest and best-preserved salt wetland reserves on the Lower Swan. The undredged shallows provide habitat for waders and waterbirds. In 1970 George Seddon observed that black swans do not appear on the broadwater parts of the Swan. Black swans seen on Perth and Melville Water in late nineteenth-century photographs were said to be pinioned birds that had been brought from lakes to ornament the river. Yet today fleets of twenty or thirty black swans can be seen cruising the river at Alfred Cove and Attadale.

The bird life should not be disturbed of course, but *Earnest* loves to tear past the Attadale shore where strong south-westerlies funnel over a relatively low saddle of the limestone ridge and blast out from the shore over perfectly smooth water allowing us to scorch along at the greatest possible speed heading towards Point Walter.

Point Walter was named by Stirling. He had an uncle Walter (Sir Walter Stirling) and a grandfather of the same name and title. Stirling would have called the point 'Walter point', the lower case 'point' always coming after the name by naval convention. Some of the Swan River (properly 'Swan river') points retain the naval word order, some points get named indiscriminately — Point Heathcote or Heathcote Point — while Point Walter and Point Dundas have definitely reversed their original order.

Alfred Waylen got the Point Walter land allocation in 1830. He immediately started building and applied for a liquor licence. His intention was to establish an inn and ferry station approximately halfway between Fremantle and Perth. The colonial authorities were not keen to grant Waylen a ferry licence. They seem to have wanted to control a monopoly. I have found no evidence whatsoever that any impecunity motivated them. Rather, there was not enough business for even one regular ferry service.

In 1831 Waylen first proposed a canal through the sand spit at Point Walter which would shorten the voyage from Fremantle to Perth by a couple of miles. Boats rounding the spit were sometimes delayed by wind and tide, and accidents

Whaleboats were used as ferries on the Swan River
Courtesy Ross Shardlow

caused by cutting the corner too closely, or by the steep chop in the tide race, were frequent. Thomas Puckrin lost a boat and three tons of wheat in 1833. John Smith and James Elliot drowned when they capsized one of Partridge's fishing boats in 1836.

Waylen's proposal was that he would cut the channel in exchange for a land grant on the Point Resolution side of the river, but it was not accepted by the government. Some sources say a channel was dug through the sand, but it silted up in 1833. A (second?) channel was definitely cut through the land at Point Walter and opened in 1837.

Waylen did build a hostelry at Point Walter and obtained a liquor licence. When he left the colony in 1832 the inn was run by W H Smithe. When the 1837 channel was dug, the inn was leased along with the channel to John and Henrietta Gresswell. The fee to transit the channel was six pence or 1 shilling after dark. The inn and channel changed hands frequently until they were leased in 1843 by the Caporn family — Samuel, Ann and fourteen kids — and became known unofficially as the Cape Horn Inn, although its real name was the Vauxhall Tavern and it had been known as the Waterman's Retreat.

The Caporn boys all became boatmen and ferrymen well known for experience, skill and tenacity, but not unblemished sobriety. They were also boatbuilders. Fredrick, with two brothers and a friend, won the first rowing race on the river in their four-oar gig.

The gig, which they used as a ferry or passage boat making the run from Perth to Fremantle and back daily, could carry about a ton (1.02 t) of cargo plus passengers.

In 1853 William Lawrence (who was married to Elizabeth Caporn) contracted to make the daily run with the mails from Perth to Fremantle and from Fremantle to Perth, weather permitting, for two shillings per day.

On a day in July 1856, William Lawrence and Samuel Caporn junior went on a bit of a binge, as river boatmen were more or less expected to do, but on that occasion it led to a serious mess-up with the mails and ultimately to their conviction for the theft of gold sovereigns from the mail. Lawrence got eight years and Caporn got six. Both men earned tickets-of-leave for good behaviour. William Lawrence went on to set up one of the most successful and respected shipyards on the Swan. On the Perth foreshore they built steam ferries, racing and cruising yachts, steam and motor launches, pearling schooners and cargo vessels.

The Caporns left Point Walter in 1852, moving to Rocky Bay and then to Fremantle.

In 1856 the publican's licence for the Point Walter inn was withdrawn because the channel was not being maintained. That was before the introduction of steam ferries but most of the river boats by that time were too large to go through the channel.

Dr Alfred Waylen sold Point Walter to the government in 1895 and it was then declared an A-Class Reserve. It was not easily accessible by road, but on weekends and holidays, excursion ferries took hundreds of picnickers and holiday-makers to Point Walter from Fremantle and Perth. I particularly like the sound of a picnic held by 250 members of the Perth Greek Orthodox congregation before Lent of 1906. They started with oysters and chablis before getting stuck into the spit-roast sheep and goats.

Many families went to camp at Point Walter during the summer school holidays. There were no facilities and the area became rather despoiled from overuse. Melville Roads Board took over the management and control of the reserve from the state government in 1912. They put in a caretaker and levied camping fees of two shillings a week or ten shillings for the whole summer. The caretaker was required to provide hot water at all times for threepence per teapot or one shilling per kerosene tin.

By-laws prohibited campers from all forms of riotous and indecent behaviour, swearing, riding their bicycles at over twelve miles per hour, and bathing in anything less than a neck-to-knee costume for both sexes. Camping remained popular despite the prohibitions and increased in popularity in 1914 when a tramway to Point Walter was laid.

In 1916 further regulations prohibited smoking in shelter sheds, access to the jetty while wearing a bathing costume between 7 am and 8 pm and, almost unbelievably, loitering on the foreshore while wearing a bathing costume. Even those prohibitions didn't make people stay away, so a whole range of amenities, facilities and entertainments were provided, drastically changing the character of

The big-budget view across Point Walter to
Melville Water from Mosman Park

the point: there were tearooms with hundreds of coloured lights strung around them, bands played for dancers on a packed dance floor in the evenings and other entertainments were provided at an open-air playhouse. There were fruit stalls, merry-go-rounds, weighing machines, photographers, acres of lawns, cricket pitches and ten tennis courts, and in 1922 flush toilets were installed. All of which pushed the camping fee up to five shillings a week — and yet Point Walter ran at a significant loss, much to the irritation of the local ratepayers.

In 1934 Point Walter was handed back to the state government who ran it in a more low-key style for the next forty years. A military training camp was established there during the Second World War and from 1948 until 1972 the scruffy camp provided temporary accommodation for immigrants, sometimes sheltering more than twice the number of people it was designed for. After 1972 it was used as a holiday camp for children from country areas.

Rocky, muddy beaches at Point Walter (and also at Deepwater Point and at Applecross near the jetty) were 'reclaimed' by bringing in many truckloads of sand in the 1960s.

In 1976 when Melville Council were expecting to regain control of the reserve they proposed demolishing the buildings and using the area to extend the Melville golf course. The proposal met strident local opposition even from some golfers. The buildings survived for a few more years and were then replaced by 'chalet-style' accommodation.

Although proposals for a commercial fun park and restaurants were rejected for many years because of local opposition there is a smart Mediterraneanesque restaurant there now. But there is nowhere like the Cape Horn Inn for a simple boatman such as me to fuel up with a quick mug of rum, one of arrack and perhaps a few tankards of home-brewed beer, all clots and bacteria.

I often drag *Earnest* across the Point Walter sand spit rather than sail all the way around it. The spit must be approached with caution or given a wide berth. Everything that projects above water level is clearly sand but there must be a significant number of large rocks sticking up from the sand below water level. Everyone I know who has sailed around the spit, cutting the corner, believes they have run into every rock there is.

Having crossed or rounded the spit, one is back in Blackwall Reach where *Earnest* first hit the water after his major rebuild. I had wondered whether Blackwall Reach, which really looks nothing like the Blackwall Reach on the Thames, was given that name partly because it ended at the Vauxhall Inn — although Vauxhall on the Thames is nowhere near Blackwall Reach — but the name Blackwall Reach wasn't used until nearly fifty years after the Vauxhall Inn lost its licence.

There is an urban myth that the waters of Blackwall Reach are unfathomably deep. It is believed, by a woman who sometimes cuts my hair, that the murdered victims of organised crime gangs are routinely dumped in the river, strapped into their cars, to be lost forever in the abysmal depths. In truth Blackwall Reach is not as deep as parts of Freshwater Bay.

Another hairdresser who tidies my greying curls told me that when she gained Australian citizenship her friends made her gobble a meat pie, guzzle a glass of beer and plunge from the cliffs at Point Walter Reserve into Blackwall Reach to confirm her enculturation.

The left bank immediately downstream of Point Walter is natural marri, Fremantle mallee and peppermint gum forest on a ridge above low limestone cliffs. Along those cliffs there are some particularly good examples of exposed solution pipes — dense calcareous linings that formed around drainage holes in the limestone and later created needles and pinnacles of rock when the softer surrounding limestone was eroded. There is a wonderful walking and cycling track undulating and twisting through the rugged woodland with fine views of the river.

The left bank of Blackwall Reach is in the suburb of Bicton. Bicton was the name of the property of John Hole Duffield who had migrated from the village of Bicton in south Devon. He built a house and developed a very successful farm despite the poor soil on the sandstone ridges. He had 5700 vines on his Bicton farm which provided the grapes for his Fremantle winery and brewery.

Bicton wine was probably the first Western Australian wine exported to other parts of Australia. In 1849 Duffield sent a barrel of his well-respected drop to a brother-in-law in South Australia.

John Hole Duffield died in 1859 and his vineyard was leased to John Luff who died a few months later, along with one of John Hole's sons, when a hole they were digging for a well fell in.

John Duffield is not much celebrated in Bicton or anywhere in the municipality of Melville. Most pioneers have streets, reserves and even bays and headlands named after them, but nowhere in Melville is there a Duffield Walk, Duffield Parade or even a short, dead-end, Hole Close.

Downstream of the Point Walter nature reserve, the rest of the Blackwall Reach shore is more of the expensive riverside real estate. Some of the houses have been built on flat plots of land created by cruelly quarrying back into the steep limestone hill.

My least favourite piece of riverside domestic architecture anywhere on the Swan and Canning is on Blackwall Parade. I suspect the architect promised his client that the building would nestle into the hill creating a harmonious and restrained effect. It looks like a nightmare cross between Darth Vader's spaceship and a Tyrolean chalet.

The other day I heard a local architect talking on the radio describing an award-winning house design built recently in Perth, which he said was 'blank or mute to the street'. The fantastic thing was that he intended no fault-finding, he was excited by that achievement. Not with a confident statement but a muted

Thoughtlessly situated houses on the cliffs above Rocky Bay

whimper: the conclusion to several millennia of architectural history. Despite the houses, which are mostly of approximately appropriate scale if nothing else, Blackwall Reach remains a dramatic and impressive stretch of the river.

Preston Point and much of the East Fremantle reach downstream from Blackwall Reach, is lost behind rows and rows of marina jetties and the white plastic powerboats that fill the marina berths.

Looking down that relatively uninspiring reach towards North Fremantle, the view of Rocky Bay is entirely wrecked by a ribbon of houses, square geometric abstractions, silhouetted along the top of the rugged cliffs of the bay.

North Fremantle is supposed to be a model of the kind of development that should be allowed on the river's banks, and some aspects of it are good, but that single row of houses, standing out against the sky along the cliffs, is as appropriate as building a multistorey car park on top of a ruined castle or a row of fuel storage tanks on the Great Wall of China. And every time I sail down that reach, the ribbon of houses has stretched further along the crest of Cypress Hill.

In my humble opinion, no consonant tradition of architecture would even consider building there and it will serve them right if a severe winter storm blows their brick veneer boxes off the cliff into the river.

Although on the river you can't follow the East Fremantle shore from East Fremantle Yacht Club to Preston Point because of the palisades of marina pens, the East Fremantle Council does seem to have preserved a narrow public right of way along the foreshore through the several yacht clubs, marinas and on a boardwalk around the Boardwalk Restaurant.

The right of way is however blocked by a Ministry of Defence property, used by the 5 Section, 52nd Military Police Platoon, Special Investigations Branch, who seem to need game fishing boats for their investigations, and the Royal Australian Navy Reserve Cadets, whose need for boats and canoes is more understandable.

I suspect that the public right of way irks the leaseholders and quite likely they emphasise their potential exposure to public liability in arguing that they should be relieved of those risks. There are plenty of signs phrased in ungrammatical legalese intended to disclaim liability.

IMPORTANT PUBLIC NOTICE

All users of these Facilities do so entirely at their own risk and responsibility and to the maximum extent permitted by law release from any liability whatsoever and indemnify the owner and its servants, or agents, or invitees in respect of any injury, loss or damage of whatever nature sustained or incurred by the users.

There are painted yellow lines showing where public way is permitted, and on a very high tide one could get one's feet wet by following them. I don't like the increasingly litigious trend in Australia, but I was tempted to slip on the wet concrete at Aquarama Marina and test the indemnity intended by that convoluted sentence.

As everyone knows, prohibition greatly inflates the value of even the most unattractive activities. A small, slightly jagged rockery beside the Boardwalk Restaurant is decorated with a sign that reads 'CHILDREN PLEASE KEEP OFF ROCKS'. I'm a grown-up now, of course, but I'm tempted to take my toy soldiers or a bunch of kids down there and climb all over the rocks with them.

At the other end of the Marina Reach a short limestone breakwater or groyne protects the corner of Swan Yacht Club's jetties from the current scouring around the point. There is a small brass plaque informing that the groyne was 'opened' by the Hon. Jim McGinty on 21 May 1995, and behind it there stands a big black, white and red sign:

DANGER NOTICE OF WARNING.

THIS BREAKWATER MAY BE DANGEROUS DUE TO POSSIBLE MOVEMENT OF ROCKS BECAUSE OF SETTLEMENT AND THE ACTION OF THE RIVER

AND OTHERWISE EVERY PERSON WHILST ON THE SAID BREAKWATER IS THERE ENTIRELY AT HIS OR HER OWN RISK

He or she shall not have or make any claim for injury or damage whether to his or her person or property including motor vehicles against the SWAN YACHT CLUB INC., their servants, agents or workmen howsoever such injury and/or damages may be occasioned whether due to any negligent act, breach of duty, default and/or omission on the part of SWAN YACHT CLUB INC. or their servants, agents or workmen.

NO FISHING

NO SWIMMING

NO DIVING

Swimming on the groyne is no more possible (or dangerous) than swimming in the car park and I doubt that the yacht club can forbid the public swimming in the river. I really can't see why they should need to ban fishing either. What did Jim McGinty open the groyne for? Surely not just as a test site for stretching the envelope of prohibition.

Preston Point was the site of one of the first large shipyards on the Swan. William Owston served his apprenticeship as a shipwright in the Royal Navy dockyards at Chatham, England. He visited Western Australia while working as a ship's carpenter in 1849 and returned to settle a couple of years later. In 1853 he set up as a shipwright at Preston Point, first building a lighter for carrying cargoes and passengers to and from ships anchored in Gage Roads. In 1857 he built *New Perseverance*, a schooner of 105 tons and went back to sea as her master. When William Owston senior launched *New Perseverance* she was certainly the largest vessel that had been built on the Swan.

TONS AND TONNES

The tonnage of a ship is not a measure of weight or mass. A schooner of 105 tons would probably be able to load more than 150 tons, or tonnes, of cargo. Tonnage was calculated from ships' dimensions according to formulae which were changed from time to time. Though tons and tonnes are nearly the same as units of mass, there is no meaning and no point in converting ships' registered tons to metric tonnes because it is an entirely notional, dimensionless measure.

Owston's son, also named William, continued shipbuilding at Preston Point. In 1876 he built a smart, yacht-like fore-and-aft schooner which he offered to the government for use as a revenue schooner.

Similarly large lighters were built just downstream in East

Fremantle by Howston and Murray and across the river at A E Brown's yard in the late nineteenth and early twentieth centuries.

As late as 1938 William Murray came out of retirement to supervise the construction of a big lighter at a yard between the Fremantle railway and traffic bridges.

Parts of the East Fremantle shore retained an industrial character until the 1980s. There were old boatyard sheds and jetties. A photograph of East Fremantle from the North Fremantle side of the river published in George Seddon's *Swan River Landscapes* is almost impossible to reconcile with the view one sees today — only two buildings are recognisable. Not only have a row of boatsheds and warehouses along the shore been removed, but an attractive limestone church has been vaporised to make way for the Stirling Highway carried across the river by the Stirling Bridge.

Below the bridge is the site of a brewery, originally Driver's Brewery and later Castlemaine Brewery. Just upstream is the one riverside building that has escaped destruction. Inside it you can see some very good old photos of the surrounding river bank from the days when there were boatyards and brewers.

Some say it was once the house of Mr Driver who owned the brewery, but it was better known as the house of Thomas and Fanny Carrol. Thomas Henry Carrol was a boatbuilder and he had a large boatbuilding shed beside the house. He built a pearling lugger in 1904 but mainly worked on building and repairing smaller boats

The Carrol's is now the Leftbank, a fashionable and popular waterside pub and restaurant. Riverside Drive runs between the Leftbank and the river so it's not strictly speaking a riverfront pub, but they make a feature of the river bank location rather than turning their back on it. In fact across the road, they lease half a jetty from the Town of East Fremantle where river-borne patrons can tie up and step ashore. That jetty has a small sign on it which I think quite the most euphonious on the river.

NO VING

O

JI MPING

A few hundred yards from my home, the Leftbank is probably the place I'd been looking for all up and down the rivers of Perth — almost the only place on the Swan where you can enjoy a drink while watching the sun sparkling on the water and the river boats going to and fro.

If I sit there on the balcony with a powerful pair of binoculars for long enough I might even catch a graffiti artist tagging *Earnest* where she lies padlocked on the opposite bank.

The old Swan Brewery under Mount Eliza

EPILOGUE

A month or two later, in the depth of winter, I approached a self-imposed deadline for finishing the *Earnest* manuscript, printing it out and showing it to a potential publisher — never an easy step, even with a short article. I was just about to load the printer with paper and start printing when I decided to make one more quick voyage up the river and back to check that I hadn't written anything that seemed hopelessly wrong or missed something blindingly obvious.

The weather was good, I had a minor cold front with a few showers to push me up the river under sail and I called in to have a chat with Ray at Maylands while the worst of the front passed.

Ray was still fired with enthusiasm for his plan to circumnavigate Australia on a raft of forty-four gallon drums powered by a Holden station wagon. His wife and son were getting ready to spend a year in Ireland while Ray built and sailed the raft.

Other things had changed: in wintry light, softened by a thin luminous drizzle, the Cenotaph and avenue of trees on Mount Eliza do no damage to the view at all. Round at Belmont, St Columbans was all Christo, wrapped in bright blue plastic for some reason. There were plenty of other changes to be noted on the way upstream and on the way back down with a cool easterly breeze, but it was time to draw a line under what I'd written.

Each part of the river has been observed on one voyage at a particular time of year. I sometimes went back, on foot, or by bike, even in a car, to check details, but not to revise what I saw. If some details seem wrong: if the trees I called marri seem to be lemon-scented gums, and the stretch of the river I said was in Vincent is in Mount Lawley, they were marri in Vincent on the day that I rowed past, if not on any other day.

But I would like to say that whatever I thought and wrote about the external appearance of the new Maritime Museum, internally it is a very exciting space, a real triumph of contemporary architecture.

That the river should change, that it should appear different on each visit, is hardly a new observation. It is two-and-a-half thousand years since Heraclitus of Ephesus pointed out that you can't step into the same river twice. But the rivers are relatively unchanging and provide a strong link to our past. As time flows, the river flows to the sea. Yet we may follow a river upstream to its source, going against the flow of time. As the river flows to the sea, it simultaneously cuts deeper and deeper into the geological past.

The Upper Swan and Canning rivers seem to be cutting back into our historical past. You may follow the rivers back through the origins of the Swan River Colony to find yourself in a time of primal solitude.

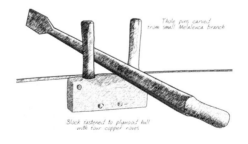

Thole pins carved from small Melaleuca branch

Block fastened to plywood hull with four copper roves

Earnest's double thole pins

REFERENCES

Appleyard, R T and Manford, T, 1979. *The Beginning: European Discovery and Early Settlement of Swan River, Western Australia*, University of Western Australia Press, Crawley.

Bourke, M J, 1987. *On the Swan (History of Swan District)*, University of Western Australia Press, Crawley.

Burton Jackson, J L, 1982. *Not an Idle Man: a biography of John Septimus Roe*. M B Roe, West Swan.

Cameron, J M R, 1973. Prelude to Colonisation: James Stirling's Examination of Swan River. *Australian Geographer* 12 (4): 309–27.

Cooper, W S and McDonald, G, 1989. *A City for all Seasons: the story of Melville*. City of Melville.

Davidson, D, 1997. *Women on the Warpath*. University of Western Australia Press, Crawley.

Dickson, R A 1998. *They Kept the State Afloat: Shipbuilders, Boatbuilders and Shipwrights of WA 1829–1929*. Hesperion Press, Perth.

Dickson, R A, n.d. *Steam Whistles on the Swan*. Report No. 70: Department of Maritime Archaeology, Western Australian Maritime Museum, Fremantle.

Doyle, M (ed.), 1834. *Extracts from the Letters and Journals of George Fletcher Moore*, London.

Erickson, R, 1987. *Dictionary of Western Australians, Vols I and II*. University of Western Australia Press, Crawley.

Fremantle, C H, 1979. *Diary and Letters of Admiral Sir C H Fremantle, GCB. relating to the Founding of the Colony of Western Australia*, 1829. Edited by Lord Cottesloe, CB, Fremantle Arts Centre Press, Fremantle (Originally published London, 1928).

Johnstone, R, 1988. *The Tranby Hardeys*. Parmelia Publishing, Serpentine.

Layman, L (ed.), 2001. *Rica's Stories: Rica Erickson*. Royal Western Australian Historical Society, Perth.

Moore, G F, 1884. *Diary of Ten Years of an Early Settler in Western Australia*. M Walbrook, London. (Facsimile 1978, University of Western Australia Press, Crawley.)

Murray, K O, 1949. From Oars to Diesel on the Swan. *Royal West Australian Historical Society Journal and Proceedings ('Early Days')*, IV, I.

Ogle, N, 1839. *The Colony of Western Australia*, James Frazer, London (Republished 1977, John Fergusson, Sydney.)

Scrimshaw, C, [1981?]. *Swan and Canning River Wrecks*. Unpublished MAAWA report.

Seddon, G, 1970. *Swan River Landscapes*. University of Western Australia Press, Crawley.

Smith, F and Barrett-Lennard, D, 1978. *A History of Houghton*. Self-published, Perth.

Tuckfield, T, 1971. Early Colonial Inns and Taverns. *Royal Western Australian Historical Society Journal and Proceedings*, VII, III.

UBD Perth Street Directory 1999. UBD, Osborne Park.

The West Australian StreetSmart, 2001 Perth Street Directory. West Australian Newspapers Ltd, and Department of Land Administration.

I NDEX

First published 2003 by
FREMANTLE ARTS CENTRE PRESS
25 Quarry Street, Fremantle
(PO Box 158, North Fremantle 6159)
Western Australia.
www.facp.iinet.net.au

Consultant Editor Ray Coffey.
Production Vanessa Bradley.
Cover Designer Marion Duke.
Typeset by Fremantle Arts Centre Press.
Printed by Craft Print International, Singapore.

National Library of Australia
Cataloguing-in-publication data

Burningham, Nick. 1954-
Messing about in earnest: exploring the Swan and Canning rivers.

Includes index.
ISBN 1 920731 25 3.

1. Burningham, Nick — Journey — Western Australia — Swan
River Region. 2. Burningham, Nick — Journey — Western
Australia — Canning River Region. 3. Swan River Region
(W.A.) — Description and travel. 4. Canning River Region
(W.A.) — Description and travel. I. Title.

994.12

The State of Western Australia has made an investment in this project through
ArtsWA in association with the Lotteries Commission.